A Tale of Two
KINGDOMS

A Tale of Two
Kingdoms

Exploring the Book of Revelation in
the Light of Other Scripture

George Hattenfield

M & T Miller Publishing
Columbus, Ohio

A Tale of Two Kingdoms
Exploring the Book of Revelation in the Light of Other Scripture
By George W. Hattenfield

Copyright © 2016 George W. Hattenfield. All rights reserved.

Published by M & T Miller Publishing.

Cover Art and Design by Tucker Media.

Scripture taken from the New King James Version®. Copyright © 1982 by Thomas Nelson. Used by permission. All rights reserved.

First Printing: 2016
ISBN: 978-0-9830929-1-9

I dedicate this book to my dear wife, Jean, who has been a faithful companion and partner in ministry for more than sixty years. Her love and support continues to be a vital part of my life and my ministry.

Contents

Acknowledgements

The people of Linworth Baptist Church have encouraged me to put these studies into a book and without their encouragement and support this book would not have been written.

I want to also acknowledge those who have had a part in helping me put this work together: Dr. Daniel Estes and Dr. Dave Warren read the manuscript and offered their thoughts. Miss Susan Stewart served as the editor for this material. Pastor Steven Smith provided the technical help needed to put it in e-book format. Matt Miller, Bob Crunelle, Debbie Chandler, and Jeremy Chandler for all of their help in getting the book printed. Mark and Leanne Tucker for designing the cover and title pages.

Introduction

WHEN OUR CHILDREN WERE GROWING UP, we enjoyed putting jigsaw puzzles together. It was always a challenge, especially when there were more than 1,000 pieces, but it was fun seeing the picture come together. At first you have just a border, the outer edge. The outer edge is important because it determines the size and the shape of the picture. It also begins to give a glimpse of the nature of the picture. Then you begin to fill in the rest of the picture, a little here and a little there. The more pieces added, the more the details of the picture begin to come together.

This is the way it is in the Book of Revelation. Some people shy away from this book and some see it as mysterious or confusing, and difficult to understand. In reality, it is the final piece of God's revelation, as He completes the picture for us, and we can see how everything fits together. God's eternal plan and purpose that begins to unfold in Genesis is brought to completion in the Book of Revelation. To fail to read and study this book is to miss the end of God's story. It is to fail to see and understand how God's creative plan and purpose comes to complete fruition.

We don't want to miss the final pieces that complete the picture and pull it all together. God's story is incomplete if we ignore or make light of the Book of Revelation. However it is also important that we see how those final pieces fit into the total picture. Therefore when we study the Book of Revelation, we need to see how it fits into God's revelation in the other Scriptures. This provides us with the necessary context to understand Revelation. One of the keys to understanding the Book of Revelation is to go back to the Book of Genesis and seek to understand God's creative purpose when He made this world and when He created humans to inhabit it. What God purposed to do in the beginning is what He will do when we come to the conclusion found in Revelation.

God is sovereign and He will ultimately accomplish all that He planned.

God made humans in His own image and gave them authority to rule over this earth and all of the created beings who are a part of this sphere. Their rebellion against God brought a curse which has affected them and their ability to fulfill what God designed for them. The question that runs through Scripture is, "Will God's original plan and purpose be fulfilled?" or "Will humans ever exercise the dominion over creation that God intended?" I believe that this question is answered in the Book of Revelation.

PART I

A TALE OF TWO KINGDOMS

A Tale of Two Kingdoms

THERE IS A THEME running through all of Scripture that finds its climax in the Book of Revelation. That prevailing theme is what might be called *A Tale of Two Kingdoms*. Before we begin to explore the Book of Revelation, it would be profitable for us to trace this theme through Scripture so that we can better understand how it all comes to a conclusion. The two kingdoms are the Kingdom of God and the Kingdom of Man. Jesus often spoke in His ministry about the Kingdom of God, and urged His hearers to invest in God's eternal Kingdom. The Book of Revelation ultimately focuses on the Kingdom of God, and how it will be established on earth (and how it will finally rule in God's New Creation). It also focuses on the Kingdom of Man, and how these two kingdoms are in conflict with each other. Before the Kingdom of God can be established, the Kingdom of Man must be defeated and destroyed.

Man's kingdom speaks of this world system and the culture that humans have developed with the intention of bringing some measure of joy and meaning to life, while seeking to live separated from God. Sin brought about separation between humans and God in the Garden of Eden, and while God has reached out in grace to humans, many people continue to seek their own way and live apart from God. Humans have developed a culture and have accomplished some good things, but an honest evaluation of this world's system points to a mixture of good and evil. The presence of good and evil in man's kingdom is vital to our understanding of the Book of Revelation.

Charles Dickens began his novel *The Tale of Two Cities* with words that called his readers to consider not only cities like London and Paris, but the prevalence of good and evil in our world, and the potential danger that is in our midst. He begins with these words:

> It was the best of times, it was the worst of times, it was the age of wisdom, it was the age of foolishness, it was the epoch of belief, it was the epoch of incredulity, it was the season of Light, it was the season of Darkness, it was the spring of hope, it was the winter of despair, we had everything before us, we had nothing before us, we were all going direct to Heaven, we were all going direct the other way — in short, the period was so far like the present period, that some of its noisiest authorities insisted on its being received, for good or for evil, in the superlative degree of comparison only.

The words of Dickens also are applicable to what we see in our world today. In some ways, this is the best of times. Man has reached new heights in the development of our culture in many areas. In the field of medicine, we have made great strides in dealing with the common illnesses that previously plagued our people, and we have added years to life expectancy. When it comes to transportation, we have automobiles that practically drive themselves, thanks to guidance systems that lead us to our selected destination. In communications, we have the capability of instant contact with others, almost anywhere in our world. We live in homes that feature all of the latest conveniences to make life better for all of us. We have an education system that provides training in almost any field we might choose. With all of these positives, however, an honest evaluation must look at the other side of the ledger.

Today we must also honestly say, "It is the worst of times." In our world, there are many who are hungry and unemployed, seeking even the basic needs of life. Even among those who have more than enough of this world's goods, there often is dissatisfaction with life, and a desire for something to satisfy their emptiness. A drug culture has developed among some who are looking for fulfillment and satisfaction. We have a problem with alcoholism that enslaves many people, destroying lives and many families. There is emptiness in many lives, and a search for meaning and purpose. Our suicide rate continues to rise. Marriage, although for many may initially seem to promise joy and satisfaction, often ends in discord. Crime is rampant in our streets, and violent crime continues to escalate at an alarming rate. Many of our criminals are of an age that we might consider them children. There has been almost constant warfare between the nations of our world. Unemployment is a serious problem in our culture, and financial stress with rising debt threatens our way of life.

During our lifetime, we have seen the development and growth of a world economy. What happens in one part of the world has an impact on all parts. When there is conflict in the oil-rich nations of our world, we all feel it at the local gas station. When an earthquake, tsunami or some other disaster strikes one country, it has an impact on the economic system of many other nations. When banks fail in some other country, the U.S. stock market is impacted. We are no longer an isolated people with our own economy.

We hear many predictions about the economic future, both of this country and of the world. We hear predictions about the sustainability of programs like Medicare and Social Security. Beyond that there are predictions that raise questions about the solvency of nations, and even of our whole-world economy. The question is, "Who can we believe, and in what can we safely invest?" In answer to these questions, God's Word has much to say about this world's economy, and there are specific predictions to guide us.

As we honestly look at our world, we see a materialistic system that is not only headed for potential disaster, but that has brought us into bondage. We no longer live the quiet life in simple freedom. Materialistic values and a love for pleasure have invaded our lives and changed our perspective. We are, for the most part, a sophisticated, worldly minded people, caught up in the philosophy and pursuits of this world system. We may be free from tyranny and political dictatorship, but are we free from the oppression of materialism?

We also live in a world of many religions, and our religious beliefs and practices separate us from one another. Religious differences have even become a threat to warfare and violent uprising in our world. Even those who do not consider themselves to be religious are often devoted to objects or people which they "worship." What we love, believe in and devote our time pursuing, can in a real sense become our religion.

In our world, there are governments that are oppressive and many people suffer under these repressive rulers. We can see a variety of political systems in which people are governed in our world, and we can find weaknesses in all of them. From the rule of a dictator or a monarch, to the democratic form of government, there are problems. This sometimes causes people to rebel, often resulting in changes in the form of government. Personal ambition and greed have motivated rulers to increase the suffering of those who are under their rule, and those who are targets of their attacks. All of this can be described as our world system.

We need to honestly consider this world system, and its ability to bring fulfillment to those who are a part of it. Our purpose in this study is first to consider what God's Word has to say about this world system, and then to explore what God's Word says about the plan and purpose He has for us, as His creation. Our desire is to develop a Biblical view of this present world system, and also seek God's perspective as we search for answers to life's questions.

The Book of Revelation helps us see the true nature of man's kingdom, as it has been under the control of Satan and his demonic kingdom. God wants us to see the evil nature of this kingdom, so that we might recognize the need for its destruction, and so we might respond to the call of Scripture to separate ourselves from this evil kingdom that is destined to destruction.

As we look at the problems that we find in this world system, and the potential for its collapse, the question that we want to consider is, "Do we have an alternative? Is there another system that we can embrace?"

In the Bible, we discover that there is an alternative to man's economic and political system. The Word of God speaks of man's kingdom, but it also presents the Kingdom of God. While this Kingdom may now appear to us in a spiritual form to be received by faith, the Word of God promises that this Kingdom is going to be established on earth, and that it will endure forever.

In order to be better prepared to understand what God is saying in the Book of Revelation, it is important for us to spend some time considering these two kingdoms and the true nature of each of them. The Book of Revelation describes how man's kingdom will come to an end, and how God's kingdom will be established as promised throughout Scripture. These two kingdoms occupy a major place in the Book of Revelation.

The Kingdom of Man

CHAPTER **2**

I N THE CREATION ACCOUNT found in the Book of Genesis, we find the record of God's purpose for man, as he was given authority to rule over this earth and over all of the things God had made on this earth.

> Then God said, "Let Us make man in Our image, according to Our likeness; let them have dominion over the fish of the sea, over the birds of the air, and over the cattle, over all the earth and over every creeping thing that creeps on the earth."
> (Genesis 1:26)

Man was given dominion, God-given authority, to rule over this earth. When Adam sinned, God did not remove that authority, but He did put a curse upon this earthly creation, making it more difficult for man to exercise authority. Humans are therefore accountable to God in fulfilling this responsibility.

Man's rule is established by God and it is under His authority, therefore those who rule in man's kingdom are accountable to God. The record of history (both secular and Biblical) shows us some rulers who tried to rule in righteousness and peace, but the record also is filled with men who have oppressed others and were hungry for power. Man's kingdom has never been able to deal with the underlying sin problem in human nature, and therefore mankind has come short of a reign of complete righteousness and peace.

The Bible gives us further insight into the evaluation of Man's Kingdom as we are made aware of the influence of Satan and the forces of evil that are at his command. The Book of Revelation helps us see the true nature of man's kingdom, as it has been under the control of Satan and his demonic kingdom. God wants us to see the evil nature of this kingdom, so that we might recognize the need for its destruction, and so we might respond to the call of Scripture to separate ourselves from this evil kingdom that is destined to destruction.

Throughout Scripture, there are two kingdoms presented: the Kingdom of Man, which has been under the control of Satan and in rebellion against God, and the Kingdom of God, as presented to us in the teaching ministry of Jesus Christ. These two kingdoms are in conflict, and in the Book of Revelation we see that conflict brought to an end with the triumph of God's Kingdom under the Lordship of His Son. From the practical side, we also need to be aware of the spiritual battle that is present, and how we can be equipped for this conflict. There are choices for us to make, and we need to be informed regarding the nature of this conflict.

This struggle began in heaven with the rebellion of Lucifer, who was joined with other angels to create the demonic kingdom. The fall of Lucifer is recorded in Isaiah 14 and in Ezekiel 28. In the Isaiah passage, Lucifer is called by name and he expresses the desire that motivated him to rebel against God:

> How you are fallen from heaven,
> O Lucifer, son of the morning!
> How you are cut down to the ground,
> You who weakened the nations!
> For you have said in your heart:
> "I will ascend into heaven,
> I will exalt my throne above the stars of God;
> I will also sit on the mount of the congregation
> On the farthest sides of the north;
> I will ascend above the heights of the clouds,
> I will be like the Most High."
> Yet you shall be brought down to Sheol,
> To the lowest depths of the Pit.
>
> (Isaiah 14:12-15)

In this passage, Lucifer is in heaven as one of God's angels, but he has a desire to exalt himself and even rise above God. It is also noted that he had an impact on others and swept a number of God's angels away in his rebellion (Revelation 12:3-4). Here is the beginning of a kingdom that stands in opposition to God, and one that ultimately will have an impact on the kingdom of man. Ezekiel 28 makes that point as the chapter begins with a message for the Prince of Tyre (the human ruler). In verse 11 and further, the message is directed to the King of Tyre, or the one who is the power behind the human ruler. Lucifer (Satan) is presented as that power behind the human ruler.

This angelic being is described as one of God's anointed cherubim, and the passage makes clear that he was created by God to serve as a holy angel, but he rebelled. The passage links with the one in Isaiah:

> Moreover the word of the LORD came to me, saying, "Son of man, take up a lamentation for the king of Tyre, and say to him, 'Thus says the Lord GOD:
> "You were the seal of perfection,
> Full of wisdom and perfect in beauty.
> You were in Eden, the garden of God;
> Every precious stone was your covering:
> The sardius, topaz, and diamond,
> Beryl, onyx, and jasper,
> Sapphire, turquoise, and emerald with gold.
> The workmanship of your timbrels and pipes
> Was prepared for you on the day you were created.
>
> You were the anointed cherub who covers;
> I established you;
> You were on the holy mountain of God;
> You walked back and forth in the midst of fiery stones.
> You were perfect in your ways from the day you were created,
> Till iniquity was found in you.
>
> By the abundance of your trading
> You became filled with violence within,
> And you sinned;
> Therefore I cast you as a profane thing

Out of the mountain of God;
And I destroyed you, O covering cherub,
From the midst of the fiery stones.

Your heart was lifted up because of your beauty;
You corrupted your wisdom for the sake of your splendor;
I cast you to the ground,
I laid you before kings,
That they might gaze at you.
You defiled your sanctuaries
By the multitude of your iniquities,
By the iniquity of your trading;
Therefore I brought fire from your midst;
It devoured you,
And I turned you to ashes upon the earth
In the sight of all who saw you.
All who knew you among the peoples are astonished at
you;
You have become a horror,
And shall be no more forever.""""

                                                (Ezekiel 28:11-19)

Having been cast down to earth, we see Satan tempting Adam and Eve, challenging God's Word, and encouraging them to rebel against God's command. Satan and his kingdom had an impact on the humans in the Garden, and this conflict of kingdoms began to include humans. In Genesis 3:15, we find God speaking of this conflict and its ultimate result, as these two kingdoms collide. This prediction sets the stage for the rest of the message of Scripture and for the history of humanity. Consider the words of this important statement as it is directed to Satan:

And I will put enmity between you and the woman, and
between your seed and her Seed; He shall bruise your head,
And you shall bruise His heel.

As Eve was deceived by Satan working in and through the serpent, so the woman shall be used of God to bring forth the One who would conquer Satan, but this Savior also would suffer in the conflict. God indicated that, in the years ahead, there would be continual conflict between these two kingdoms. It is interesting to note that God spoke of the seed of the woman, giving us a hint of what God would do in bringing His Son into our world, conceived in the womb of a virgin without any human father.

The flood, recorded in Genesis 6-9, came as a result of man's failure to rule in righteousness and peace:

> Then the LORD saw that the wickedness of man was great in the earth, and that every intent of the thoughts of his heart was only evil continually. And the LORD was sorry that He had made man on the earth, and He was grieved in His heart. So the LORD said, "I will destroy man whom I have created from the face of the earth, both man and beast, creeping thing and birds of the air, for I am sorry that I have made them."   (Genesis 6:5-7)

In mercy God spared Noah and his family because they were seeking to live in harmony with the God who created them. In saving them from this judgment, God provided for a new beginning for the human race after the flood. In Genesis 9 we find some changes as the animal kingdom and humans become more hostile toward each other. Humans now are permitted to eat meat and some of the animals became carnivorous and began to attack humans. This is recorded in Genesis 9:2-3:

> And the fear of you and the dread of you shall be on every beast of the earth, on every bird of the air, on all that move on the earth, and on all the fish of the sea. They are given into your hand. Every moving thing that lives shall be food for you. I have given you all things, even as the green herbs.

Genesis 9:5 adds the following:

> Surely for your lifeblood I will demand a reckoning; from the hand of every beast I will require it, and from the hand of man. From the hand of every man's brother I will require the life of man.

God also gave authority to humans to exercise capital punishment when one person commits murder against another human. This additional authority was given to man in order that evil might be restrained by human government. We find this in Genesis 9:6:

> Whoever sheds man's blood, by man his blood shall be shed;
> For in the image of God He made man.

The authority for human government to exercise capital punishment is restated in the New Testament:

> For rulers are not a terror to good works, but to evil. Do you want to be unafraid of the authority? Do what is good, and you will have praise from the same. For he is God's minister to you for good. But if you do evil, be afraid; for he does not bear the sword in vain; for he is God's minister, an avenger to execute wrath on him who practices evil.
>
> (Romans 13:3-4)

Throughout the Old Testament, we can trace this conflict as Satan focuses his attack upon this godly line that is to bring forth the Seed of the Woman. There were times when Satan attempted to destroy the entire nation of Israel, and other times when his attack was narrowed on the royal line that would lead to the Messiah. As God narrowed His choice to Abraham, Isaac and Jacob, the attack was on the people of Israel as when the Pharaoh attempted to kill all the baby boys born to Israeli families. Much later, in the days of Queen Esther under Persian rule, an edict was enacted with the purpose of annihilation of all Jews. God worked through Esther to thwart that edict and bring deliverance to His people.

With God's selection of David as the family line from whom the Messiah would be born, Satan narrowed his attack on that line to either kill or corrupt that line so that God could not bring His Son into the world. On one occasion, all the boys in the royal line were killed by a wicked queen (Athaliah), but God spared one boy to carry on the line. When the time came for Jesus to be born, Satan inspired King Herod to make his attempt to kill Jesus by killing all the boys born in Bethlehem around that time.

When Satan could not destroy the people of Israel, he enticed them into the worship of false gods so that God's wrath might be turned upon them. Even on their way out of Egypt, while Moses was on Mount Sinai receiving the law from God, Aaron and the people were engaged in the worship of a golden calf. The history of Israel in the Old Testament is filled with many occasions when God's people departed to worship idols, resulting in God's wrath. Idolatry and immorality reared its ugly head, even in the lives of godly men who succumbed to Satan's temptation. God judged His people and sent them into exile under the control of Assyria and Babylon but, in faithfulness to His covenant, He did not destroy them.

As we read the Biblical account of the Kings who ruled Israel and Judah, we again discover spiritual conflict as the people often departed from God, led by leaders who introduced idolatry and a departure from God's law. God appointed prophets to confront His people about their sin and rebellion, and warn them of God's impending judgment. These prophetic messages were often rejected, and God finally sent His people into exile. The ten tribes of Israel were taken captive by the Assyrians and, at a later time, the two tribes of Judah were exiled in Babylon.

In spite of the unfaithfulness of Israel in those days, God remained faithful to His promises that He had made to Abraham, Isaac and Jacob. God will restore Israel to a place of blessing and He will bring His promised Messiah into the world. God would call out a remnant people in Israel and preserve the Messianic line through these difficult times.

When Israel failed to drive out the Canaanites, they left themselves and their families open to the ungodly influence of the world around them. This began a challenge that continued through New Testament times and into the present day. God's people live in an ungodly world, and the challenge for us is to be light and salt, to impact our world for God and the message of Jesus Christ. Beginning in the New Testament with the redemptive work of Christ and the indwelling presence of the Holy Spirit, God has equipped the followers of Christ to have an impact on our world for His cause. This world system, however, is still present with us, and Satan uses it to entice God's people to compromise Biblical principles in a way that allows the world system to have an impact upon God's people.

Paul reminds us in Ephesians 6:10-18 that we are in a spiritual conflict with the kingdom of Satan, and the allurements of this world are used to draw us away from God. God has provided all of the armor and the weapons that we need to be victorious in this battle, but the struggle is real. Jesus warned His followers that there would be conflict since we live in a hostile world. In John 15:18-21, Jesus said:

> If the world hates you, you know that it hated Me before it hated you. If you were of the world, the world would love its own. Yet because you are not of the world, but I chose you out of the world, therefore the world hates you. Remember the word that I said to you, "A servant is not greater than his master." If they persecuted Me, they will also persecute you. If they kept My word, they will keep yours also. But all these things they will do to you for My name's sake, because they do not know Him who sent Me.

In the parable of the wheat and the tares found in Matthew 13:24-30, Jesus spoke of the fact that the enemy would infiltrate God's wheat with tares (weeds) bringing about a mixture that would make it difficult to determine those who truly belonged to God from those who did not:

> Another parable He put forth to them, saying: The kingdom of heaven is like a man who sowed good seed in his field; but while men slept, his enemy came and sowed tares among the wheat and went his way. But when the grain had sprouted and produced a crop, then the tares also appeared. So the servants of the owner came and said to him, "Sir, did you not sow good seed in your field? How then does it have tares?" He said to them, "An enemy has done this." The servants said to him, "Do you want us then to go and gather them up?" But he said, "No, lest while you gather up the tares you also uproot the wheat with them. Let both grow together until the harvest, and at the time of harvest I will say to the reapers, First gather together the tares and bind them in bundles to burn them, but gather the wheat into my barn."   (Matthew 13:24-30)

Jesus explained this parable to His disciples in Matthew 13:36-43, and identified the enemy responsible for this mixture as Satan:

> Then Jesus sent the multitude away and went into the house. And His disciples came to Him, saying, "Explain to us the

parable of the tares of the field." He answered and said to
them: "He who sows the good seed is the Son of Man. The
field is the world, the good seeds are the sons of the kingdom,
but the tares are the sons of the wicked one. The enemy who
sowed them is the devil, the harvest is the end of the age, and
the reapers are the angels. Therefore as the tares are gathered
and burned in the fire, so it will be at the end of this age. The
Son of Man will send out His angels, and they will gather
out of His kingdom all things that offend, and those who
practice lawlessness, and will cast them into the furnace of
fire. There will be wailing and gnashing of teeth. Then the
righteous will shine forth as the sun in the kingdom of their
Father. He who has ears to hear, let him hear!"

(Matthew 13:36-43)

Before Jesus suffered and died for our sins, He told His disciples that
He would build His church (Matthew 16:18), and with this He also
promised that the gates of hell would not prevail against it. While this
promise focuses on the ultimate outcome, it also implies that Satan
and His kingdom would do all that they could to have an impact on
the Lord's Church. Satan and his kingdom would not prevail, but they
would exert all of the power at their disposal to do harm to the church.

As the Book of Acts records the birth of the church, it also records
the conflict that rises up against God's people. There is persecution,
martyrdom and hostility from religious groups and from governments.
Some of the greatest damage to the church however comes from the
infiltration of Satan and his forces within the visible church. Consider
the warning of Paul to the Ephesian elders in Acts 20:28-31:

Therefore take heed to yourselves and to all the flock, among
which the Holy Spirit has made you overseers, to shepherd
the church of God which He purchased with His own blood.
For I know this, that after my departure savage wolves will
come in among you, not sparing the flock. Also from among
yourselves men will rise up, speaking perverse things, to
draw away the disciples after themselves. Therefore watch,
and remember that for three years I did not cease to warn
everyone night and day with tears.

Peter also spoke in 2 Peter 2:1-3, about this infiltration in the church that will corrupt the church and its impact for Christ:

> But there were also false prophets among the people, even as there will be false teachers among you, who will secretly bring in destructive heresies, even denying the Lord who bought them, and bring on themselves swift destruction. And many will follow their destructive ways, because of whom the way of truth will be blasphemed. By covetousness they will exploit you with deceptive words; for a long time their judgment has not been idle, and their destruction does not slumber.

The Apostle John warns of this infiltration of "tares among the wheat" as the church is impacted by Satan and this world system. John writes in 1 John 2:18-19 the following words:

> Little children, it is the last hour; and as you have heard that the Antichrist is coming, even now many antichrists have come, by which we know that it is the last hour. They went out from us, but they were not of us; for if they had been of us, they would have continued with us; but they went out that they might be made manifest, that none of them were of us.

In 2 Corinthians 11:13-15, the Apostle Paul speaks of the deceptive work of Satan and his human ministers as they infiltrate the church:

> For such are false apostles, deceitful workers, transforming themselves into apostles of Christ. And no wonder! For Satan himself transforms himself into an angel of light. Therefore it is no great thing if his ministers also transform themselves into ministers of righteousness, whose end will be according to their works.

God will judge those who have sought to overthrow the Church of Christ, and the gates of hell will not prevail against His church.

As Jesus evaluates the seven churches in Revelation 2 and 3, we see some of the evidence of this infiltration. These seven churches were literal churches in the Roman province of Asia, which is now part of the country of Turkey. These churches were started by the Apostle

Paul, or begun by the outreach of churches that his team began. Of the seven, only two (Smyrna and Philadelphia) did not receive any words of condemnation. As the Lord commended the seven churches for what they had done, He also spoke of things that were not pleasing to Him. There were various levels of compromise and departure in five of these seven churches.

Some had lost their first love for Christ, while others were embracing false doctrine or showed very little evidence of any spiritual life. We see how the church has been impacted by the world's system and by Satan's kingdom when we read some of what Jesus said to them. Consider the following statements:

> But I have a few things against you, because you have there those who hold the doctrine of Balaam, who taught Balak to put a stumbling block before the children of Israel, to eat things sacrificed to idols, and to commit sexual immorality. Thus you also have those who hold the doctrine of the Nicolaitans, which thing I hate.   (Revelation 2:14-15)

> Nevertheless I have a few things against you, because you allow that woman Jezebel, who calls herself a prophetess, to teach and seduce My servants to commit sexual immorality and eat things sacrificed to idols   (Revelation 2:20)

> And to the angel of the church in Sardis write, "These things says He who has the seven Spirits of God and the seven stars: I know your works, that you have a name that you are alive, but you are dead."   (Revelation 3:1)

The final church in this group being evaluated by Christ is Laodicea. There is little to commend this church but there is a serious condition in that church that is found in many churches today. The following passage demonstrates how Satan and the world have impacted the church. Revelation 3:14-19:

> And to the angel of the church of the Laodiceans write, "These things says the Amen, the Faithful and True Witness, the Beginning of the creation of God: I know your works, that you are neither cold nor hot. I could wish you were cold or hot. So then, because you are lukewarm, and neither

cold nor hot, I will vomit you out of My mouth. Because you say, 'I am rich, have become wealthy, and have need of nothing'—and do not know that you are wretched, miserable, poor, blind, and naked— I counsel you to buy from Me gold refined in the fire, that you may be rich; and white garments, that you may be clothed, that the shame of your nakedness may not be revealed; and anoint your eyes with eye salve, that you may see. As many as I love, I rebuke and chasten. Therefore be zealous and repent."

(Revelation 3:14-19)

While these seven churches were actual churches in the time when John wrote, they also provide a picture of churches throughout the ages. There are some churches that are faithful and true like Smyrna and Philadelphia, but there are others that have been corrupted by Satan and the influence of this world, or that have cooled in their love for Christ or are unaware of their true spiritual poverty. What Jesus said in Matthew 13 is seen in Revelation as Jesus evaluates the church. With all that Satan has done to diminish the impact of the church, and even to bring the judgment of Christ on some in it, we need to know that the words of Jesus in Matthew 16:18 are still true, "the gates of hell shall not prevail against it" (His Church).

The Lord will separate the tares from the wheat so that the false will be removed into judgment, but the true followers of Christ will prevail in the end. Those who are faithful and true in their faith in Christ will enter into His kingdom, and the Lord will bring judgment upon this world and upon Satan for what has been done to the people of God. Our Lord has said "vengeance is mine," and He will bring justice to those who have suffered at the hands of Satan and the forces of this world system. This is what is presented to us in the Book of Revelation. The Lord brings judgment upon Satan and man's system that has persecuted and corrupted a portion of the Lord's church, and His church is seen as ultimately triumphant in God's plan.

It is important to take note of the order that we find in the Book of Revelation. It begins with a vision of Jesus Christ in all of His glory, as He is standing in the midst of His Church represented by these seven lampstands. After His words of commendation and condemnation as He evaluates His church, we next find a scene in Heaven (Revelation 4 and 5) where He, as the conquering Lamb of God, is found worthy to carry out the eternal plan of God, in which His Kingdom will ultimately be established and His church will prevail.

The next portion of the book, beginning in Revelation 6, pictures Christ as the Lamb, opening the seals on God's plan. When it unfolds, it will bring judgment on the world system and on Satan's kingdom. We are told in the Ten Commandments (Exodus 20:4-5; 34:6-7) that our God is a jealous God and He will defend His name and avenge His people. Satan and the kingdom of this world must be held accountable for their blasphemy against God and for what they have done to His people. It is interesting to note what we read in the opening of the fifth seal:

> When He opened the fifth seal, I saw under the altar the souls of those who had been slain for the word of God and for the testimony which they held. And they cried with a loud voice, saying, "How long, O Lord, holy and true, until You judge and avenge our blood on those who dwell on the earth?" Then a white robe was given to each of them; and it was said to them that they should rest a little while longer, until both the number of their fellow servants and their brethren, who would be killed as they were, was completed.   (Revelation 6:9-11)

As we continue on through the Book of Revelation, it is important to remember this passage for what happens when the wrath of God is poured upon the kingdom of this world, in response to the cry of those who have suffered and have even been martyred for the cause of Christ. The church of Christ, as seen in the church at Smyrna, has suffered. As seen in other churches, Satan has been able to make inroads. He will, however, not prevail and God will avenge His people. When God's judgment is poured out, there is no sign of repentance, and when Christ appears to claim His throne, the rulers of this world fight against Him. In light of all of this, the only possible end is total destruction and eternal judgment in the Lake of Fire.

As we focus on the cries of the martyrs, we also must note that what is taking place in the Book of Revelation is related to the prayers of God's people throughout the ages. In Revelation 5:8, we see the celebration of worship is linked to the prayers of God's people:

> Now when He had taken the scroll, the four living creatures and the twenty-four elders fell down before the Lamb, each having a harp, and golden bowls full of incense, which are the prayers of the saints.

The opening of the seals and the fulfilling of God's stated purpose is connected to the prayers of God's people.

In Revelation 8:1-5, we find another link between the judgment that comes upon this world and the prayers of God's people:

> When He opened the seventh seal, there was silence in heaven for about half an hour. And I saw the seven angels who stand before God, and to them were given seven trumpets. Then another angel, having a golden censer, came and stood at the altar. He was given much incense, that he should offer it with the prayers of all the saints upon the golden altar which was before the throne. And the smoke of the incense, with the prayers of the saints, ascended before God from the angel's hand. Then the angel took the censer, filled it with fire from the altar, and threw it to the earth. And there were noises, thunderings, lightnings, and an earthquake.
>
> (Revelation 8:1-5)

God's people have been told that they should not seek vengeance on those who oppressed or persecuted them, but rather they should put it in God's hands, with the promise that He will avenge them. In the Book of Psalms, we find many imprecatory psalms where the writer cries to God for vengeance on his enemies. The prayers of God's people will be answered as God's judgment is poured upon the wicked.

Think also of how many people have prayed over the years, in words like those given to us by our Lord when He taught His followers to pray, "Thy kingdom come, thy will be done on earth as it is in heaven" (Matthew 6:10). This prayer for the establishment of God's kingdom and for the fulfilling of His will on earth as it is in heaven, implies God's judgment of all evil. God's kingdom cannot be established and His will cannot be totally fulfilled without the judgment of man's kingdom and its wickedness and oppression of God's people. This prayer will be answered in the Book of Revelation.

The conflict between these two kingdoms must end, and the Word of God assures us that it will not only end, but will end in a glorious victory won by our Lord Jesus Christ. Satan's head will be crushed and human rebellion will be totally destroyed so that righteousness and peace can prevail in the New Heaven and the New Earth. Jesus Christ will reign forever in the Eternal Kingdom of God and those who are His people, through faith in Christ, will reign with Him. Knowing this should cause us to shun the ways of this evil world and the allurements of what it offers, and set our heart on God's Eternal City.

As the world system, a part of Satan's kingdom is destroyed, we note what is said as a response to God's judgment on this world system pictured as Babylon the Great:

> Rejoice over her, O heaven, and you holy apostles and prophets, for God has avenged you on her!
> (Revelation 18:20)

Add to this the words found in Revelation 18:23-24:

> The light of a lamp shall not shine in you anymore, and the voice of bridegroom and bride shall not be heard in you anymore. For your merchants were the great men of the earth, for by your sorcery all the nations were deceived. And in her was found the blood of prophets and saints, and of all who were slain on the earth.

Immediately following the destruction of this system, which has persecuted and slain God's people seeking to thwart the plan of God and corrupt His church, we find the great Hallelujah chorus as God's victory is celebrated in Revelation 19:1-9:

> After these things I heard a loud voice of a great multitude in heaven, saying, "Alleluia! Salvation and glory and honor and power belong to the Lord our God! For true and righteous are His judgments, because He has judged

the great harlot who corrupted the earth with her fornication; and He has avenged on her the blood of His servants
shed by her." Again they said, "Alleluia! Her smoke rises up
forever and ever!" And the twenty-four elders and the four
living creatures fell down and worshiped God who sat on
the throne, saying, "Amen! Alleluia!" Then a voice came
from the throne, saying, "Praise our God, all you His servants and those who fear Him, both small and great!" And
I heard, as it were, the voice of a great multitude, as the
sound of many waters and as the sound of mighty thunderings, saying, "Alleluia! For the Lord God Omnipotent
reigns! Let us be glad and rejoice and give Him glory, for
the marriage of the Lamb has come, and His wife has made
herself ready." And to her it was granted to be arrayed in fine
linen, clean and bright, for the fine linen is the righteous acts
of the saints. Then he said to me, "Write: 'Blessed are those
who are called to the marriage supper of the Lamb!'" And
he said to me, "These are the true sayings of God."
(Revelation 19:1-9)

The church prevails as the Bride of Christ, arrayed in His Righteousness,
and Christ comes to establish His Kingdom upon the earth. Ultimate
victory is won, as promised in God's Word, and this should encourage
God's people as we continue to face the conflict in this present time. Our
Lord assures us of victory in Him, and He encourages us to withdraw
from this world system and invest our resources in the Kingdom of
God. Note the words that are found in Revelation 18:4-5:

And I heard another voice from heaven saying, "Come out
of her, my people, lest you share in her sins, and lest you
receive of her plagues. For her sins have reached to heaven,
and God has remembered her iniquities."

God calls on His people to be set apart unto Him and set apart from
this world, believing that this world system is headed for destruction
and that God's eternal Kingdom will prevail.

CHAPTER 3

Identity of Babylon the Great

HAVING BRIEFLY TRACED THE CONFLICT between man's kingdom and God's kingdom recorded in Scripture, it is important that we see in what form this world system is represented in the Book of Revelation. One of the keys to understanding the Book of Revelation is to identify what is meant by the term "Babylon the Great." This term has a major part in the book and the destruction of this Babylon brings great rejoicing to God's people. The nature of this Babylon gives rise to the judgment of God that we see poured out in the book. Several times we find an announcement is made linking this Babylon with God's judgment. Before we look at the Book of Revelation it is important that we get some understanding of "Babylon the Great." We want to begin by looking at the passages in Revelation that speak of this Babylon.

> And another angel followed, saying, "Babylon is fallen, is fallen, that great city, because she has made all nations drink of the wine of the wrath of her fornication."
> (Revelation 14:8)

> Now the great city was divided into three parts, and the cities of the nations fell. And great Babylon was remembered before God, to give her the cup of the wine of the fierceness of His wrath. (Revelation 16:19)

> And on her forehead a name was written: MYSTERY, BABYLON THE GREAT, THE MOTHER OF HARLOTS AND OF THE ABOMINATIONS OF THE EARTH.
> (Revelation 17:5)

> And he cried mightily with a loud voice, saying, "Babylon the great is fallen, is fallen, and has become a dwelling place of demons, a prison for every foul spirit, and a cage for every unclean and hated bird!" (Revelation 18:2)

> Standing at a distance for fear of her torment, saying, "Alas, alas, that great city Babylon, that mighty city! For in one hour your judgment has come." (Revelation 18:10)

> Then a mighty angel took up a stone like a great millstone and threw it into the sea, saying, "Thus with violence the great city Babylon shall be thrown down, and shall not be found anymore." (Revelation 18:21)

As we look at these passage we learn a number of things about "Babylon the Great". First, in Revelation 14:8 we discover that this "Babylon" has had an impact on all nations because all nations have become intoxicated with the wine of her fornication. The fornication is a departure from a relationship with God in an attempt to find some pleasure and satisfaction in another relationship and the worship of other gods. The impact of this Babylon has been felt in every nation on earth. As we decide on how to interpret this "Babylon the Great" we must see that it is worldwide in its impact and therefore it is clear that more than one city is involved.

In Revelation 16:19 we learn that cities of the nations fell with the destruction of Babylon. Again, our interpretation of this Babylon must be broad enough to involve all the nations on earth. We are also told in this passage that this great city is divided into three parts. We will consider those three parts of Babylon later in this study but for now we simply must include in our interpretation the fact that the cities of the nations are included with the destruction of Babylon.

Next we learn in Revelation 17:5 that this title is given to the harlot woman as well as to the city of Babylon. Both the city and the harlot are linked together as part of this Babylon. This is clearly stated as we read Revelation 17:18. In this passage the harlot woman is identified with the city: "And the woman whom you saw is that great city which reigns over the kings of the earth." The city and the harlot woman are clearly linked so that our interpretation must include this fact.

In the three passages quoted from chapter 18 we are given further information about this city and its destruction by the judgment of God. In verse 2 we learn that this city is full of all kinds of evil spirits and wickedness. It is the seat of the full manifestation of evil and judgment is therefore announced in verse 10. God has been longsuffering with the wickedness of this Babylon but ultimately the Day of Judgment must come. In verse 21 we are told that the judgment comes with violent overthrow as it is compared to casting a great millstone into the sea. Our interpretation of Babylon the Great must fit with the facts brought out in these verses.

Babylon is often interpreted to refer to a literal city. Those who interpret Babylon as being a literal city are divided as to what city is intended. Some have suggested that the ancient city of Babylon in Iraq is to be rebuilt before the end comes. Others have identified this city with Rome, London, Paris, New York or some other major city in our world. Rome is favored by many because the harlot woman is said to be seated on seven mountains (the interpreter links this to the seven hills of Rome). However in Revelation 17:9-10 these seven mountains are linked to the seven heads of the beast and those heads are said to be seven kings (or kingdoms) according to verse ten. "Here is the mind which has wisdom: The seven heads are seven mountains on which the woman sits. There are also seven kings. Five have fallen, one is, and the other has not yet come. And when he comes, he must continue a short time." We will say more about these seven kings (or kingdoms) later but for now we simply respond to those who interpret Babylon the Great as Rome.

As we seek to identify Babylon the Great it is important that we also note that the destruction of this city is widespread. With the destruction of the city the entire world appears to be shut down as all shipping on the seas comes to a halt. In Revelation 18:22-24 we also note the end of music, the end of industry and the end of all social life. "The sound of harpists, musicians, flutists, and trumpeters shall not be heard in you anymore. No craftsman of any craft shall be found in you anymore, and the sound of a millstone shall not be heard in you anymore. The light of a lamp shall not shine in you anymore, and the voice of bridegroom and bride shall not be heard in you anymore. For your merchants were the great men of the earth, for by your sorcery all the nations were deceived. And in her was found the blood of prophets and saints, and of all who were slain on the earth."

In this passage there is again great breadth as the entire world is impacted by the fall of Babylon. As the reason for this judgment is given in verse 24 there is an emphasis upon all nations and the entire earth. The merchants are considered to be great because they were successful in their business and in their merchandise people from all nations were deceived by thinking that possession of material things is success. Note also that this judgment comes because this Babylon is responsible for the persecution and martyrdom of God's prophets and His saints. Add to this the charge that this city is responsible for the deaths of many who were murdered or killed because of human greed.

The rejoicing and glorious worship that is recorded in Heaven (Revelation 19:1-6) and the return of Christ that follows, points to the fact that this judgment and destruction is much wider than one city. In that passage we see a great multitude in heaven giving thanks for a glorious victory in which this city has been destroyed and the harlot has been judged. Before the Kingdom of Christ can be established on earth this kingdom, called Babylon the Great, must be destroyed by God's judgment.

Before we arrive at another interpretation of Babylon the Great we must take note of Revelation 18:4 where God's people are urged to flee from this city and separate from its wickedness. "And I heard another voice from heaven saying, 'Come out of her, my people, lest you share in her sins, and lest you receive of her plagues.'" In this passage God calls upon those who belong to Him to come out of this Babylon and be set apart from all of its wickedness. Judgment will be poured out upon all who are a part of this city and God warns His own people to flee.

This admonition and warning becomes impractical if the city of

Babylon has not yet been built or the city intended is not one in which we live. The message of the Book of Revelation becomes less applicable for us if it is about a city in which we do not live or about a city that is not clearly identified. In the introduction to the book our Lord pronounces a blessing in Revelation 1:3 "Blessed is he who reads and those who hear the words of this prophecy, and keep those things which are written in it; for the time is near." This blessing is for those who read, those who hear and those who keep what is written in this prophecy. There is a message in this book that is intended to impact the way we live. This book is intended to be very practical as we live in view of the end times.

This blessing is repeated at the end of the book as the Lord urges us to pay attention to the message that is revealed for us. Note the words of Revelation 22:7: "Behold, I am coming quickly! Blessed is he who keeps the words of the prophecy of this book." There is something to be learned in the Book of Revelation that will affect the way we live as we await the return of our Savior, but we can miss the message that God has for us if we cloud the interpretation of this Babylon from which we are to flee.

Before we suggest another interpretation we call attention to the fact that there is another part that is linked to the city and the harlot who are both given this name Babylon. In Revelation 17:3 the harlot is pictured sitting (riding on) the seven-headed beast:

> So he carried me away in the Spirit into the wilderness. And I saw a woman sitting on a scarlet beast which was full of names of blasphemy, having seven heads and ten horns.

We will show in a later chapter how this beast can be traced through Scripture with its seven heads but here we simply note that the beast is linked with the harlot who is also linked to the city and when judgment comes all three will be destroyed.

It is not just one city, one harlot or even one head of this awful beast. All three are linked together to be the fullness of evil upon which God's judgment must fall. I believe that there is an interpretation that is not only consistent with what we find in Revelation but which fits with the entire message of Scripture. I believe that Babylon the Great refers

to the system of this world, of which believers are constantly warned
throughout Scripture. It is man's kingdom and that kingdom stretches
back into the Book of Genesis.

The system began in Babylon where man rebelled against God. Man's
rebellion was judged in the great flood that swept away all of humanity
except Noah and his family (Genesis 6-9). After the flood God told
Noah and his family to replenish the earth but Genesis 11:1-4 records
the response of humans:

> Now the whole earth had one language and one speech. And
> it came to pass, as they journeyed from the east, that they
> found a plain in the land of Shinar, and they dwelt there.
> Then they said to one another, "Come, let us make bricks and
> bake them thoroughly." They had brick for stone, and they
> had asphalt for mortar. And they said, "Come, let us build
> ourselves a city, and a tower whose top is in the heavens; let
> us make a name for ourselves, lest we be scattered abroad
> over the face of the whole earth."

Note in this passage man's stated purpose as together they built a city
(Babel) and a tower. It was to make a name for humanity and to resist
being scattered over the earth. With it they built a tower to establish
contact with heaven by their own effort. They began a religious system
that provided some measure of spiritual contact with heaven and their
concept of god. Babylon's pantheon of gods was later adopted by many
of the nations of the earth. God's judgment came upon this rebellion
by confusing their language and thus scattering them all over the earth.

This world's system can be traced throughout human history as
humans continue to rebel against God and against His truth. This
kingdom of man is in reality the kingdom of Satan as he has tempted
and drawn humans away from God. Satan is called the god of this
world in 2 Corinthians 4:3-4:

> But even if our gospel is veiled, it is veiled to those who are
> perishing, whose minds the god of this age has blinded, who
> do not believe, lest the light of the gospel of the glory of
> Christ, who is the image of God, should shine on them.

When this system is judged in the end, the dragon (Satan) is the one who empowers this system and he is worshipped by those who are a part of this world system:

> Now the beast which I saw was like a leopard, his feet were like the feet of a bear, and his mouth like the mouth of a lion. The dragon gave him his power, his throne, and great authority. So they worshiped the dragon who gave authority to the beast; and they worshiped the beast, saying, "Who is like the beast? Who is able to make war with him?"
>
> (Revelation 13:2, 4)

In both Old and New Testament God warned His people of the impact that this world system can have in drawing them away from God. Israel was intoxicated with the wine of this system as they embraced the gods of this world. In Proverbs the first nine chapters warn of the harlot woman who would draw the readers away from God and His truth. The Book of Ecclesiastes records Solomon's attempt to find meaning and purpose in what the world has to offer. He spoke of his search as vanity and a meaningless pursuit. His final admonition was for people to fear God and keep His commandments. Many times, as in the Book of Hosea, the prophets spoke of Israel's departure from God as spiritual adultery.

Jesus challenged His hearers telling them that no man can serve two masters. He said that you cannot serve God and mammon (what this world has to offer). In His Parable of the Prodigal Son (Luke 15) He pointed out the folly of seeking joy in what we find in this world. In His parables found in in Matthew 13 He spoke of Satan's attempt to snatch away the good seed or to draw people away by the things of this world. He spoke about the world's rebellion and hatred of God and His people and He challenged His hearers to turn away from what the world has to offer and follow Him.

In Ephesians 6:10-18 Paul warned believers of the conflict they face with Satan and this world system. In this passage they are also told of the nature of the conflict we face in this world. Paul urged his readers in Romans 12:2 not to be conformed to this world, its philosophy, its value system and its ways. His heart was grieved as he spoke of one of his team members (Demas) who forsook Paul because he loved this present world (2 Timothy 4:10).

We could multiply passages of Scripture in which God calls us away from this world system as He also tells us of its ultimate destruction in judgment. 1 John 2:15-17 is one that certainly fits here:

> Do not love the world or the things in the world. If anyone loves the world, the love of the Father is not in him. For all that is in the world, the lust of the flesh, the lust of the eyes, and the pride of life, is not of the Father but is of the world. And the world is passing away, and the lust of it; but he who does the will of God abides forever.

James spoke about a relationship with the world as spiritual adultery and this fits with the harlot woman:

> Adulterers and adulteresses! Do you not know that friend-ship with the world is enmity with God? Whoever therefore wants to be a friend of the world makes himself an enemy of God.   (James 4:4)

James would see this world system to be like a prostitute who seeks to entice God's people to find satisfaction in what the world has to offer. Believers are referred to as the bride of Christ. Therefore when a believer falls in love with material things or other activities that draw them away from Christ it is spiritual adultery. Psalm 16:11 tells us that the true source of joy and pleasure is to be found in a relationship with God:

> You will show me the path of life; In Your presence is fullness of joy; At Your right hand are pleasures forevermore.

Another key to our interpretation of Babylon the Great as the world system is to note that Scripture indicates that the system that brings forth the antichrist in Revelation was already present as New Testament writers penned their epistles. In 1 John 2:18 the writer of the Book of Revelation tells us that the antichrist's system is already present:

> Little children, it is the last hour; and as you have heard that
> the Antichrist is coming, even now many antichrists have
> come, by which we know that it is the last hour.

Again in 1 John 4:3 he speaks of the "spirit of antichrist" being already
present in his time:

> And every spirit that does not confess that Jesus Christ has
> come in the flesh is not of God. And this is the spirit of the
> Antichrist, which you have heard was coming, and is now
> already in the world.

John also closes his epistle with the words:

> Little children, keep yourselves from idols. Amen.
>   (1 John 5:21)

The Apostle Paul writes about the coming of the "man of sin" (antichrist) in 2 Thessalonians 2:3-7. In that passage he says in verse 7
that "the mystery of iniquity is already at work." The system is already
present and we are to be alerted to this reality. We do not have to wait
for the rebuilding of an ancient city or further identification of some
other city. The system that is opposed to God and to His Christ is
present and Satan uses this world system to draw people away from
God and from finding fullness in a relationship with God. This is the
message of Scripture and before God's Kingdom can be established this
system must be destroyed.

Having identified Babylon the Great as this world system (man's
kingdom) we want to look more closely at the way it is presented in the
Book of Revelation. This world system is made up of three parts and
they are pictured in this book so as to show us the true nature of the
world system and why it must come under God's judgment. It is like a
glamorous city with all of its excitement and its material possessions. It
is like a harlot woman who seeks to entice humans to fulfill their desire
in some love other than in God. And it is like a ravenous beast that
oppresses those who come under its rule and persecutes God's people.
Consider how this world system is pictured in the Book of Revelation.

CHAPTER 4

The Kingdom of Man Pictured as a Great City

T HE FIRST ANALOGY THAT GOD'S WORD USES is that our world system is like a great city, a place where humans have developed a somewhat sophisticated system that is designed to provide for the needs of its citizens. This city is designed so that humans can pool their resources and create a lifestyle that allows them to find some measure of satisfaction and meaning apart from dependence upon God. The city described here has lots of glamour and glitter, but the real question is: What will happen to this great city?

In the previous chapter we sought to identify the city in Revelation 18 as part of this world system. It is a system that is built upon materialistic values and one that is created by man for his own enjoyment. God created humans to live in fellowship with Him, but as they turn away from God, they need to find some other alternative to fill their lives and provide some measure of satisfaction. Many people of this world have become intoxicated with the wine of Babylon, as suggested in Revelation 18:3:

> For all the nations have drunk of the wine of the wrath of her fornication, the kings of the earth have committed fornication with her, and the merchants of the earth have become rich through the abundance of her luxury.

From both the Bible and secular history, we learn that this world system started in ancient Babylon and, therefore, that is the name that appears in this passage. Note what is said in Isaiah 21:9; Jeremiah 51:6-9 and in Revelation 14:8. In each of these passages, we find a prediction of the fall of Babylon. In each passage, the entire world is included in the fall because the entire world has participated with the system that began in Babylon. As an example of what Scripture has to say, consider the words of Jeremiah 51:6-9:

> Flee from the midst of Babylon, And every one save his life! Do not be cut off in her iniquity, for this is the time of the LORD's vengeance; He shall recompense her. Babylon was a golden cup in the LORD's hand, That made all the earth drunk. The nations drank her wine; Therefore the nations are deranged. Babylon has suddenly fallen and been destroyed. Wail for her! Take balm for her pain; Perhaps she may be healed. We would have healed Babylon, But she is not healed. Forsake her, and let us go everyone to his own country; For her judgment reaches to heaven and is lifted up to the skies.

As we considered the judgment of this city in Revelation 18:21-23 we noted the destruction of man's system and with God's judgment nothing remains culturally, materially or economically:

> Then a mighty angel took up a stone like a great millstone and threw it into the sea, saying, Thus with violence the great city Babylon shall be thrown down, and shall not be found anymore. The sound of harpists, musicians, flutists, and trumpeters shall not be heard in you anymore. No craftsman of any craft shall be found in you anymore, and the sound of a millstone shall not be heard in you anymore. The light of a lamp shall not shine in you anymore, and the voice of bridegroom and bride shall not be heard in you anymore. For your merchants were the great men of the earth, for by your sorcery all the nations were deceived.

The music industry is included along with the commercial industry, when this system collapses. The normal celebrations such as weddings are impacted by this. Man's attempt to build a culture, a system that would provide some measure of satisfaction apart from God will be totally destroyed in the day of God's judgment.

When this great city falls, it is seen for what it truly was: the habitation of demonic spirits (Revelation 18:2). Satan is the god of this world (2 Corinthians 4:4) and he has inspired humans to build this city. In Revelation 18:3, we see the impact that this world system has had on all nations as they are seduced by the allurements of this world. Through this system, people have been enslaved by their own desires for what this world has to offer. This system is also steeped in idolatry, as humans try to find a connection with the supernatural by worshipping false gods.

To understand this world system as a city, we need to go back to the very beginning of the Bible. It is interesting to note that when Cain "went out from the presence of the Lord" in Genesis 4:16-22, the first thing he did was to build a city and develop a culture that would bring some measure of accomplishment and pleasure, as he lived apart from God:

> Then Cain went out from the presence of the LORD and dwelt in the land of Nod on the east of Eden. And Cain knew his wife, and she conceived and bore Enoch. And he built a city, and called the name of the city after the name of his son— Enoch. To Enoch was born Irad; and Irad begot Mehujael, and Mehujael begot Methushael, and Methushael begot Lamech. Then Lamech took for himself two wives: the name of one was Adah, and the name of the second was Zillah. And Adah bore Jabal. He was the father of those who dwell in tents and have livestock. His brother's name was Jubal. He was the father of all those who play the harp and flute. And as for Zillah, she also bore Tubal-Cain, an instructor of every craftsman in bronze and iron. And the sister of Tubal-Cain was Naamah.

This culture is described as including the development of commercial enterprises, music and the building of what might be called "the finer things of life." Cain and his descendants turned away from God and sought to develop a cultural system that would provide some measure of joy and satisfaction away from the "presence of the Lord." This is the spirit that we find in the world system of our present time. There is a desire to keep God out and ignore any thought of dependence upon Him. Man desires to build a society where he believes his needs will be met, and where he can enjoy life away from the "presence of the Lord."

After the destruction of the flood, described in Genesis 6-9, men gathered in Babel (Babylon) to build a tower. In Genesis 11:4, we read that they also built a city. God's purpose for humans to repopulate the earth was stated in Genesis 9:1, as God sent Noah and his family out with His blessing: "So God blessed Noah and his sons, and said to them: Be fruitful and multiply, and fill the earth." The words were "Be fruitful and multiply, and replenish the earth." The plan was to repopulate the earth after the destruction of all mankind. But they, again in rebellion, decided that they should gather together in the area of Babylon. Men built a city, and within that city, a tower that was intended to reach heaven.

Men attempted to gather together and create something that would connect them to heaven, having some concept and desire for contact with God, the supernatural, or the gods of their own creation. In doing so, humans wanted to make a name for themselves and create something for their own glory. They also wanted to avoid being "scattered abroad upon the face of the whole earth" (Genesis 11:4). Obviously this was in contrast to what God wanted for them, as clearly seen by God's response to this event.

God judged man's attempt at Babel by confusing their languages, and thus forcing them to separate from one another and scatter into various parts of the world. In Genesis 11:1, we are told that "the whole earth was of one language, and of one speech." As a result of man's rebellion against God, the people could not understand each other, causing them to scatter to various parts of the earth. This ultimately resulted in the development of different ethnic groups.

Man's concept has continued to focus on gathering together to pool resources and create a culture where they might find some fulfillment living apart from God. This is rebellion against God, since He created humans for fellowship and intended for them to find fulfillment and purpose through a relationship with Him.

The next reference to a city in Scripture is in Genesis 13, the city of Sodom, with its sister city of Gomorrah. When Abraham and Lot found that there was a need for them to separate, Abraham gave Lot the first choice of where he would choose to live. Lot chose the well-watered plain along the Jordan River and near the city of Sodom. Genesis 13:12-13 tells us that Lot pitched his tent toward, or facing to, the city of Sodom. We also are told that the men of Sodom were wicked and sinners before the Lord:

> Abraham dwelt in the land of Canaan, and Lot dwelt in the cities of the plain and pitched his tent even as far as Sodom. But the men of Sodom were exceedingly wicked and sinful against the LORD.   (Genesis 13:12-13)

In Genesis 14, we find that Lot and his family are evidently living in Sodom because when the city is under attack and the people are taken in captivity, Lot is among them. Abraham and his men go into battle against the forces that have taken the people of Sodom, and they successfully rescue Lot and the captives from Sodom. The interesting thing is that Lot and his family chose to return to Sodom. In Genesis 19:1, Lot is actually sitting in the gate of the city, which was the place where commercial and official business was conducted in ancient cities. The city was enticing for even a man like Lot (called a righteous man in 2 Peter 2:7-9), for he and his family returned to this place that is described as evil.

When God was determined to destroy this city because of its wickedness, He spared Lot and his family because of the intercession of Abraham. Lot could not convince his sons-in-law to leave the city, and even he and his immediate family had to be almost dragged away from this place. In fact, Lot's wife was compelled to look back on this city, even though she had been warned about the consequence. She could not let go, and was turned into a pillar of salt.

The impact of this city continued to have its hold on Lot and his daughters, as they left the area. At first they asked the Lord permission to go into another smaller city (Genesis 19:17-21). The city concept had become so much a part of them that they could not think of living without at least a small city. They ultimately ended up living in a cave, but the impact of the city was still felt in the hearts of the daughters.

Realizing that they lost their husbands, and that there was no hope for having children, they chose to do what they had undoubtedly learned living in the city of Sodom. They got their father drunk, and each had a son with their own father. These sons, Moab and Ammon, later would become a source of trouble for God's people, Israel.

In contrast to these men in Genesis who sought to build cities or live in them, we find that Abraham and the patriarchs were content to live in tents and trust God to supply their needs. They lived contented lives, finding satisfaction in following God's direction for their lives. In Hebrews 11:9-10, we discover that they had their eyes fixed upon a city – but it was not a city built by humans here on earth, rather it is said to be the City of God.

> By faith he dwelt in the land of promise as in a foreign country, dwelling in tents with Isaac and Jacob, the heirs with him of the same promise; for he waited for the city which has foundations, whose builder and maker is God.

This eternal city is described in Revelation 21 as it comes down from God out of heaven, and is joined to the earth. In this New Creation, we find that God's purpose is fulfilled as God and humans dwell together eternally. While man's city is to be destroyed, the eternal city of God will become a reality forever.

In Revelation 18:5-8, we hear what God has to say about this system that humans have built:

> For her sins have reached to heaven, and God has remembered her iniquities. Render to her just as she rendered to you, and repay her double according to her works; in the cup which she has mixed, mix double for her. In the measure that she glorified herself and lived luxuriously, in the same measure give her torment and sorrow; for she says in her heart, "I sit as queen, and am no widow, and will not see sorrow." Therefore her plagues will come in one day – death and mourning and famine. And she will be utterly burned with fire, for strong is the Lord God who judges her.

God is just and holy and cannot allow this evil system to escape His condemnation. The angel announces God's judgment on this city and this system. God has seen "her" sins and He remembers all of her iniquities. As a just God, He must deal with this evil system. Instead of glorifying God, this system has glorified man and his accomplishments. She has lived for the luxuries of life, trying to find fulfillment apart from God. She has elevated herself to the status of a queen and sought to avoid all that is unpleasant. Material values are at the heart of this system, and lives are evaluated by these materialistic standards. God will rain His plagues upon this city, and this world system will totally collapse under His mighty hand of judgment. Because God is just and holy, He cannot allow this evil system to escape condemnation.

The people who have lived by this system, and built their lives around what this world has to offer, will grieve greatly when the whole system is destroyed (Revelation 18:9-19). The rulers of this world have lived luxuriously, and have sold themselves in order to gain power, possessions and pleasure. They have been exalted by the system but, when it all collapses, they will suffer great loss.

The merchants in this passage are the people who have benefited greatly from this materialistic system. There are honest merchants in our world whose intention is not to exploit people for personal gain, but much of this system is built on the love of money as recorded in 1 Timothy 6:6-11. In that passage, we learn that "the love of money is the root of all kinds of evil." Humans are tempted by their desire for materialistic gain to do things that are not just, honest and certainly not fair. In this same passage, Paul urges his readers to find contentment in the basic things of life, and not allow their hearts to be drawn away by the pursuit of riches:

> Now godliness with contentment is great gain. For we brought nothing into this world, and it is certain we can carry nothing out. And having food and clothing, with these we shall be content. But those who desire to be rich fall into temptation and a snare, and into many foolish and harmful lusts which drown men in destruction and perdition. For the love of money is a root of all kinds of evil, for which some have strayed from the faith in their greediness, and pierced themselves through with many sorrows.

It is also significant to note in Revelation 18:11-19, that the listed items go beyond the basic necessities of life. The list of merchandise found in this city is that of earthly treasure: fancy apparel, rich furnishings, personal luxuries, fine foods, means of transportation and servants. God's Word encourages us to be content with what God has given us, but the merchants of this world try to convince us that we need far more than these basic necessities. The message is that joy comes in how many possessions we own. The merchants want us to believe that we cannot live without these worldly possessions. Many have sold themselves or neglected their families in order to have the finer things of life. In pursuit of the world's values, some have shut God out of their lives.

In verses 17-19, we read about those people who have made a good profit in transporting the goods that will be sold by the merchants. The one thing that seems to be most important in this world is the gross national product. Imports and exports are a vital part of the system. When this materialistic system fails, many will cry and lament. In 1929, when the stock market fell apart, many people committed suicide. Collapse of the economic system gave them no reason to live. Their lives were so wrapped up in profit and loss that they could not continue living.

Those who have embraced the system have often become ensnared in it, and have even become slaves to it. This is man's system, as he seeks to find meaning and joy in life apart from God. Like Cain in Genesis 4:16-17, who went out from the presence of the Lord, men have chosen to build a city and a system that would provide for their needs, so that they might live apart from dependence upon God.

This chapter (Revelation 18) ends with rejoicing in heaven as recorded in Revelation 18:20-24:

> Rejoice over her, O heaven, and you holy apostles and prophets, for God has avenged you on her! Then a mighty angel took up a stone like a great millstone and threw it into the sea, saying, Thus with violence the great city Babylon shall be thrown down, and shall not be found anymore. The sound of harpists, musicians, flutists, and trumpeters shall not be heard in you anymore. No craftsman of any craft

shall be found in you anymore, and the sound of a millstone shall not be heard in you anymore. The light of a lamp shall not shine in you anymore, and the voice of bridegroom and bride shall not be heard in you anymore. For your merchants were the great men of the earth, for by your sorcery all the nations were deceived. And in her was found the blood of prophets and saints, and of all who were slain on the earth.

This world system has been part of Satan's kingdom, and it is an enemy of God. It has seduced many people and turned their hearts away from God. It has provided many idols for humans to worship. It has opposed God and His people, and it has been responsible for much of the violence in our world.

In Revelation 19:1-6, we learn more about God's righteous judgment, as we are permitted to hear the celebration in heaven:

After these things I heard a loud voice of a great multitude in heaven, saying, Alleluia! Salvation and glory and honor and power belong to the Lord our God! For true and righteous are His judgments, because He has judged the great harlot who corrupted the earth with her fornication; and He has avenged on her the blood of His servants shed by her. Again they said, Alleluia! Her smoke rises up forever and ever! And the twenty-four elders and the four living creatures fell down and worshiped God who sat on the throne, saying, Amen! Alleluia! Then a voice came from the throne, saying, Praise our God, all you His servants and those who fear Him, both small and great! And I heard, as it were, the voice of a great multitude, as the sound of many waters and as the sound of mighty thunderings, saying, Alleluia! For the Lord God Omnipotent reigns!

This passage shows God's destruction of the system that has enslaved humans. The system itself is destroyed, as well as everything that is part of it. The world's music is gone (verse 22). The industry that produced the things that helped to entice humans is gone (verse 22). The bright lights and the festivities that brought a false sense of joy and pleasure are gone (verse 23).

Psalm 16:11 tells us God designed man to find his joy and fullness in fellowship with his Creator:

> You will show me the path of life; In Your presence is fullness of joy; At Your right hand are pleasures forevermore.

Man has tried to invent all kinds of alternatives so he can find some source of pleasure in this world. In reality, these alternatives are all hollow and empty. They are like soap bubbles that will soon be gone. Solomon wrote about the vanity of trying to find meaning and satisfaction in the things of this world system. Jesus spoke of this in the Parable of the Prodigal Son where this young man spent his entire inheritance seeking satisfaction and pleasure in this world, ending up hungry and empty, feeding pigs.

In Revelation 18:23-24, we see further reason why this system must be destroyed. It has brought greed and introduced all kinds of evil. Motivated by a love for pleasure and profit, many have built their lives based on this world system. The consequences of their love of material things led to evil behavior including many murders and thefts. God's people have suffered greatly from an attraction to the world system.

Before we leave this chapter, and what God says about this city, it is important that we note the challenge that is given to God's people in verse 4. It is a challenge that is found many times in Scripture:

> And I heard another voice from heaven saying, Come out of her, my people, lest you share in her sins, and lest you receive of her plagues.

God warns His people of the dangers of letting themselves get enamored with this system. Look at Jeremiah 50:8, 51:6-9, Isaiah 52:11, 2 Corinthians 6:17 and Romans 12:2 where God calls His people to live here on earth without getting caught up in the philosophy of the world and seeking fulfillment from materialistic things. Our sufficiency is in God, and the true riches are those that are eternal. Why would you want to invest in a system that you know is going to be destroyed?

We should not share in the sins of this system or we will share the consequence as Lot's wife did. Jesus cautioned His followers not to collect treasures on earth where moth and rust corrupt and thieves break in and steal. Investing in this world system will come to an end when we die or when the final collapse comes. Either way, those treasures will be lost. Christ encourages us to invest in eternity, building treasure in heaven, where our investments are not only safe, but will bring eternal dividends. This is the wisest financial counsel we can get.

There is another city recorded in Revelation 21 and it is called the City of God. That city is the eternal city that Abraham and the patriarchs sought as they lived as pilgrims here on earth (Hebrews 11:9, 10). That city is described for us in all of its glory in Revelation 21-22. Before that city can descend from God, out of heaven, this earthly city of man must be destroyed. This world system must be destroyed because it is used by Satan to entice people from the pursuit of God and the reality that is discovered in that relationship.

In Pilgrim's Progress John Bunyan pictured this concept as he wrote of the journey of a christian on his way to the Celestial City. On the way he comes to Vanity Fair where all of the glitter and glamor of this earthly city sought to entice him and deter him on his journey.

CHAPTER 5

Man's Kingdom Pictured as a Harlot Woman

In Revelation 17:18, we discover that the city of Babylon is also described as a harlot woman who seeks to entice the people of this world to find satisfaction in an illicit relationship that promises pleasure, possessions and power. In this passage, we are specifically told that the woman and the city are one and the same: "And the woman whom you saw is that great city which reigns over the kings of the earth." The world's materialistic system that offers human enjoyment, pleasure and some sense of satisfaction is like a prostitute that appeals to man's human desires. James 1:14 tells us that sinful humans have desires that respond to the enticement that the world sets before them. This temptation produces all kinds of sinful behavior. So man has been enticed by this harlot system to seek some measure of satisfaction and enjoyment in what man's system (the world) has to offer.

God created man in His own image in order that He might fellowship with humans in a loving relationship. His plan was that humans find their joy and satisfaction in this relationship with God. In Psalm 16:11, David expresses this, "In your presence is fullness of joy; at your right hand there are pleasures evermore." When sin entered the human race with Adam and Eve, this relationship was affected, and man and God were separated.

God's love for humans has not changed and His desire is to see that relationship restored. That cannot happen as long as sin is present. Therefore God's love motivated Him to send His Son into our world as a human, in order that Christ might go to the cross and fully pay the penalty of sin that separated us from God. Through the death and resurrection of Christ, sin has been put away and we can now be reconciled to God through faith in Christ. When we come to faith in Christ, we discover the joy of living in fellowship with God. As we grow in our relationship with God, the fullness of joy becomes more and more a reality.

Satan is still intent on interfering with that relationship, however, and he offers humans some alternatives of joy and pleasure, to draw them away from God. The world system, with all of its allurements, is one of the powerful ways that he seeks to draw people away from God. Scripture speaks of this approach as that of a harlot woman who offers pleasure and some measure of joy in what the world has developed in its system. The enticement of possessions, pleasure and power are designed to meet with the sinful desires of humans. They find response in the "lust of our eyes, in the desires of our flesh and in the pride of life," the desire for control. In idolatry and false worship, this harlot offers some measure of fulfillment and satisfaction for man's spiritual desire apart from a relationship with the true God.

In Revelation 18:3, we see the impact that this world system had on all nations, as they were seduced by the allurements of this world:

> For all the nations have drunk of the wine of the wrath of her fornication, the kings of the earth have committed fornication with her, and the merchants of the earth have become rich through the abundance of her luxury.

Through this system, people have been enslaved by their own desires for what this world has to offer. Jesus described people who turn from God, seeking satisfaction from some other love relationship, as fools. The Prodigal Son in Luke 15 demonstrates the emptiness that one finds when he departs from the father and seeks satisfaction in what the world has to offer.

Solomon also wrote about this in the first nine chapters of Proverbs. Before he recorded the proverbial truth of God's wisdom beginning in chapter 10, he challenged his readers to embrace God's truth as a man falls in love with his wife. In this section, God's wisdom is pictured as a pure and lovely lady who provides all that a man needs to bring fulfillment and satisfaction to his life. In the same section of the book, Solomon also pictures the world's wisdom as a prostitute called "Woman Folly." She seeks to entice men and draw them away from the wisdom of God's truth. The challenge is for men to resist the temptation of being enticed by the philosophy and way of the world. We are told that the path of human wisdom may at times seem right to us, but the path ends in death and it is to be avoided. Psalm 1 encourages us to resist the way of the world and man's wisdom, in order that we might focus and meditate on what God says in His Word. What God teaches us in His Word produces stability and true success in life.

It might be helpful to review what Solomon wrote as he summed up the final part of the first nine chapters of Proverbs. He presents the appeal of Lady Wisdom, who urges readers to choose God's way, and then he gives the message of Woman Folly, who seeks to entice people to choose the way of this world. This passage is so clear that it is helpful to review it again now.

Way of Wisdom
Wisdom has built her house,
She has hewn out her seven pillars;
She has slaughtered her meat,
She has mixed her wine,
She has also furnished her table.
She has sent out her maidens,
She cries out from the highest places of the city,
"Whoever is simple, let him turn in here!"
As for him who lacks understanding, she says to him,
"Come, eat of my bread
And drink of the wine I have mixed."
Forsake foolishness and live,
And go in the way of understanding.
He who corrects a scoffer gets shame for himself,
And he who rebukes a wicked man only harms himself.
Do not correct a scoffer, lest he hate you;
Rebuke a wise man, and he will love you.
Give instruction to a wise man, and he will be still wiser;

Teach a just man, and he will increase in learning.
The fear of the LORD is the beginning of wisdom,
And the knowledge of the Holy One is understanding.
For by me your days will be multiplied,
And years of life will be added to you.
If you are wise, you are wise for yourself,
And if you scoff, you will bear it alone.

(Proverbs 9:1-12)

The Way of Folly
A foolish woman is clamorous;
She is simple, and knows nothing.
For she sits at the door of her house,
On a seat by the highest places of the city,
To call to those who pass by,
Who go straight on their way:
"Whoever is simple, let him turn in here;"
And as for him who lacks understanding,
she says to him, "Stolen water is sweet,
And bread eaten in secret is pleasant."
But he does not know that the dead are there,
That her guests are in the depths of hell.

(Proverbs 9:13-18)

In Revelation 17, we see the way and wisdom of this world described as a prostitute who seeks to entice humans to find their satisfaction in what she has to offer, rather than finding satisfaction through a relationship with God. Throughout Scripture, God speaks of departure from His way as spiritual adultery. God made us for Himself, and He wants to be the love of our lives. The world seeks to draw us into an illicit relationship. Enticement may take a number of different forms. Some people are enticed by the desire for material wealth, some by the desire for political power, success or fame, and some by the pursuit of pleasure.

As we seek to understand what John is saying in the Book of Revelation, it is helpful to note the connection that we find between Revelation 17:1- 3 and Revelation 21:9-10. The wording in these two passages is so similar that we are intended to note the connection. Both passages

present two women and two cities. One of the seven angels introduced
John to these two women. The woman in Revelation 17:1-3 is this
harlot woman who seeks to entice people to find satisfaction with her.
The woman presented to us in Revelation 21:9-10 is the chaste bride of
Christ.

Revelation 17:1-3, 18 states:

> Then one of the seven angels who had the seven bowls came
> and talked with me, saying to me, Come, I will show you the
> judgment of the great harlot who sits on many waters, with
> whom the kings of the earth committed fornication, and the
> inhabitants of the earth were made drunk with the wine of
> her fornication. So he carried me away in the Spirit into the
> wilderness. And I saw a woman sitting on a scarlet beast
> which was full of names of blasphemy, having seven heads
> and ten horns. . . . And the woman whom you saw is that
> great city which reigns over the kings of the earth.

Revelation 21:9-10 says:

> Then one of the seven angels who had the seven bowls filled
> with the seven last plagues came to me and talked with me,
> saying, "Come, I will show you the bride, the Lamb's wife."
> And he carried me away in the Spirit to a great and high
> mountain, and showed me the great city, the holy Jerusalem,
> descending out of heaven from God.

In both references to a woman, Revelation 17:18 and Revelation 21:10,
the woman is identified with a city. One is the city of God, the New
Jerusalem, which will come down from heaven, and the other is Babylon, the city of this world. Before the Bride can be seen in all of her glory
and her purity, the seductress must be destroyed. Before God's Holy
City can be revealed, the world's city of Babylon must be destroyed.

In Revelation 17:1, the harlot is described as sitting upon many
waters. We do not have to guess the interpretation of this, because
in verse 15 we are told that these many waters are peoples, multitudes,
nations and tongues:

> Then he said to me, The waters which you saw, where the
> harlot sits, are peoples, multitudes, nations, and tongues.

This woman has had a great impact upon multitudes of people from all nations of this earth. Many have fallen in love with this world and with all of its allurements. This harlot has been enticing humans throughout all of the ages of human history. In His justice, God must deal with a system that has such an impact on so many lives.

The rulers of this earth have lusted after all that this harlot has to offer: possessions, power and pleasure (Revelation 17:2). Many kings and other rulers have sold themselves to the system and compromised moral principles, in order that they might gratify their own desires with this harlot woman. It is not just the rulers, for the common people of this world have also become intoxicated with the wine of her fornication. People have been intoxicated with the love of this world and all that it has to offer. They seek satisfaction and fulfillment in the things of this world, and in pleasure that is available to them.

We will examine the beast later, but we note here that verse 3 tells us that this harlot rides the beast. The seven-headed system that has ruled on this earth in a number of different forms has always been dominated by this harlot woman. Whatever form the political system has taken, the harlot has been in the saddle, with her enticements for the rulers of this world. So again, this is not one specific city or one period in history, but rather it is a system that has been a part of human history from the beginning of sin in the Garden of Eden.

As a harlot, she has arrayed herself in such a fashion to make her attractive, alluring and seductive. Like the harlot in the Book of Proverbs, she does all that she can to entice people to come under her spell. She is deceptive and successful in enticing people to find pleasure in what she, as the world's system, has to offer. Just as Satan tempts in attractive ways, this harlot entices us with her beauty and her seduction.

In verse 5, she is called "Babylon the Great, the mother of harlots and abominations of the earth." Both the city and the woman are identified with Babylon. This seductive system goes way back and has its roots in Babylon, the place where idolatry first flourished. The pantheon of gods, with all of its immorality, began in Babylon and has been adopted into every succeeding culture in this world. This harlot woman seeks to entice people to satisfy their religious desire in the worship of false gods. God declared that He is the only true and living God. He said that the worship of other gods was spiritual adultery and would come under His condemnation. In spite of God's warnings, this harlot has drawn many people away from God to worship other things.

In Revelation 17:6, we are reminded that this idolatrous system has long been the enemy of God and of His people (Genesis 3:15). Many of God's people have been persecuted and martyred by this harlot woman. She has wielded great power over the various rulers of this world, and she is opposed to God's people. Many have been martyred by the leaders of some religious system that is in opposition to the true and living God.

The Scripture makes it clear that we are to love the Lord God with all of our being, as stated by Jesus in Matthew 22:35-38:

> Then one of them, a lawyer, asked Him a question, testing Him, and saying, Teacher, which is the great commandment in the law? Jesus said to him, "You shall love the LORD your God with all your heart, with all your soul, and with all your mind. This is the first and great commandment."

This world system, represented by the harlot woman, seeks to entice men to fall in love with the gods and the pleasures that this system has to offer.

God will bring judgment upon this woman, as described in Revelation 17:16-18. This world system is both an idolatrous religious system pictured by the harlot, and a commercial system pictured in the great city. The third analogy that we will explore is the likeness of this system to a ravenous beast. This beast-like analogy is used to describe the nature and the actions of the world's great empires and the rulers that have oppressed God's people.

In the last form of that beast, we will find a confederation of rulers who turn against this harlot and destroy her. The Lord will use these evil rulers to destroy this idolatrous part of the system (Revelation 17:16-17), and then God Himself will judge and destroy this ravenous beast.

This entire system is headed for destruction, whether it is the economic and cultural side of the city, the idolatrous side of the harlot woman or the beastly side of oppressive world rulers. All will come to an end.

Man's Kingdom Pictured as a Beast

G OD WANTS US TO UNDERSTAND the true nature of this world system. It is indeed attractive, like a beautiful and glorious city with all of its sophistication, and all that it has to offer humans to fulfill their desire for possessions. It is also like a seductress, a harlot woman who offers some measure of pleasure and satisfaction, but who also makes humans captives to her lures. She entices humans to find joy and pleasure in things other than in God, the source of true joy and pleasure. She entices men to worship things and false gods rather than the true and living God. In addition, God's Word describes this system as a beast which seeks to devour humans and bring them to destruction. The ravenous nature of a beast is used to speak of the true nature of men who are hungry for power and exploit others as they rule over them.

God established human government after the flood, giving humans the authority to rule over nations so that evil might be restrained. God's judgment came upon the world in the great flood because of the unrestrained evil that had erupted in the human race (Genesis 6). When the flood ended, God told Noah that He was granting to mankind the authority to execute judgment upon those who did evil:

> Surely for your lifeblood I will demand a reckoning; from the hand of every beast I will require it, and from the hand of man. From the hand of every man's brother I will require the life of man. Whoever sheds man's blood, By man his blood shall be shed; For in the image of God He made man.
> (Genesis 9:5, 6)

The authority given to human government is more fully described in Romans 13:1-7. This passage explains that rulers are given their authority by God, and the principal reason for this authority is to restrain evil in the world. Human government is given authority from God, to make laws that will help to restrain evil. These laws define what activity will bring judgment upon those who are found guilty. The purpose is to bring about a system of justice, protecting those citizens against whom crimes have been committed.

While this authority is necessary to restrain evil and execute justice, there are human rulers who become hungry for power and go beyond the purpose established by God. These rulers, in reality, deal unjustly and even cruelly with their own people and neighboring nations. The hunger for power has resulted in human rulers who have been oppressive and who, like ravenous beasts, have caused much suffering to other humans. This is what John describes as he speaks of the beast in the Book of Revelation.

John begins his description of this beast in Revelation 13, as he sees it rise up out of the sea of humanity. It is a beast unlike anything that we have ever seen in nature, telling us that it is in reality truly hideous. This beast speaks of rulers who have sought to extend their normal national boundaries and build empires that bring other nations under their control. The Bible specifically deals with this beast-like system as it impacts the people of God, oppressing and persecuting them. There have been many oppressive rulers over the course of human history, but God speaks to His people specifically about those who will impact them.

The beast described in Revelation 13 has seven heads and ten horns. On each of these ten horns, there is a crown which indicates that this beast-like creature will seize power and rule over many, bringing them under his control. Note also that upon each of these seven heads, there is a "name of blasphemy." This tells us immediately that this beast is in opposition to God. This beast speaks against God and all that is holy and righteous. He will also oppress and persecute the people of God.

In Revelation 13:2, we discover that this beast has some likeness to a leopard, and feet like a bear and a mouth that is similar to a lion. It is important to note that this beast is a composite of several different ravenous animals, and each of these animals is capable of preying upon humans. The very term "beast" indicates that the creature presents a threat to anyone who gets in its path or seeks to tame it.

It is interesting to note that Daniel uses these same three beasts in his prophecy in Daniel 7. In that passage, he is told by God's messenger that three kingdoms would come to world- empire status and bring trouble to God's people, Israel. The three beasts in Daniel 7 are Babylon, Persia and Greece. As John sees them in Revelation 13, he is looking back and therefore he sees them in reverse order, Greece (leopard), Persia (bear) and Babylon (lion).

We discover the true beast-like nature of this system in Revelation 13:2, as we read that the dragon (Satan) gave him his power, his throne and great authority. This beast-like system ascends out of the bottomless pit, and it is destined to go into perdition. It is Satan's system, his kingdom on this earth. It is opposed to God, and all those who are part of God's kingdom. God's people are warned many times in Scripture of the danger of this world system. This world system, with its beast-like nature, is under the control of Satan and therefore is in opposition to God. In verse 4, we learn that Satan is worshipped in and through this system. Satan is the god of this world (2 Corinthians 4:4). The final stage of this beast eventually will be seen in the Antichrist, and the supernatural power of Satan will become more evident at that time.

The beast introduced in Revelation 13 is further identified in Revelation 17:8-18. We learn that this beast seems to be more dominant at specific times. The Scripture says that it "was and it is not but it will rise again" (verse 8). Even when this beast-like system is not as dominant, especially how it relates to God's people, be assured that it will rise up again. This beast-like system reminds us of a monster in Greek mythology named Hydra, which had nine heads. When one was cut off, two others appeared, unless the wound was cauterized. Hydra was finally slain by Hercules. The beast in Revelation is like Hydra. It has appeared in many forms over the years, and it has been subdued by God, and even thought to be defeated by God's people – only to rear its ugly head later in some other form.

We are first introduced to the conflict that takes place between the beast and God's people in Genesis 3:15. Satan approached Eve in the form of a beautiful serpent. The true nature of that reptile was not seen in its original form. That change came as a result of the serpent's part in the temptation. After the sin of Adam and Eve, God said that there would be enmity, hatred and hostility between Satan and the Seed of the woman. Conflict was predicted and God said that the Seed of the woman would crush the serpent's head and in the conflict, this Messiah would be wounded in his heel.

When God called Abraham, He promised to make of him a great nation, and from his descendants one would come who would bring blessing to all nations. Abraham was chosen to be the line from whom the Messiah would come. When God made this promise to Abraham, Satan's attack heightened on that family and nation. When God promised David that this Messianic King would come from his line, Satan again narrowed his attack on this line of descendants. There were attempts to corrupt and to destroy this line, hoping to thwart God's plan. This battle between Satan (and his forces), and God (with His people), increases in intensity throughout history.

Revelation 17:9 adds information that helps us understand and better identify this beast as a system that has long been used of Satan, in opposition to God and His people. We are told that there are seven heads on this beast, and the seven heads are seven mountains. Some biblical scholars have interpreted these mountains by linking them to the seven hills of Rome, but a closer look at the context and the total destruction of this beast indicates that it is more than just Rome or any other one city. It is more fitting that we see it as the world system under the control of Satan.

Mountains in Scripture speak of strong kingdoms (Isaiah 2:2; Jeremiah 51:25; Daniel 2:35; Zechariah 4:7). In Revelation 17:10, we see that seven kings or kingdoms are connected to these mountains. It appears that this aspect of the world system has to do with strong rulers who have dominated the system and have specifically been oppressive to God's people. Five of these kingdoms who fought against God's people are in the past, one is current as John writes, and one is yet to come in the future.

The description of the beast in Revelation 13:2 is the same as Daniel 7:3-6 (lion, bear, leopard). This helps us identify three of the kingdoms who persecuted God's people as Babylon, Persia and Greece. Daniel's vision only spoke of what was in the future for Israel after his time, and did not include two other empires used of Satan to harass God's people. Daniel's people were under Babylon when he wrote, and the time of captivity was about to end with the rise of Persia. God wanted His people to know, however, that their return to their land did not mean the end of trouble for Israel. Trouble would continue under the Persian Empire, Greek Empire, and then under Roman domination. Since Rome was dominating Israel when John wrote, Rome is the kingdom spoken of as being in the present.

A study of the Old Testament appears to suggest that Egypt and Assyria are the other two kingdoms to join Babylon, Persia and Greece, resulting in the five kingdoms that were in the past from John's perspective. When we add these two kingdoms to our understanding of this great beast it is significant to note that this beast began to appear as soon as the family of Jacob became the nation of Israel. This began in Egypt and the first oppression and persecution of God's people began there.

Certainly Egypt oppressed and enslaved the people of Israel under the rule of the pharaoh. This pharaoh did speak against God in Exodus 5:2,

> And Pharaoh said, "Who is the LORD, that I should obey His voice to let Israel go? I do not know the LORD, nor will I let Israel go."

Pharaoh would not respond, not even to God's miracles. His magicians were able to do some supernatural things, and so he refused to listen to the God of Israel. Not only did Pharaoh harden his heart against God, but he made an attempt to wipe out the seed line by ordering the death of all the newborn boys in Jewish families. We know of one, Moses, who was spared, but many other boys died under Pharaoh's edict. This attempt to destroy the seed line fits the pattern that we find in other places in Old Testament history.

As we compare the plagues that are predicted in the Book of Revelation, we find some similarity with those described in Egypt. I believe that the same beast-like system that appeared in Egypt in the days of Moses is the one that will rise again many times in the course of human history. It is Satan's system, and he will work through human leaders who have a hunger for power and a desire to build for themselves a great empire. God intervened and this beast-like regime was destroyed as Pharaoh and his army was drowned in the Red Sea.

While there were other nations in the Old Testament that opposed God and oppressed His people, the next great empire would be the Assyrian Empire. Assyria was the empire that took the ten tribes of Israel into captivity and also harassed the city of Jerusalem in the time of King Hezekiah. Sennacherib, the King of Assyria, not only put Jerusalem under siege, but he blasphemed the name of God in 2 Kings 19:9-13:

> And the king heard concerning Tirhakah king of Ethiopia, "Look, he has come out to make war with you." So he again sent messengers to Hezekiah, saying, "Thus you shall speak to Hezekiah king of Judah, saying: 'Do not let your God in whom you trust deceive you, saying, "Jerusalem shall not be given into the hand of the king of Assyria." Look! You have heard what the kings of Assyria have done to all lands by utterly destroying them; and shall you be delivered? Have the gods of the nations delivered those whom my fathers have destroyed, Gozan and Haran and Rezeph, and the people of Eden who were in Telassar? Where is the king of Hamath, the king of Arpad, and the king of the city of Sepharvaim, Hena, and Ivah?'"

As we add the Assyrian empire to this list, we are able to identify the five nations that are past as Egypt, Assyria, Babylon, Persia and Greece.

The beast-like Assyrian empire felt the hand of God in judgment as the angel of the Lord brought death to their camp, as recorded in 2 Kings 19:35:

> And it came to pass on a certain night that the angel of the LORD went out, and killed in the camp of the Assyrians one hundred and eighty-five thousand; and when people arose early in the morning, there were the corpses—all dead.

The passage goes on in 2 Kings 19:36-37 to tell us of the death of King Sennacherib:

> So Sennacherib king of Assyria departed and went away, returned home, and remained at Nineveh. Now it came to pass, as he was worshiping in the temple of Nisroch his god, that his sons Adrammelech and Sharezer struck him down with the sword; and they escaped into the land of Ararat. Then Esarhaddon his son reigned in his place.

The next empire to arise and have an impact on God's people was the kingdom of Babylon. Babylon was responsible for the destruction of Jerusalem and the Temple of God. The people of Judah were carried into exile by Babylon. Before God humbled Nebuchadnezzar, he required that people bow down and worship his great image under threat of death (Daniel 3). God intervened and spared the lives of Shadrach, Meshach and Abednego, overpowering the king's edict. During the reign of Belshazzar (Daniel 5), the holy vessels that were taken from the Temple of God were desecrated in a drunken party. God intervened again bringing this kingdom to an end in one night.

Under Persian rule, the people of Israel were allowed to return to the land of Israel, but there was still oppression and there were attempts to exterminate Israel. One of the Persian rulers, under the guidance of Haman, issued an edict calling for the death of all Jews, as recorded in the Book of Esther. If God had not intervened through Queen Esther, Satan would have been successful in destroying the line that would bring Christ into our world. This deliverance from God is still celebrated today in the Jewish feast of Purim. The pattern continued as another form of the beast arose and God intervened and brought an end to that empire.

The empire of Alexander the Great was next to emerge on the scene of human history, as Alexander brought God's people in Israel under the control of Greece. It was Alexander's plan to Hellenize the world by bringing all people under Greek culture, including speaking the Greek language. While God used some of this to later speed the spread of the Gospel, it caused great stress to those who were Hebrews living under God's law. This became more intense after the death of Alexander and the division of his empire. The empire of Alexander the Great was divided into four parts, with each part ruled by one of Alexander's generals. One of the kings in the dynasty of Seleucus was a man named Antiochus Epiphanes. He was the person who desecrated the temple by offering a sow on the altar in God's Temple, referred to as the "abomination of desolation." Again God had to deliver His people from Greek oppression under the leadership of the Maccabees. This victory is celebrated in the Jewish feast of Hanukkah.

The beast-like empire that was present when John wrote was certainly the Roman Empire, and we are familiar with its oppression of God's people. It was under Roman rule that King Herod made his attack on all the boys born in Bethlehem, two years old and under. He felt threatened by the birth of this new king and, undoubtedly inspired by Satan, sought to put Him to death. It was the Roman Governor Pilate who issued the sentence for the crucifixion of Jesus, and it was Rome that finally destroyed the city of Jerusalem and the temple, scattering the people of Israel all over the world. Later, Roman emperors like Nero persecuted Christians and were responsible for many who were martyred. God's people suffered under Roman rule. Each of these strong kingdoms was used by Satan to persecute the people of God. Each of these kingdoms also was linked with the harlot, and each was opposed to God's people.

The great statue in Daniel 2 described these same empires from man's viewpoint, picturing them as great empires and constructed of precious metals. However, as we look at this statue, we see a decline in the value of the metals described in that passage, with the value lessening from head to foot. The description begins with a head of gold, representing the kingdom of Babylon, and next are the chest and arms of silver, referring to the Medes and the Persians. The third empire, Greece, is represented by the belly and thighs of brass, and finally the legs of iron depict the Roman Empire. The two legs may symbolize the division between east and west that took place in the later days of the Roman Empire. This division has continued to the present day, as the nations of our present world are divided between east and west. As the description goes down to the feet and toes of the image, we discover that there is further decline in the value of the metals. The feet are described as being a mixture of iron and clay.

While there are no more Great Empires that will dominate the world until the final one under the Antichrist, there have been other rulers who have sought to rise to that status. In the west, we have seen Great Britain build an empire of which it was said, "The sun never set upon the British Empire." Colonies were ruled under Great Britain in all five of the continents on earth. Many of the nations that were under the British flag now have become independent nations. The French also sought empire status under the rule of Napoleon, and Spain, along with Portugal, had a great impact, particularly in South America. Germany sought to build an empire under the Kaiser and later under Adolf Hitler, whose reign brought about the Jewish Holocaust.

When you consider the history in the eastern world, you find rulers and nations who have oppressed people and sought to build empires. Russia created the Soviet Union and in it there was persecution of both Jews and Christians. Japan aggressively sought to extend the Emperor's rule, bringing other people under their control. China also has spread its kingdom, and along with the growth, has persecuted God's people. Christians were persecuted and Christianity was forced underground as Communism ruled. Muslim rule has spread throughout the Middles East into Africa, and also in other parts of Asia. It is yet to be seen how far that impact will be extended.

There is, however, one final phase of this world system yet to come.

The Antichrist will come out of that final phase. The Antichrist will be the strong leader who will oppose God and oppress His people. At the beginning of his reign, he is linked with ten other rulers who make up the ten horns on the beast. They will support the Antichrist and give power to him. There is a coalition of evil in this final phase. The great kingdoms of this world have always been opposed to God and His people. The system has appeared in many forms, but it is the same system. God will allow evil to come to its fullest form before God's judgment falls upon this beast-like system. The final form may be coming together now or in the near future. We know from Scripture that this beast certainly will raise its ugly head again.

CHAPTER 7

The Final Rise of the Beast in the Antichrist

THIS WORLD SYSTEM has, from the beginning, been in opposition to God and to His Son Jesus Christ. When Cain built the first city mentioned in Scripture (Genesis 4:16-17), his intention was to get away "from the presence of the Lord." He decided to live his life apart from God, and he began to build a city and a culture that would provide some sense of satisfaction, leaving God out of his life. God had offered him an opportunity to repent, but he chose to turn away from the Lord and begin a life of his own.

When we get to the Tower of Babel in Genesis 11, we find men are gathered together with a stated desire to build a name for themselves and to rebel against God's directive that they should spread out and replenish the earth after the flood. Genesis 11:4 records the following:

> And they said, "Come, let us build ourselves a city, and a tower whose top is in the heavens; let us make a name for ourselves, lest we be scattered abroad over the face of the whole earth."

We learn in this passage that, along with the famous tower, they also were building a city and developing a culture where they could have their desires met. The fact that their desire with the tower was to make some connection with the heavens tells us that there was some religious intent, but it was not focused on God. This becomes obvious when we consider God's judgment upon them. Their rebellion against God's directive was met with judgment as God caused them to speak different languages, so that they would be forced to scatter and populate the earth.

With the different languages, we also see the development of different ethnic groups.

Psalm 2 speaks about the leaders of this world system, and their attitude toward God and His sovereign rule over them. In verses 1-3 we read the following:

> Why do the nations rage
> And the people plot a vain thing?
> The kings of the earth set themselves,
> And the rulers take counsel together,
> Against the LORD and against His Anointed, saying.
> "Let us break their bonds in pieces
> And cast away their cords from us."

The rulers of this world seek to go their own way, and they desire to be free from all restraint that God might put upon them. They are against God and against His anointed Messiah, Jesus Christ.

God's response to human rebellion is seen in the following verses in this Psalm.

> He who sits in the heavens shall laugh;
> The Lord shall hold them in derision.
> Then He shall speak to them in His wrath,
> And distress them in His deep displeasure:
> "Yet I have set My King
> An My holy hill of Zion."

God laughs, not because man's rebellion is not serious, but because of man's puny attempt to overthrow and thwart the plan of Almighty God. He will judge those who rebel against Him and He will establish His King upon His holy hill of Zion. Humans cannot thwart the eternal plan of God, yet they still rebel and make their attempt.

In Psalm 2:7-9, we hear God setting forth His plan:

> I will declare the decree:
> The LORD has said to Me,
> "You are My Son,
> Today I have begotten You.
> Ask of Me, and I will give You
> The nations for Your inheritance,

> And the ends of the earth for Your possession.
> You shall break them with a rod of iron;
> You shall dash them to pieces like a potter's vessel."

God will carry out His plan, and His Son Jesus Christ will rule and reign over the earth in God's Kingdom. Humans may be in opposition, but they cannot overthrow the plan of God.

In the last three verses of this Psalm, we find good advice given to all who would stand in opposition to God. In these verses we read,

> Now therefore, be wise, O kings;
> Be instructed, you judges of the earth.
> Serve the LORD with fear,
> And rejoice with trembling.
> Kiss the Son, lest He be angry,
> And you perish in the way,
> When His wrath is kindled but a little.
> Blessed are all those who put their trust in Him.

Any opposition to God is futile in the long run, for God will prevail and those who rebel will be judged. The wise person is one who submits to God and to His Son, Jesus Christ. The Son will surely reign, and a person is wise if they bow their knee to Him, lest they suffer the King's wrath in the future.

God told Satan that he would have conflict with his own forces, but ultimately the Lord would prevail and crush the head of the serpent (Genesis 3:15). In spite of this predicted outcome, Satan is determined to war against God, and specifically against God's Son, Jesus Christ. In this battle, he will enlist human leaders to stand in opposition to God and to Jesus Christ. This world system is described as a beast in Revelation 13:2-4, and there we learn that Satan empowers the human rulers that are part of this beast-like system. In that passage we also discover what motivates Satan:

> Now the beast which I saw was like a leopard, his feet were like the feet of a bear, and his mouth like the mouth of a lion. The dragon gave him his power, his throne, and great authority. And I saw one of his heads as if it had been mortally wounded, and his deadly wound was healed. And all

> the world marveled and followed the beast. So they wor-
> shiped the dragon who gave authority to the beast; and they
> worshiped the beast, saying, "Who is like the beast? Who is
> able to make war with him?"

Satan's rebellion against God began with a desire to be like God and to
be worshipped. Through the beast, Satan is able to achieve that goal
(at least for a time), as people will worship him and the system that he
has created.

The origin of this beast-like world system also is made clear as we
read the words of Revelation 17:8:

> The beast that you saw was, and is not, and will ascend out
> of the bottomless pit and go to perdition. And those who
> dwell on the earth will marvel, whose names are not written
> in the Book of Life from the foundation of the world, when
> they see the beast that was, and is not, and yet is.

Here we are told that this beast ascends out of the bottomless pit, as it
is a part of Satan's kingdom. The end result of this beast is said to be
destined to go to perdition. God's judgment will surely come upon this
wicked system.

God's judgment has fallen upon this beast-like system in the past.
This can be seen as we consider what happened to the first six heads of
this beast. God brought judgment upon Egypt because of their dealings
with the people of Israel. The ten plagues brought devastation to the
land, and to the people of Egypt while God miraculously spared His
people from most of these plagues. The death of the first-born children in Egypt finally brought deliverance for Israel's people, although
Pharaoh and his army still pursued them. God brought final deliverance and a fatal blow to this beast when they were destroyed in the Red
Sea.

God brought judgment upon Assyria and their ruler when the death
angel went through their camp, and when the king was slain by his own
sons as recorded in 2 Kings 19:35-37. A similar fate came upon Babylon
in the reign of Belshazzar when the kingdom fell to the Medes and the
Persians in one night, recorded in Daniel 5. God then used Greece

and Alexander the Great to bring judgment on the Persian Empire. In turn, the Greek Empire also was conquered by the Romans. God later brought judgment on the Roman Empire because of their oppression of His people. Each of these heads were defeated and ceased to exercise power, but this beast would rise again.

The final phase of this system is yet to come, as is recorded for us in Revelation 17:10:

> There are also seven kings. Five have fallen, one is, and the other has not yet come. And when he comes, he must continue a short time.

This final head will be dominated by the one who is called in Scripture the "Antichrist" or the man of sin. We want to look more in depth at this final head of this beast yet to come. It is encouraging for us to note in this verse that his reign will be for just a short period of time.

Jesus spoke of the fact that this man's rule will be shortened by God's mercy, because of the intensity and the nature of his reign. In Matthew 24:15-22, we read about the intense wickedness that will prevail, and of the shortness of the time by God's mercy. Consider these words:

> "Therefore when you see the 'abomination of desolation,' spoken of by Daniel the prophet, standing in the holy place" (whoever reads, let him understand), "then let those who are in Judea flee to the mountains. Let him who is on the housetop not go down to take anything out of his house. And let him who is in the field not go back to get his clothes. But woe to those who are pregnant and to those who are nursing babies in those days! And pray that your flight may not be in winter or on the Sabbath. For then there will be great tribulation, such as has not been since the beginning of the world until this time, no, nor ever shall be. And unless those days were shortened, no flesh would be saved; but for the elect's sake those days will be shortened."

The words of Jesus send us back to the prophecy of Daniel, and what is recorded in Daniel 9. As the people of Israel were about to return home after their exile in Babylon, God wanted them to know that their time of trouble was not yet over. Their exile would be over in the 70 years promised by Jeremiah, but the period in which God would continue to judge them under Gentile rule would continue for a period of time described as 70 times seven. God did, however, promise an end, and a fulfillment of His promises to the patriarchs and the establishment of a kingdom:

> Seventy weeks are determined
> For your people and for your holy city,
> To finish the transgression,
> To make an end of sins,
> To make reconciliation for iniquity,
> To bring in everlasting righteousness,
> To seal up vision and prophecy,
> And to anoint the Most Holy.
>
> (Daniel 9:24)

God will fulfill His promises and bring His plan to completion, but there would be an extended period of time in which Israel would still suffer under Gentile domination.

This prophecy goes on to speak of the rebuilding of Jerusalem after the return from Babylon, and it gives a timetable leading up to the coming of Messiah. Jesus referred to this as He wept over Jerusalem, because they did not know when He was to appear (Luke 19:41-44). It goes on to speak of the death of the Messiah, and the fact that His death was not for himself, but for the sake of others. It also spoke of the destruction of the Temple and of the city of Jerusalem. This was fulfilled in 70 A.D. by the Roman Empire under Titus.

Daniel also was told of a prince who would rule over Israel, and would be related to those who destroyed the city and the temple. This statement has led many Bible students to think that this prince would be from what was formerly the Roman Empire. Another possible interpretation of this statement may simply be that he is part of this same seven-headed beast. The final ruler who is yet to come is connected to those who have opposed God in the past. He will be part of this beast-like world system.

Daniel 9:27 records details about this prince (and Jesus refers to this passage in Matthew 24):

> Then he shall confirm a covenant with many for one week; but in the middle of the week He shall bring an end to sacrifice and offering. And on the wing of abominations shall be one who makes desolate, even until the consummation, which is determined, is poured out on the desolate.

There are several items to note in this passage. What we first learn is that this prince (ruler) will make a covenant with Israel for seven years (referred to as one week in Daniel). We are not told the specifics of this covenant, but the purpose possibly could be to resolve the Middle East conflict. It also may give Israel permission to build a new temple. As we shall see, this man is a deceiver, yet Israel may be willing to accept this treaty as a way to restore and rebuild their temple.

The verse goes on to tell us that he will break his covenant in the middle of those seven years. This divides this period into two segments of three and one-half years each. We will find that this period corresponds with what the Bible says about the period of time called the Tribulation, with a prince who is called the "Antichrist" in the New Testament. The Antichrist breaks his covenant by causing sacrifices to cease, which seems to confirm that the Temple in Jerusalem will be rebuilt, possibly as a result of this treaty. Jesus spoke of this as "the abomination of desolation" and said that this would signal the final three and one-half years, which He refers to as the Great Tribulation.

Antiochus Epiphanes (175-163 B.C.) desecrated the Temple under Greek rule when he offered a sow on the altar, thus making the Temple unholy and in need of cleansing after his defeat. So this final ruler will do something in the Temple that will desecrate it in such a way that the Lord calls it an abomination. In 2 Thessalonians 2:4, we find information that certainly would fulfill this prophecy of Daniel. The passage says the final ruler is called "that man of sin, the son of perdition." Take note of what Paul says he will do:

> who opposes and exalts himself above all that is called God or that is worshiped, so that he sits as God in the temple of God, showing himself that he is God.

The Apostle John in Revelation 12:11-15 adds to what Paul said about the False Prophet:

> Then I saw another beast coming up out of the earth, and he had two horns like a lamb and spoke like a dragon. And he exercises all the authority of the first beast in his presence, and causes the earth and those who dwell in it to worship the first beast, whose deadly wound was healed. He performs great signs, so that he even makes fire come down from heaven on the earth in the sight of men. And he deceives those who dwell on the earth by those signs which he was granted to do in the sight of the beast, telling those who dwell on the earth to make an image to the beast who was wounded by the sword and lived. He was granted power to give breath to the image of the beast, that the image of the beast should both speak and cause as many as would not worship the image of the beast to be killed.

In this passage, it appears that this second beast (later identified as the False Prophet) is promoting the ruler, who is also called the Antichrist. The focus of this passage is worship. Satan empowered this False Prophet with the ability to perform miracles, and these miracles cause an image of the beast to be able to speak, and to demand worship of all people. Satan has this desire for worship, and his design here is that man be worshipped. If this image is set up in the Temple for people to worship, this would be an abomination that would desecrate that sanctuary. Note also that those who will not worship this image are put to death.

When we go back to what Jesus said in Matthew 24:15-22, we can understand why He told His followers that such an abominable act would trigger the awful days of what is called the Great Tribulation. People should flee because persecution of God's people will become so intense when worship of this image is required under threat of death. It also is the reason why God, in mercy, will shorten the time period in which this man of sin will rule to just three and one-half years.

We turn next to Revelation 12, where we find another location where Scripture helps us put this all together. In that chapter, we read about the conflict between Satan and the seed of the woman that was predicted in Genesis 3:15. This woman is a symbolic picture of the people of Israel, with the twelve stars representing the twelve tribes. God promised Abraham and the patriarchs that the Messiah would come into the world from the line of Israel, and we find this in the genealogy of Jesus Christ, listed in Matthew 1 and Luke 3. In Revelation 12:1-4, we see Satan in combat with the woman and with her seed:

> Now a great sign appeared in heaven: a woman clothed with the sun, with the moon under her feet, and on her head a garland of twelve stars. Then being with child, she cried out in labor and in pain to give birth. And another sign appeared in heaven: behold, a great, fiery red dragon having seven heads and ten horns, and seven diadems on his heads. His tail drew a third of the stars of heaven and threw them to the earth. And the dragon stood before the woman who was ready to give birth, to devour her Child as soon as it was born.

The dragon is clearly identified for us in verse 9 of chapter 12:

> So the great dragon was cast out, that serpent of old, called the Devil and Satan, who deceives the whole world; he was cast to the earth, and his angels were cast out with him.

In this passage we also see this seven-headed beast connected to the dragon, for it is Satan's system, and he controls these rulers who attack Jesus Christ and persecute God's people. It was Satan who motivated King Herod to attempt to put Jesus to death shortly after he was born.

The baby that is born to this woman (Israel) is identified in Revelation 12:5 as the one "who would rule all nations with a rod of iron," speaking of Jesus Christ, the Messiah. Satan sought to kill Jesus as a baby, as prompted by King Herod, and also as the people of Nazareth tried to cast Him over a cliff. Satan also tried to corrupt Him, tempting Him by offering to give Him rule over this world system if He would bow down and worship him (Matthew 4:8-9). Finally Satan caused Christ's heel to be bruised in the conflict on the cross. Christ, however, prevailed in that conflict, crushing the head of the serpent. His triumph is seen in His resurrection from the dead and His ascension into heaven, where He sits upon the throne.

Even though Satan has been defeated, he continues to do all that he can in opposition to Christ by attacking the woman who gave birth to this man-child (Revelation 12:6):

> Then the woman fled into the wilderness, where she has a place prepared by God, that they should feed her there one thousand two hundred and sixty days.

Note in this verse that Satan's attack on Israel will last for 1260 days, which is another way of saying three and one-half years. When Satan can no longer touch Christ as He sits upon the throne, he will turn his attention to the people of Israel – to whom God is committed in His covenant with the patriarchs.

This attack is what Scripture calls "the Great Tribulation," and it will bring intense suffering as Satan persecutes the people of Israel, knowing that his time is limited according to Revelation 12:12. Satan has been defeated by the angel Michael and God's heavenly army, according to verses 7-12 in this chapter. He is totally expelled from heaven, and his area of operation is limited to the earth only. Verse 12 tells of great celebration in heaven, but it also warns that those who dwell on earth will experience intensity in Satan's attack:

> Therefore rejoice, O heavens, and you who dwell in them! Woe to the inhabitants of the earth and the sea! For the devil has come down to you, having great wrath, because he knows that he has a short time.

In the remaining verses of Revelation 12, we read about the increase of persecution that is aimed at this woman (Israel), and we also read of God's protection of her in miraculous ways. The power of God was seen in Egypt when God protected His people from the attacks of that phase of the beast. God will again protect the people of Israel in the time of this tribulation when they are under attack by the last phase of the same beast. Revelation 12:13-17 describes this for us:

> Now when the dragon saw that he had been cast to the earth,

he persecuted the woman who gave birth to the male Child. But the woman was given two wings of a great eagle, that she might fly into the wilderness to her place, where she is nourished for a time and times and half a time, from the presence of the serpent. So the serpent spewed water out of his mouth like a flood after the woman, that he might cause her to be carried away by the flood. But the earth helped the woman, and the earth opened its mouth and swallowed up the flood which the dragon had spewed out of his mouth. And the dragon was enraged with the woman, and he went to make war with the rest of her offspring, who keep the commandments of God and have the testimony of Jesus Christ.

Not only does God miraculously protect His people when they are under attack from the beast and Satan, but Revelation 7:1-8 tells us that before Satan is permitted to begin his attack, God puts a seal on 144,000 people in Israel so that Satan will not be able to kill them even when the persecution becomes intense. Consider what God's Word says about this:

After these things I saw four angels standing at the four corners of the earth, holding the four winds of the earth, that the wind should not blow on the earth, on the sea, or on any tree. Then I saw another angel ascending from the east, having the seal of the living God. And he cried with a loud voice to the four angels to whom it was granted to harm the earth and the sea, saying, "Do not harm the earth, the sea, or the trees till we have sealed the servants of our God on their foreheads." And I heard the number of those who were sealed. One hundred and forty-four thousand of all the tribes of the children of Israel were sealed:

of the tribe of Judah twelve thousand were sealed;
of the tribe of Reuben twelve thousand were sealed;
of the tribe of Gad twelve thousand were sealed;
of the tribe of Asher twelve thousand were sealed;
of the tribe of Naphtali twelve thousand were sealed;
of the tribe of Manasseh twelve thousand were sealed;
of the tribe of Simeon twelve thousand were sealed;
of the tribe of Levi twelve thousand were sealed;
of the tribe of Issachar twelve thousand were sealed;

of the tribe of Zebulun twelve thousand were sealed;
of the tribe of Joseph twelve thousand were sealed;
of the tribe of Benjamin twelve thousand were sealed.

While Satan is the power behind this attack on God's people, it is the Antichrist (as ruler of this final phase of this beast) who carries out this attack. Revelation 13:5-8 describes his attack and his blasphemy against God. In this passage, we again discover his desire for the people of this world to worship him. When God's people refuse to give him that worship, he makes war against them:

> So they worshiped the dragon who gave authority to the beast; and they worshiped the beast, saying, "Who is like the beast? Who is able to make war with him?" And he was given a mouth speaking great things and blasphemies, and he was given authority to continue for forty-two months. Then he opened his mouth in blasphemy against God, to blaspheme His name, His tabernacle, and those who dwell in heaven. It was granted to him to make war with the saints and to overcome them. And authority was given him over every tribe, tongue, and nation. All who dwell on the earth will worship him, whose names have not been written in the Book of Life of the Lamb slain from the foundation of the world.

This Antichrist becomes the personification of this beast-like system, as God permits the evil of man to come to fullness before He brings judgment upon this world system. While there were other heads of this beast who sought the worship of other humans, this aspect comes to fullness under this final head. With the Antichrist, there will be ten kings, the ten horns on the beast, but they will support the Antichrist and give power to him. Revelation 17:12-13 says,

> The ten horns which you saw are ten kings who have received no kingdom as yet, but they receive authority for one hour as kings with the beast. These are of one mind, and they will give their power and authority to the beast.

All human governmental power appears to be consolidated in this one head under the rule of the Antichrist.

The harlot woman is the one who seeks to entice humans to find pleasure and satisfaction, so that humans focus their love and worship on the things of this world. As a part of this world system, she seems to represent the religions of this world as alternatives to the worship of the one True and Living God. The religions of this world all provide some means by which humans can appease their god and find some acceptance by what they do, in all of their religious activity. Like Cain, they seek to offer their best, but as sinners they have nothing to offer a Holy God. Jesus Christ offered Himself as our sin-bearer, and we find our acceptance before God in the finished work of Christ.

In Revelation 17:16-17, this harlot woman (who has offered religious systems to the people of this world) is now destroyed by those who join with the Antichrist to bring all worship under one image, the worship of the beast. In this passage, the harlot is destroyed and all other forms of worship are brought under this one directive to worship the beast and the dragon, Satan, who is behind this beast:

> And the ten horns which you saw on the beast, these will hate the harlot, make her desolate and naked, eat her flesh and burn her with fire. For God has put it into their hearts to fulfill His purpose, to be of one mind, and to give their kingdom to the beast, until the words of God are fulfilled.

God also will use the Antichrist, and the rulers with him, to destroy the harlot who represents all the false gods of this world. The Antichrist will cause the world to turn from all others gods to worship him, under the teaching of the False Prophet and the miracle-working power of Satan.

As we study what the Bible says about this world system under Satan's control, we see this concept of consolidation in each area so that all human power is brought under one head. This beast, with his group of other rulers, brings unification to government control. As we previously saw, the harlot aspect of the world system also is swallowed up by the beast. In Revelation 13:16-17, we learn that this final ruler will exercise control over the commerce of the world. We have seen in Revelation 18 how this materialistic system finally will collapse, but before it does, it comes under the control of the beast. We see this control described in Revelation 13:16-17:

> He causes all, both small and great, rich and poor, free and slave, to receive a mark on their right hand or on their foreheads, and that no one may buy or sell except one who has the mark or the name of the beast, or the number of his name.

All trade, buying and selling are under the control of this ruling system and no one can be involved without his mark, under his authority.

The dream of mankind, as expressed in Genesis 11 at the tower of Babel, is to see a unified system where humans and their accomplishments are exalted. This unified system will become a reality under the rule of the Antichrist. Governmental control will be unified under this final head of the beast, and with it all worship and religious activity will be focused on the image of the beast. Satan is the power behind this world system, and man will blaspheme the name of God and rebel against God's authority. Those who do not bow to this beast-like system will be killed unless miraculously protected by God.

In Revelation 16 we see the angels of God pouring out vials of wrath upon this earth, and especially on this beast-like system. Note in verse 2 that God's wrath is poured upon those who "had the mark of the beast on them and who worshipped his image." In verse 10, God's wrath is directed upon the "throne of the beast and his kingdom." In these passages, we see the rebellion of man as "They blasphemed the God of heaven because of their pains and their sores, and did not repent of their deeds." A similar statement is found at the end of verse 9 where we read,

> And men were scorched with great heat, and they blasphemed the name of God who has power over these plagues; and they did not repent and give Him glory.

Even though rebellious humans know that these plagues come from God, and that He has power over them, the people refuse to submit to His authority. Instead, they blaspheme His name and do not repent and give God the glory that belongs to Him. As Psalm 2 made clear, there is nothing more that God can do when men have rebelled against Him and His Son, Jesus Christ. When they spurn God's love and grace, there is nothing more to do but allow them to experience His wrath and His judgment. This is seen as we look at Revelation 19, where the return of Christ to earth is recorded for us. Christ comes as the conquering king to establish the Kingdom of God upon the earth.

When Christ returns to earth to sit upon the throne and rule with God's authority, He comes in power and in great glory. Consider the words of Scripture as they describe this event in Revelation 19:11-16:

> Now I saw heaven opened, and behold, a white horse. And He who sat on him was called Faithful and True, and in righteousness He judges and makes war. His eyes were like a flame of fire, and on His head were many crowns. He had a name written that no one knew except Himself. He was clothed with a robe dipped in blood, and His name is called The Word of God. And the armies in heaven, clothed in fine linen, white and clean, followed Him on white horses. Now out of His mouth goes a sharp sword, that with it He should strike the nations. And He Himself will rule them with a rod of iron. He Himself treads the winepress of the fierceness and wrath of Almighty God. And He has on His robe and on His thigh a name written: KING OF KINGS AND LORD OF LORDS.

As the Lord returns in all of His glory, we might think that the men of earth would bow to Him, but this is not the case. Here again we see the true nature of the heart of man and why Jesus said in John 3, "except a man be born again he cannot enter into the Kingdom of God." Note the reaction to the rulers of earth and their followers as recorded in Revelation 19:19:

> And I saw the beast, the kings of the earth, and their armies, gathered together to make war against Him who sat on the horse and against His army.

The end comes as the beast and the false prophet are cast into the Lake of Fire, and those who followed them are slain by the sword out of the mouth of Christ.

Unbelieving humans refuse to acknowledge the Lordship of Jesus Christ, and openly rebel against God's Kingdom. This is further seen in what is described in Revelation 20. In that chapter, Jesus Christ is seen establishing God's Kingdom on earth, and ruling over it for one thousand years. This kingdom is described in both Old and New Testament as one of righteousness and justice. It also is a time of peace and prosperity, and a time of extended life span for those who live in that time. All creation is restored under the control of Christ, so that:

> The wolf also shall dwell with the lamb, The leopard shall lie down with the young goat, The calf and the young lion and the fatling together; And a little child shall lead them.
>
> (Isaiah 11:6)

During that period of time, Satan is bound in the bottomless pit so that he cannot interfere with the reign of Christ, and cannot seduce men to follow him in rebellion.

By His nature, God is a loving and gracious being, but He will not force men to love Him or follow His ways. God created humans with the ability to choose, so that they might worship and love Him because that is their desire. However, giving humans a choice opens the door to the possibility that they might choose not to respond to God, choosing their own way instead. This is what happened in the Garden of Eden, and this is what happens again and again in this world. In Revelation 20:7-9, we discover that God will again give humans the opportunity to make their own choice. Having lived for 1,000 years under the righteous and peaceful reign of Christ, we might think that all people will choose for this reign to continue forever, but such is not the case.

In this passage are the following solemn words: Now when the thousand years have expired, Satan will be released from his prison and will go out to deceive the nations which are in the four corners of the earth, Gog and Magog, to gather them together to battle, whose number is as the sand of the sea. They went up on the breadth of the earth and surrounded the camp of the saints and the beloved city. And fire came down from God out of heaven and devoured them. When given an alternative, humans reject God's Kingdom and the rule of His Son.

It is interesting to me that many people speak of heaven and indicate that they would like to enter God's Kingdom, but they often define heaven in accordance with their own desires. The truth is that this passage tells us that humans will be given the opportunity to live in this perfect kingdom where righteousness and peace reign. In spite of what they have experienced of what we might call "a little taste of heaven right here on earth," many will still reject God's rule and rebel with Satan against the Lordship of Jesus Christ. As it was when He was on earth, many will still refuse to submit to Him as their king.

The only alternative that remains when men reject God's rule is that they be forever separated from God in the Lake of Fire. God has done all He can in providing salvation and the gift of eternal life in His Son Jesus Christ. If people reject God's grace and mercy, there is no alternative but to be separated forever from God in eternal darkness. As Cain chose to go away from the presence of the Lord, so many others will make that same choice eternally, by rejecting what Christ has done for them on Calvary. God was willing to give His Son as a sacrifice for human sin, but those who refuse to accept that gift by faith in Christ are essentially choosing to live apart from God forever.

This final separation of rebellious humans from God is recorded for us in Revelation 20:11-15, when God calls them into account for what they have done at what is called the Great White Throne Judgment. Man's works are examined and then his response to the salvation provided in God's Son is considered. In this passage we read:

> Then I saw a great white throne and Him who sat on it, from whose face the earth and the heaven fled away. And there was found no place for them. And I saw the dead, small and great, standing before God, and books were opened. And another book was opened, which is the Book of Life. And the dead were judged according to their works, by the things which were written in the books. The sea gave up the dead who were in it, and Death and Hades delivered up the dead who were in them. And they were judged, each one according to his works. Then Death and Hades were cast into the lake of fire. This is the second death. And anyone not found

written in the Book of Life was cast into the lake of fire.

When men stand before the Holy God, the books containing their works are opened. Here again it is proven in the record that "all have sinned and come short of the glory of God." In Romans 6:23, God's Word reminds of the penalty of sin when we read, "The wages of sin is death." It is not a matter of whether one's good works outweigh their bad, the only question is, "Have you sinned?" After guilt is established from the record books, the Book of Life is opened to see if that person's name is recorded in that book.

The Book of Life is the record of all those who have acknowledged their sin and rested their faith in Jesus Christ, who made a sacrifice for them on the cross. While all have sinned, Christ died to fully pay the penalty of all their sin. This makes the real issue to be, "What have you done in response to the gift of eternal life that God offers to you in His Son?" God is willing to accept you and forgive you for all of your sin, if you will come to Christ and put your faith and trust in Him, and in what He has done for you. If you spurn His love, grace and the gift that He offers, there is nothing more that God can do. The ultimate end of those who reject God's grace in His Son is eternal separation in the Lake of Fire.

CHAPTER 8

The Kingdom of God and His Christ

THE BOOK OF REVELATION must be seen as the fulfillment of God's eternal purpose as it was stated in His creative acts. God's plan for man is described in Genesis 1:26:

> Then God said, "Let Us make man in Our image, according to Our likeness; let them have dominion over the fish of the sea, over the birds of the air, and over the cattle, over all the earth and over every creeping thing that creeps on the earth."

God did as He planned, creating humans in His own image, and giving them dominion over all of God's earthly creation. All of God's created beings on earth were put under Adam's control, and he was also directed to tend the Garden of Eden.

When Adam rebelled against God and was no longer in harmony with the One in whose image he was made, he hid from God – realizing that sin had separated him from his creator. As a result of this sin, God cursed the creation over which Adam was to have dominion, thus limiting man's ability to exercise dominion over this natural world. God cursed the ground because of human sin. He caused thorns and thistles to grow so that man would have to labor by the sweat of his brow in order to make a living, because this earth would not submit to his authority without a struggle. Humans have rebelled against the authority of God, and now the earth, which man was to rule, would be in rebellion against him.

The flood, in the days of Noah, came upon the earth because humans continued to rebel against God, and this rebellion became even more intense. Genesis 6:5 says:

> Then the LORD saw that the wickedness of man was great in
> the earth, and that every intent of the thoughts of his heart
> was only evil continually.

After the flood, God established human government to put some
restraint on evil, but humans have continued to fall short of bringing
about a rule of righteousness and peace. Various forms of government
have been implemented during the history of man, but all have fallen
short of establishing a rule of righteousness and peace.

Romans 13:1-7 speaks of this God-given authority and the responsibility of rulers to restrain evil by bringing the guilty to justice:

> Let every soul be subject to the governing authorities. For
> there is no authority except from God, and the authorities
> that exist are appointed by God. Therefore whoever resists
> the authority resists the ordinance of God, and those who
> resist will bring judgment on themselves. For rulers are not a
> terror to good works, but to evil. Do you want to be unafraid
> of the authority? Do what is good, and you will have praise
> from the same. For he is God's minister to you for good.
> But if you do evil, be afraid; for he does not bear the sword
> in vain; for he is God's minister, an avenger to execute wrath
> on him who practices evil. Therefore you must be subject,
> not only because of wrath but also for conscience' sake. For
> because of this you also pay taxes, for they are God's minis-
> ters attending continually to this very thing. Render there-
> fore to all their due: taxes to whom taxes are due, customs to
> whom customs, fear to whom fear, honor to whom honor.

God established human government as a means of restraining evil, and
human rulers must be held accountable for how they have exercised
this God-given authority. Humans have failed to rule in justice and
righteousness, and the authority has often been misused and abused.
Humans have been drunk with a desire for power, and have bowed to
Satan and to the materialistic values of this world system. Power can
cause rulers to be consumed by pride and to rule over their subjects
in a self-serving way. At their very best, human rulers have not been

able to resolve many of the basic problems of society, because they have no ability to deal with the underlying problem: the problem of sin. Human government continues to change, as people try to bring justice and peace to this earth by their methods. During the course of human history, man has tried various types of government, yet none has been successful in bringing peace and righteousness to this world.

After the flood, God directed the family of Noah in Genesis 9:1 to begin to replenish (repopulate) the earth. Not long after that, we find men choosing to rebel against the directive God had given. Instead of replenishing the earth, they chose to gather together in the land of Shinar and build a city and a tower. The Bible records their motive in this project in Genesis 11:1-4,

> Now the whole earth had one language and one speech. And it came to pass, as they journeyed from the east, that they found a plain in the land of Shinar, and they dwelt there. Then they said to one another, "Come, let us make bricks and bake them thoroughly." They had brick for stone, and they had asphalt for mortar. And they said, "Come, let us build ourselves a city, and a tower whose top is in the heavens; let us make a name for ourselves, lest we be scattered abroad over the face of the whole earth."

Their stated purpose in building the tower was to stay together, not to be scattered throughout the earth. This was in contrast to what God had said to Noah. The people also wanted to build a city to develop a culture that would provide for their needs, and they wanted to erect a tower to connect them with heaven. This appears to be an attempt to build some kind of spiritual edifice that would lead to a religious experience. Turning from God, they attempted to develop their own religious system that would provide for their spiritual desires.

God was displeased with man's rebellion, and He judged them as we discover in Genesis 11:5-9,

> But the LORD came down to see the city and the tower which the sons of men had built. And the LORD said, "Indeed the people are one and they all have one language, and this is what they begin to do; now nothing that they propose to do

will be withheld from them. Come, let Us go down and there confuse their language, that they may not understand one another's speech." So the LORD scattered them abroad from there over the face of all the earth, and they ceased building the city. Therefore its name is called Babel, because there the LORD confused the language of all the earth; and from there the LORD scattered them abroad over the face of all the earth.

This event is a significant event in human history because it explains the creation of various ethnic groups, including diverse languages and cultures. Man's rebellion against God is the cause for this diversity and the resulting hostility that has often developed between various ethnic groups because of an inability to fully understand each other. God used the confusion of language to force men to scatter and replenish the earth.

God again intervened in human history as He called Abraham to leave his home land and go to a new place that God had for him. In this call, God made a promise to Abraham, as found in Genesis 12:1-3:

Now the LORD had said to Abram:
   "Get out of your country,
   From your family
   And from your father's house,
   To a land that I will show you.
   I will make you a great nation;
   I will bless you
   And make your name great;
   And you shall be a blessing.
   I will bless those who bless you,
   And I will curse him who curses you;
   And in you all the families of the earth shall be blessed."

God not only promised to bless Abraham, but He also promised to bring a new nation from his descendants. This new nation would ultimately be the people through whom the Messiah would come into the world. All families of the earth would be blessed through this promised Messiah.

Later God delivered this people (Israel) from bondage in Egypt and led them through the wilderness to the land He had promised to Abraham. On their journey, they spent time at Mount Sinai, where God gave Moses the laws that would govern this nation. The form of government that was established at that time is what can be called a "theocracy." There was no king and no legislative branch in the theocracy because God would rule His people, and they would obey His Law. Moses was appointed as God's representative, and Aaron was consecrated to be the priest. God made provision for the failures of humans, and He set laws regarding sacrifices and established a Day of Atonement. In this we have an earthly form of the Kingdom of God. God had delivered His people and had blessed them as their gracious king.

But humans again rebelled under God's rule and, in the days of Samuel, the people of Israel demanded a king to rule over them like all the nations of earth. God permitted them to have a king, although He warned of the result of rebellion, and what some of their kings would do. God graciously provided for them in their rebellion by sending His Holy Spirit to help their king to rule and enforce the Law of God. Their first king, Saul, started well, but ended in rebellion against God. He was replaced by David, "a man after God's own heart." David was a good king, and God promised to bring the Messiah from his descendants, yet even David was not perfect in his reign.

David's son, Solomon, was given wisdom from God so that he might lead the nation in God's way. His kingdom enjoyed peace and prosperity, but he also did not obey God in all his ways. He relied upon a strong military and he amassed great wealth, but he also married many wives from other nations. These wives came with their gods and their own system of worship, which Solomon began to embrace. Because of his idolatry, God divided the kingdom during the lifetime of Solomon's son. Idolatry continued to grow, both in the northern kingdom of Israel and the southern kingdom of Judah. Evil invaded this earthly form of God's Kingdom (the theocracy) and God had to judge His people by sending them into exile. God allowed Assyria and Babylon to conquer these two kingdoms and take them captive to foreign lands.

God's plan and purpose, however, did not change. God spoke through prophets to warn His people of the fact that judgment would come, but He also promised to send the Messiah who would, in truth, establish God's Kingdom and rule over it forever. God's purpose is clearly stated in Psalm 2 where we read the following:

> Why do the nations rage,
> And the people plot a vain thing?
> The kings of the earth set themselves,
> And the rulers take counsel together,
> Against the LORD and against His Anointed, saying
> "Let us break their bonds in pieces
> And cast away their cords from us."
> He who sits in the heavens shall laugh;
> The Lord shall hold them in derision.
> Then He shall speak to them in His wrath,
> And distress them in His deep displeasure:
> "Yet I have set My King
> On My holy hill of Zion."
> "I will declare the decree:
> The LORD has said to Me,
> 'You are My Son,
> Today I have begotten You.
> Ask of Me, and I will give You
> The nations for Your inheritance,
> And the ends of the earth for Your possession.
> You shall break them with a rod of iron;
> You shall dash them to pieces like a potter's vessel.'"
> Now therefore, be wise, o kings;
> Be instructed, you judges of the earth.
> Serve the LORD with fear, and rejoice with trembling.
> Kiss the Son, lest He be angry,
> And you perish in the way,
> When His wrath is kindled but a little.
> Blessed are all those who put their trust in Him.

In Revelation 4 and 5, we see a scene in Heaven prior to God's judgment falling upon the earth's people and rulers who must be held accountable before God. In that scene, we see God seated upon His throne, with the angels and the saints gathered around His throne. As the record of that scene continues in Revelation 5:2, a question is asked that demands an answer. The question is given to us in the words of an angel:

> Then I saw a strong angel proclaiming with a loud voice, "Who is worthy to open the scroll and to loose its seals?"

The sealed scroll represents God's creative plan in which He determined to give man authority to rule as God's agent on this earth. God's plan was for man to rule under His authority, but the angel's question is, "Who is worthy to fulfill the plan of God?"

In Revelation 5:3, a thorough search is conducted for a human who can fulfill this role and bring God's plan into reality:

> And no one in heaven or on the earth or under the earth was able to open the scroll, or to look at it.

As a result of this search, no one was found worthy to assume this role. When it speaks of those "under the earth," it refers to those who are in the place of departed spirits waiting God's judgment. These surely are not worthy to rule in righteousness, but the search also included those presently living on earth – they also were found to be unworthy. As the angel reveals the results of this search, we learn that humans who are in heaven were included, as well. We might think of them as among the best and the most worthy of consideration, but even they are not worthy.

The Apostle John weeps when he learns that there is not one person in the entire human race worthy to rule and bring God's plan to fulfillment. Paul tells us in Romans 3:23, "all have sinned and come short of the glory of God." There is no one who can claim to meet God's holy standard and accurately reflect His image. There is no human ruler who can be found who is perfect and worthy to carry out God's plan. There is no system of human government that is without flaw because, as mentioned earlier, men cannot deal with the basic issue of human sin and all of its consequences. The rulers also are sinful humans who are prone to act in ways that are not in the best interests of their people, and certainly not in harmony with God's holy standard.

Thankfully, God's Word does not leave us without hope. One of the elders in heaven encouraged John, telling him that his tears are no longer warranted. There is someone who meets all of the qualifications necessary to fulfill God's plan; there is a man (Jesus) who is worthy. As promised to David in 2 Samuel 7, this man is one of his descendants, here called "the Lion of the tribe of Judah, the Root of David." Not only is He worthy to open this sealed scroll and carry out God's plan, He has already "prevailed to do so." As John turns his attention to look at this one, the only hope of all mankind, what he sees in the midst of God's throne is not exactly what he expected. Consider the words of Revelation 5:6:

> And I looked, and behold, in the midst of the throne and of the four living creatures, and in the midst of the elders, stood a Lamb as though it had been slain, having seven horns and seven eyes, which are the seven Spirits of God sent out into all the earth.

The Lion of whom the elder spoke is now seen as a Lamb that has been slain. This is the Lamb of God who suffered and died upon the cross of Calvary, as a sacrifice for the sins of the whole human race. He has "prevailed" because He has dealt with the sin problem for mankind. He is the one ruler who can transform the sinful heart of humans, and He is a ruler without sin of His own.

Christ also meets the necessary qualifications to rule for God over His creation, because He is fully, as a man, under the control of God's Holy Spirit. This is the interpretation of the seven horns and the seven eyes that are seen here. The horns speak of power and the number seven is the number of perfection or completion. This is a symbolic way of saying that the fullness of God's power rests upon Him and equips Him to rule over God's creation. Before Jesus left His disciples to return to the Father, He told them in Matthew 28:18, " All power (authority) is given unto me in heaven and in earth." He is also said to have seven eyes, symbolic of full discernment. He sees things as they really are. He is able to perfectly assess every situation, and to make wise decisions with discernment.

Christ is one who is worthy to fulfill the eternal plan of God, and to rule over God's Kingdom. He has offered Himself as a sacrifice for human sin, and has therefore reconciled those who believe in Him, bringing them back into a relationship with God. By His sacrifice, He also has provided for restoration, so that the image of God can be seen in mankind again. When He returns in God's New Creation, every consequence of sin will be removed and all creation will be restored, so that God and humans will dwell together in unity forever. Christ is equipped to rule because He has all power and complete discernment. He alone is the one who is worthy to rule over God's creation.

In Hebrews 2:5-10, the writer speaks to this same point, as he quotes from Psalm 8 regarding the fact that God gave man the authority to rule over this earth. God put all of the living creatures of earth under man's control. However the writer goes on to tell us, "But now we see not yet all things put under him." He acknowledges that creation is in rebellion against man's attempt to have control, as a result of the sin of humans and the curse upon creation. Humans struggle to bring nature and the animal kingdom under their control, but as Scripture says, this has not happened to this point. In the verse that follows, the writer turns our attention to the fact that there is one man who is worthy to exercise authority.

Hebrews 2:9-10 expresses the hope of all mankind:

> But we see Jesus, who was made a little lower than the angels, for the suffering of death crowned with glory and honor, that He, by the grace of God, might taste death for everyone. For it was fitting for Him, for whom are all things and by whom are all things, in bringing many sons to glory, to make the captain of their salvation perfect through sufferings.

As will later be addressed in this study, not only is Jesus Christ worthy to rule and reign, but His sacrifice provides the opportunity for believers ultimately to reign with Him.

Returning to our passage in Revelation 5, we see the response of all those who are gathered around the throne of God, both angels and men. What follows is a glorious scene of all of the redeemed, along

with the angels, worshiping the Lamb and giving praise for what He
has done. Their praise is found in verses 9 and 10:

> And they sang a new song, saying: You are worthy to take
> the scroll, and to open its seals; for You were slain, and have
> redeemed us to God by your blood out of every tribe and
> tongue and people and nation, and have made us kings and
> priests to our God; and we shall reign on the earth.

Jesus Christ is qualified to rule and fulfill God's plan, not only because
He became a man, one with us, but also because He has redeemed and
reconciled us to God. His redemptive work on Calvary has paid in-full
the penalty of sin, and now God can restore all things and bring His
eternal plan to completion.

This praise continues through the rest of this passage, as the Lamb is
found worthy to rule. Not only do the followers of Christ praise Him,
but every "created being in heaven, on earth and under the earth" join
in acknowledging Him as being worthy of all honor and glory and
worthy to rule and reign. In Philippians 2:9-11, we see this acknowl-
edgement of Christ as every knee is bowed to Him and every tongue
confesses that He is Lord. As a result of the Son of God being willing
to humble Himself, and as a man sacrificing Himself for us, we read:

> Therefore God also has highly exalted Him and given Him
> the name which is above every name, that at the name of
> Jesus every knee should bow, of those in heaven, and of those
> on earth, and of those under the earth, and that every tongue
> should confess that Jesus Christ is Lord, to the glory of God
> the Father.

The Lamb of God is found worthy to bring God's plan to completion
and is worshipped as God, In the very first verse of the next chapter
in Revelation (Revelation 6), we see the Lamb opening the seals on
the scroll (the unveiling of the creation plan). This plan establishes
a kingdom of righteousness and peace with Jesus Christ as King, and
begins with God's judgment of man's system and those who have ruled
over it. Righteousness and peace cannot be established until sin is put
away, and Christ accomplished this (put away sin) on the cross. The

next thing that must happen, before He returns to establish this kind of rule, is the putting away of man's system that is out of harmony with God's plan. Therefore we see the Lamb opening the seals and setting in motion the judgment of this world's system, which has been under Satan's power.

After this judgment has taken place, including the harlot woman judged and the materialistic system represented by the city of Babylon destroyed, we see heaven preparing for Jesus Christ's return to earth, to claim His throne and establish His kingdom. Revelation 19:1-6 records this scene in Heaven for us:

> After these things I heard a loud voice of a great multitude in heaven, saying, Alleluia! Salvation and glory and honor and power belong to the Lord our God! For true and right-eous are His judgments, because He has judged the great harlot who corrupted the earth with her fornication; and He has avenged on her the blood of His servants shed by her. Again they said, Alleluia! Her smoke rises up forever and ever! And the twenty-four elders and the four living crea-tures fell down and worshiped God who sat on the throne, saying, Amen! Alleluia! Then a voice came from the throne, saying, Praise our God, all you His servants and those who fear Him, both small and great! And I heard, as it were, the voice of a great multitude, as the sound of many waters and as the sound of mighty thunderings, saying, Alleluia! For the Lord God Omnipotent reigns!

The words of this passage prompted George Frederick Handel to com-pose his great work, *The Hallelujah Chorus*. It is the people of Heaven who sing these words of praise to God, giving thanks that man's Satan-inspired system is destroyed. Looking at Revelation 18:24 we discover that this system of man has been responsible for the deaths of many of God's people. Again the angels join with the saints in giving praise to God. There is a thunderous sound as God is worshipped and praised for the system's destruction.

The hallelujahs end with "the Lord God omnipotent reigns," signi-fying the destruction of all that is opposed to God. Satan is defeated, the world's system is destroyed, and the way is clear for Christ to return to earth and establish a kingdom of righteousness and peace. When Christ returns in all of His glory, the beast that opposes Him is cast into the Lake of Fire, and the False Prophet with him. All those who followed the beast are slain and their carcasses become a feast for the birds of prey. All who have opposed Christ, along with the Anti-Christ, are brought to judgment preparing the way for the Kingdom of God and His Christ to become a reality. There is a man (Jesus Christ) who will rule in righteousness and peace as God designed in His original creation, recorded in the Book of Genesis.

The return of Christ is recorded in Revelation 19:11-16:

> Now I saw heaven opened, and behold, a white horse. And He who sat on him was called Faithful and True, and in righteousness He judges and makes war. His eyes were like a flame of fire, and on His head were many crowns. He had a name written that no one knew except Himself. He was clothed with a robe dipped in blood, and His name is called The Word of God. And the armies in heaven, clothed in fine linen, white and clean, followed Him on white horses. Now out of His mouth goes a sharp sword, that with it He should strike the nations. And He Himself will rule them with a rod of iron. He Himself treads the winepress of the fierceness and wrath of Almighty God. And He has on His robe and on His thigh a name written: KING OF KINGS AND LORD OF LORDS.

The identity of this King riding on a white horse cannot be in doubt as we consider the words of this passage. He is called "Faithful and True," one who is totally true and reliable. He is the one who came to reveal God to us, and His words are without any error or pretense. He is the one ruler who can be trusted implicitly. We also are told that He comes "in righteousness." He is holy and the only man who has ever lived without sin. He is totally committed to the righteous standard of God and He will "judge and make war" on the basis of this righteous standard. He is furthered described as having penetrating fiery eyes that see into the very heart of those whom He will judge. His robe has been dipped in blood, referring to the sacrifice He made for us on the cross. John is told that His name is called "The Word of God." This is the title that John used of the Son of God when he wrote his Gospel (John 1).

The description continues as it speaks of His authority to rule and reign. There are many crowns upon His head, for He alone is found worthy and all authority is given unto Him. In verse 16, we are told that there is a name, a title written on His robe that says, "King of kings and LORD of lords." All other rulers bow to Him because He is supreme. In the previous verse (verse 15) we are told that He will rule with a rod of iron, indicating that He will exercise sovereign control and a sword proceeds out of His mouth to enforce His rule. A sword from His mouth indicates that He can exercise judgment by a spoken word. As the Creator God, this One brought all things into being by a spoken word. Surely His word is powerful enough to bring judgment to those who oppose Him. This is also seen at the end of chapter 19 in verse 21.

This glorious victory of Christ is shared with those who have chosen to follow Him and put their faith and trust in Him. In Revelation 19:14 we read, "And the armies in heaven, clothed in fine linen, white and clean, followed Him on white horses." The "fine linen, white and clean" appears to refer back to verse 7 and 8 of this chapter, where it is identified with the saints, those who are believers in Jesus Christ, His bride:

> Let us be glad and rejoice and give Him glory, for the marriage of the Lamb has come, and His wife has made herself ready. And to her it was granted to be arrayed in fine linen, clean and bright, for the fine linen is the righteous acts of the saints.

Note here that the linen robe is given to her because those believers making up the bride of Christ have no righteousness of their own. As they come to Christ by faith, they are clothed in His righteousness. These believers come with Christ and they will reign with Him.

This earthly millennial reign of Christ fulfills all the kingdom promises that we find in the Old Testament and allows humans the opportunity to experience a righteous and peaceful reign for 1,000 years. However as we see in Revelation 20:7-9, God allows Satan to be released for a short time to give humans a choice whether or not to live under the reign of Christ. It is here that we discover the truth of Jesus' statement to Nicodemus when He said, "Except a man be born again, he cannot enter into the Kingdom of God." Unless a person is born of the Spirit in regeneration, he is not prepared to live in God's Kingdom.

This millennial rule of Christ removes the curse that was upon the earth because of sin. Satan is confined in the pit so that he cannot tempt men to sin, allowing humans the opportunity to live under a reign of righteousness and peace without these problems. This reign of Christ gives humans another opportunity to make a choice for God without some of the excuses that they may offer in this present time. It also makes the final judgment of God at the Great White Throne appear absolutely just when unbelieving men are separated from God in the Lake of Fire. This is not God's vindictive choice, as many might say, but it is a choice that humans make in the full light of having lived under the perfect rule of Jesus Christ. Some would say that a good God could never send people to hell, but as we examine this passage, we see that God has graciously done all He could, and it is they who makes this choice.

With this judgment passed and humans allowed their choice of eternal separation from God, it is time for God to bring His eternal plan to completion. The Book of Revelation closes with the final two chapters describing the establishment of God's Eternal Kingdom. Before this perfect creation and Kingdom can be established, every vestige of sin must be removed from this present earth. Sin began in heaven with the rebellion of Lucifer and the angels who followed him, so both heaven and earth have been marred and stained with sin. Therefore John begins in Revelation 21:1 by testifying to what he saw,

> Now I saw a new heaven and a new earth, for the first heaven and the first earth had passed away. Also there was no more sea.

Peter describes this same scene in 2 Peter 3:10-13 as follows:

> But the day of the Lord will come as a thief in the night, in which the heavens will pass away with a great noise, and the elements will melt with fervent heat; both the earth and the works that are in it will be burned up. Therefore, since all these things will be dissolved, what manner of persons ought you to be in holy conduct and godliness, looking for and hastening the coming of the day of God, because of which the heavens will be dissolved, being on fire, and the elements will melt with fervent heat? Nevertheless we, according to His promise, look for new heavens and a new earth in which righteousness dwells.

Scripture tells us that God is going to create a new heaven and a new earth, one that is perfect without the effects of sin. One of the things that John notes is that there is no sea. The seas have long divided the people of earth and helped to establish boundaries for nations, so that their excessive desire for conquest might be restrained. In the new creation, there will be no need for seas to separate, because peace and righteousness will reign. The seas also speak of unrest and the turmoil often found in the heart of men (Isaiah 57:20-21). With the curse removed, and the existence of a new creation, God's creative plan can come to fulfillment.

The Holy City, called New Jerusalem, comes down from God out of heaven in all of its glory and beauty. This heavenly city is linked to the earth, and God dwells with men and lives in fellowship with them, fulfilling the reason for creating them in His image. Just as God came down to fellowship with Adam and Eve, recorded in Genesis 3:8-10, God and man will dwell together eternally because of the sacrifice of Christ. John's record in Revelation 21:2-3 says,

> Then I, John, saw the holy city, New Jerusalem, coming down out of heaven from God, prepared as a bride adorned for her husband. And I heard a loud voice from heaven saying, Behold, the tabernacle of God is with men, and He will dwell with them, and they shall be His people. God Himself will be with them and be their God.

In Revelation 21:4-8, we are clearly assured that every vestige of the old marred creation will be removed, and every consequence of sin will be forever put away.

> And God will wipe away every tear from their eyes; there shall be no more death, nor sorrow, nor crying. There shall be no more pain, for the former things have passed away. Then He who sat on the throne said, "Behold, I make all things new." And He said to me, "Write, for these words are true and faithful." And He said to me, "It is done! I am the Alpha and the Omega, the Beginning and the End. I will give of the fountain of the water of life freely to him who thirsts. He who overcomes shall inherit all things, and I will be his God and he shall be My son. But the cowardly, unbelieving, abominable, murderers, sexually immoral, sorcerers, idolaters, and all liars shall have their part in the lake which burns with fire and brimstone, which is the second death."

The glorious city is described in all of its beauty and stability in Revelation 21:9-21:

> Then one of the seven angels who had the seven bowls filled with the seven last plagues came to me and talked with me, saying, "Come, I will show you the bride, the Lamb's wife." And he carried me away in the Spirit to a great and high mountain, and showed me the great city, the holy Jerusalem, descending out of heaven from God, having the glory of God. Her light was like a most precious stone, like a jasper stone, clear as crystal. Also she had a great and high wall with twelve gates, and twelve angels at the gates, and names written on them, which are the names of the twelve tribes of the children of Israel: three gates on the east, three gates on the north, three gates on the south, and three gates on the west.
> Now the wall of the city had twelve foundations, and on them were the names of the twelve apostles of the Lamb. And he who talked with me had a gold reed to measure the city, its gates, and its wall. The city is laid out as a square; its length is as great as its breadth. And he measured the city with the reed: twelve thousand furlongs. Its length, breadth, and height are equal. Then he measured its wall: one hundred and forty-four cubits, according to the measure of a

> man, that is, of an angel. The construction of its wall was of jasper; and the city was pure gold, like clear glass. The foundations of the wall of the city were adorned with all kinds of precious stones: the first foundation was jasper, the second sapphire, the third chalcedony, the fourth emerald, the fifth sardonyx, the sixth sardius, the seventh chrysolite, the eighth beryl, the ninth topaz, the tenth chrysoprase, the eleventh jacinth, and the twelfth amethyst. The twelve gates were twelve pearls: each individual gate was of one pearl. And the street of the city was pure gold, like transparent glass.

Following this passage, there are some notations made about things that are not present in this new creation (Revelations 21:22-27). They are not present because they are no longer needed. God Himself will be the source of these things. First there is no temple because "The Lord God Almighty and the Lamb are the temple of it." (The earthly temple was a place where God could dwell with His people in a glory cloud called the "shekinah"). When God and Christ are personally present, there is no need for a symbolic representation.

In verse 23, we are told that there is no need for the sun or for the moon because "the glory of God will fill the place with light and the Lamb is the light of it." In the creation account of Genesis, we are told that God created the sun to provide light for humans during the day, and he also made the moon to give light for night (Genesis 1:14-19). God is light and with His presence we will have no need of some other source. His glory will radiate, and there will be no darkness. Revelation 22:5 further states,

> There shall be no night there: They need no lamp nor light of the sun, for the Lord God gives them light. And they shall reign forever and ever.

In Genesis 1:14-19 we discover that God made the lights in the heavens to enable humans to divide day from night, to enable them to tell time and to know the various seasons that are a part of our present earthly experience. Living in eternity, there will be no need for any of these things. Since there is no night or darkness in this new creation, we are also told that the gate of the city, giving access to God, will never be shut. The kings of earth will bring their glory to the God who is worthy. Another reason the gates can remain open is because there is nothing to hinder perfect peace and security. All evil has been eliminated, according to Revelation 21:27,

> But there shall by no means enter it anything that defiles, or causes an abomination or a lie, but only those who are written in the Lamb's Book of Life.

We discover a number of interesting statements about this new creation in Revelation 22:1-5:

> And he showed me a pure river of water of life, clear as crystal, proceeding from the throne of God and of the Lamb. In the middle of its street, and on either side of the river, was the tree of life, which bore twelve fruits, each tree yielding its fruit every month. The leaves of the tree were for the healing of the nations. And there shall be no more curse, but the throne of God and of the Lamb shall be in it, and His servants shall serve Him. They shall see His face, and His name shall be on their foreheads. There shall be no night there: They need no lamp nor light of the sun, for the Lord God gives them light. And they shall reign forever and ever.

In this passage we discover that God is the true source of life, and with sin removed there is no reason for death. There are two things present in this passage that encourage us to see God's provision for life that is everlasting. First there is a "pure river of water of life, clear as crystal, proceeding from the throne of God and of the Lamb." The water of life flows from God's throne and we share His life which is eternal. Secondly, "on either side of the river was the tree of life." This tree is mentioned as we read about the Garden of Eden, and it was there to sustain human life forever. Genesis 3:22 makes this fact clear:

> Then the LORD God said, Behold, the man has become like one of us, to know good and evil. And now, lest he put out his hand and take also of the tree of life, and eat, and live forever, therefore the LORD God sent him out of the garden of Eden to till the ground from which he was taken.

God's love for humans is so great that He could not let them live forever in their sinful, fallen state. God had a plan of redemption that involved the sacrifice of His Son for our sin, so that with the penalty of sin paid in-full, God could give us eternal life. The Tree of Life, originally in the Garden of Eden and mentioned in Revelation 22:2, is present to assure us that God will fulfill His promise. It also provides an everlasting fruitfulness which is renewed every month, bringing healing to those people who rest their faith and trust in what God's Son has done for them. The curse is gone and life is truly everlasting.

This passage closes as it speaks of the joy that we shall experience in the presence of our Lord and Savior. We will serve Him, giving us meaningful activity, and we will reign with Him so that, in Christ, God's purpose is fulfilled. Man will have the dominion in the New Creation that was lost because of sin in the old one. Our greatest joy, however, is expressed in verse 4 where we read that "they shall see His face, and His name shall be on their foreheads." To enjoy a face-to-face relationship with Jesus Christ, and to know that we bear His name, is the greatest joy. God created us to live in fellowship with Him, and we will be fulfilled as we live in His presence. God is sovereign and His plan cannot be thwarted. What He purposed to do in creation, as recorded in the Book of Genesis, will be completely fulfilled as we discover in the Book of Revelation.

The plan and purpose of God to establish His Kingdom with a man exercising dominion over this creation is proclaimed throughout Scripture and is brought to fulfillment in the Book of Revelation. Jesus Christ will rule as King of kings and Lord of lords but, until that time comes, we must note what God's Word says about the Kingdom of Man and its opposition to God's Kingdom. However, before we consider the attempt of humans to oppose and thwart God's plan it is important to consider what Jesus Christ had to say about the Kingdom of God.

CHAPTER 9

The Kingdom of God in the Teaching of Jesus

THE NEW TESTAMENT BEGINS in Matthew chapter one with the genealogy of Jesus Christ linking Him to the royal line of King David, to whom God had promised an eternal right to the throne in 2 Samuel 7. He is also a descendant of Abraham with whom God made a covenant promising to build a nation that would ultimately bless all nations (in the Messiah). At the birth of Jesus He is announced as King to the Magi, who traveled a great distance to honor Him.

When John the Baptist began his ministry as the forerunner of Messiah his message was "Repent, for the kingdom of heaven is at hand" (Matthew 3:2). Jesus began His public ministry with the identical announcement concerning God's Kingdom in Matthew 4:17. His teaching ministry called attention to the spiritual nature of God's Kingdom as He focused on internal transformation as a necessary prerequisite for entrance into God's Kingdom. In the Sermon on the Mount He spoke of the heart issues that are part of God's law in contrast to external religious activity.

When we look at what is called "The Beatitudes" in the Sermon on the Mount we see the emphasis put on internal transformation as Jesus talks about the attitude of heart that is essential for those who would enter God's kingdom (Matthew 5:1-12). In that sermon Jesus speaks of the heart righteousness that is required in God's Kingdom. This is a righteousness that is not found in sinful men, but Scripture tells us that it comes with the new birth by faith in Jesus Christ.

In what we know as *The Lord's Prayer* Jesus taught His followers to pray for the coming of God's Kingdom and He describes that as a time when God's will is done on earth as it is in heaven. This prayer makes it clear that there is a sense in which God's Kingdom can be a reality when we believe God's Word and live in harmony with Him but the total fulfillment of this prayer must wait for a future fulfillment when God's Kingdom is established on earth and Christ reigns as King. Jesus spoke of this final establishment of God's Kingdom on earth.

In His discussion with Nicodemus, Jesus made it clear that the new birth (regeneration) was essential if anyone was to be a part in God's Kingdom. In John 3:3 He said, "Most assuredly, I say to you, unless one is born again, he cannot see the kingdom of God." It is not enough that we are alive physically; in order to function in God's Kingdom, our spirit must also be given new life. The discussion in that passage makes it clear that our spirit is regenerated by faith in Jesus Christ and His work of redemption on the cross. John 1:12-13 confirms the fact that we can be born into God's family by faith in Jesus Christ.

The teaching of Jesus on the Kingdom of God is found many times in the parables that He used. A good example of this is found in Matthew 13 where six parables all begin with the words "The Kingdom of Heaven is like." The first parable in this group of seven is used to challenge people to listen and respond to the message that follows in the other six. In what many call the Parable of the Sower the emphasis is really on the soils into which the seed is sown and to the response of each soil to the seed that is sown. Jesus challenges His hearers to act upon what they hear.

The six parables that follow can be linked together in three couplets. Two parables form a couplet as they communicate the same message using another analogy for the sake of emphasis. The message in each of these couplets is important for those who would enter into God's kingdom and therefore the Lord repeats the message in two different forms.

The first and the last of these parables form a couplet as they both speak of the fact that good and evil will both exist together in the visible kingdom at this time. The first is the parable of the wheat and the tares

(Matthew 13:24-30) and it is an analogy taken from agricultural life. The message of the last will be better understood by those who were fishermen. In the first the Son of Man (Jesus) is the sower and the seed is the Word of God. This, of course, is all good. The tares (weeds) were sown at night by an enemy (Satan). The servants of the master wanted to pull up these tares but the master said no because in doing so they might uproot some of the wheat with them. The master said that when harvest comes He will separate the wheat from the tares. The wheat will be gathered into his barn and the tares will be consumed by fire.

The last parable in this series likens the kingdom of God to a large fishing net that gathers in a great number of fish (Matthew 13:47-50). There are good fish in the net but there are also other fish which the fisherman does not want. Therefore when the net is full and he drags the net to shore He sits down and sorts out what is in his net. The good fish he puts in his vessels and the bad he throws away. The message is the same as in the first parable. At the end of the age God will send His angels to separate the righteous from the wicked. The wicked will be cast into the fiery furnace and the righteous will enter into God's kingdom. The present form of the kingdom of God as men see it may contain good and evil but do not let that deter you from making your choice. God will sort it all out at the end and only those who are righteous will enter His Kingdom.

The parable of the mustard seed (Matthew 13:31-32) and the parable of the leaven (Matthew 13:33) form another couplet as both of them speak of something that is small but has the potential to become great. The little mustard seed has the potential to become a rather large bush and the little bit of leaven put into a lump of dough has the potential for greatly increasing the size of the dough. Jesus is again teaching about the kingdom which may appear to be small in its present form. However the truth is that it will become great. God's Kingdom challenges men to make a by-faith investment based upon the fact that God has promised that His Kingdom will become great and that it will reign eternally.

Another couplet is found in the parable of the treasure hid in the field (Matthew 13:44) and the parable of the pearl of great price (Matthew

13:45-46). In the first of these two parables the one who finds the treasure hid in the field sells everything he has in order that he might purchase the field and claim the treasure hid there. In the second parable in this couplet a gem merchant finds a pearl that is of great price, having outstanding value. He also sold everything he owned in order that he might purchase this one pearl. Both of these parables speak of the kingdom of God and they emphasize the great value that is to be found in the kingdom. It is so superior to anything that has value in this world that a wise person will be willing to give up everything in order to have a part in God's kingdom.

Jesus impressed upon His hearers the great value to be found in God's kingdom when He compared it with the material values in this present world. He challenged them and us with His question: "For what will it profit a man if he gains the whole world, and loses his own soul?" The values that one might find in this earthly life are insignificant when compared with what God has promised in His kingdom. There is eternal glory in the kingdom of God but even in its present form God's kingdom offers spiritual blessings with a sense of purpose and fulfillment in this life.

In the last week before his crucifixion Jesus spoke with His disciples in Matthew 24-25 in what is often called *The Olivet Discourse*. In this passage Jesus reassured His disciples that the Kingdom of God would finally be established on earth but it must wait for the time of His return. In this discourse He spoke of the judgment that must come upon man's kingdom before God's Kingdom could be established. He spoke also of the "Time of Great Tribulation" that would precede His return. Our purpose is not to explore these two chapters but simply to note that while Jesus spoke of the spiritual aspect of God's Kingdom He also clearly taught that the kingdom would literally be established at His return. The message was for humans to be prepared for his return so that they might be a part of His kingdom.

As Jesus stood before Pilate He was asked about His kingdom as recorded in John 18:33-38 and in His response He spoke of the nature of God's kingdom and of the reality of His future reign:

Jesus answered, "My kingdom is not of this world. If My kingdom were of this world, My servants would fight, so that I should not be delivered to the Jews; but now My kingdom is not from here." Pilate therefore said to Him, "Are You a king then?" Jesus answered, "You say rightly that I am a king. For this cause I was born, and for this cause I have come into the world, that I should bear witness to the truth. Everyone who is of the truth hears My voice."

After His resurrection Jesus spoke to His disciples about things "pertaining to the kingdom of God" (Acts 1:3). In response to the disciples question as to when God's kingdom would be established Jesus told them that they did not need to know the time when God would establish His kingdom (Acts 1:7) but rather they needed to focus on the mission He had given them. The time for establishing the kingdom is linked to His return to earth as predicted in Acts 1:11.

As we look at the Book of Revelation we note in Revelation 1:1 and again in Revelation 22:6-16 that it is Jesus who is revealing the future truth to John and it Jesus who is certifying its accuracy. To discredit or to ignore what we find in the Book of Revelation is to discredit or ignore the teaching of Jesus Christ.

The *Tale of Two Kingdoms* provides us with a context that helps us better understand the Book of Revelation. The conflict between these two kingdoms is recorded in the Scriptures, beginning in the Book of Genesis and the Garden of Eden. Revelation is the last chapter of this tale and it is vital that we do not neglect the message in this final book. We need to know how this conflict will end so that we make a wise choice as to which kingdom is the best investment. God invites us to be a part of His Kingdom, but we must make the choice. With this viewpoint in mind as our context, you are encouraged to briefly walk through the Book of Revelation. What we have discovered about these two kingdoms and the conflict that has prevailed will help us better understand God's message in the final chapter of His Book.

Part II

Revelation of Jesus Christ

CHAPTER 10

Introduction to the Book of Revelation

THE BOOK OF REVELATION is the final chapter in God's message to humans. As the book begins, we are told that this message (revelation from God) was given to His Son, Jesus Christ. In Hebrews 1:1-3 we learn that God spoke in the Old Testament time through prophets, but He has now spoken through His Son. Consider what is found in that passage:

> God, who at various times and in various ways spoke in time past to the fathers by the prophets, has in these last days spoken to us by His Son, whom He has appointed heir of all things, through whom also He made the worlds; who being the brightness of His glory and the express image of His person, and upholding all things by the word of His power, when He had by Himself purged our sins, sat down at the right hand of the Majesty on high.

In Hebrews 2:1-4 the writer makes a point that the message of prophets and of angels came with all of the authority of God and we should respond as though God were speaking. Certainly the message that comes from God, through His own Son, Jesus Christ, should be given even greater authority. Therefore when we come to the Book of Revelation, we must note that it is introduced to us as God's message to His Son, to communicate to us things that we need to know. The things revealed in this book are of greatest importance, and they are going to come to pass.

In Scripture, we have traced the story of two kingdoms that are in conflict. These two kingdoms call upon us to make a choice of allegiance. The Kingdom of Man offers materialistic gain and various forms of pleasure to help us find happiness and satisfaction in life. On the other hand, the Kingdom of God calls us to find fulfillment in God through faith in Jesus Christ. One seems to offer some enjoyment and sense of fulfillment in the present, while the other calls upon us to focus on the fulfillment found in eternity.

As we contemplate this choice, there are additional facts that we need to know. A wise investor would want to consider not only how the investment is doing in the present, but he would want to know what the future potential is for the investment. If he could know which investments would bring great dividends and which ones would totally fail, he would possess valuable information.

The message that God gave Jesus Christ to share with His followers is about "things which must shortly come to pass." This is all about the future and what will happen to these two kingdoms. This message is intended to give us valuable information concerning how things will end. God wants us to know about things that are going to happen, so that we can make a wise choice. We may ask "What things?" and this brings us to what is to unfold in the book of Revelation.

We have already suggested that this book is all about two kingdoms, and how each of them will end. The message details the judgment of Man's Kingdom (under Satan's control) and how those who invest in that kingdom will experience great loss. The message of this book also unveils the establishment of God's Kingdom and the glorious future for those who are a part of it. All that God purposed to do in creation will be fulfilled in the New Creation and the glorious Kingdom of God.

God's plan also includes the exaltation of Jesus Christ, God's Son. Philippians 2:5-8 records the descent of the Son of God, as He humbled Himself becoming a man so that He might die as a sacrifice for the sins of all people. He not only became a man, but He was one who was described as meek and lowly. Not only did He die for us, but He experienced a form of death (crucifixion) that the Romans reserved for the worst of criminals. He was known as a humble carpenter and He was despised by many.

Philippians 2:9-11 continues the description of God's response to what His Son has done, in order to reconcile us to God:

> Therefore God also has highly exalted Him and given Him the name which is above every name, that at the name of Jesus every knee should bow, of those in heaven, and of those on earth, and of those under the earth, and that every tongue should confess that Jesus Christ is Lord, to the glory of God the Father.

God has highly exalted His Son, and the Book of Revelation allows us to see the unveiling of His true glory. Jesus Christ is King of kings, Lord of lords, and seated upon the throne. Revelation shows how He will exercise all authority over God's restored creation. Jesus told His disciples in Matthew 28:18 that "all authority has been given to me." In the Book of Revelation, we see this in its fullness as we view the unveiling of Jesus Christ. When we see Him in all of His glory, it has a transforming impact upon us. It motivates us to serve Him, and causes us to bow in worship at His feet.

One of the keys to understanding this great book is to trace the theme, the revelation of Jesus Christ, throughout the book, noting how God has highly exalted His Son, Jesus Christ. As Christ is presented in all of His glory, we also will note that the response of those who see Him as the Glorified Lord is to fall at His feet in worship. Some of the great worship scenes in Scripture are found in the Book of Revelation.

There is a series of five visions that John records for us in Revelation, and they provide a way for us to think through the book. Each vision adds something to provide a fuller picture of the exaltation of the glorified Christ.

The visions are:
1. Sovereign Lord as Head of His Church – Chapters 1-3
2. Sacrificial Lamb declared worthy to reign – Chapters 4, 5
3. Righteous Judge over all the Earth – Chapters 6-19
4. Conquering King establishing His Kingdom – Chapters 19-20
5. Eternal Son ruling over God's New Creation – Chapters 21-22

We will explore these five visions that set forth the exaltation of Jesus Christ as we go through the Book of Revelation, but it is important to note at the beginning that the exaltation of Christ is one of the main "things" that God said "must shortly come to pass." Satan does not want us to focus on the glorious triumph of Jesus Christ because it also means the final destruction of his kingdom and his eternal exile in the Lake of Fire.

The Apostle John, God's penman for this book, testifies in Revelation 1:2 to the person and integrity of Jesus Christ and to the accuracy of the message that is recorded in this book. Consider what is stated in this verse: "who bore witness to the word of God, and to the testimony of Jesus Christ, to all things that he saw."

In the introduction to this book there is further encouragement for those who would read God's message as He pronounces a special blessing upon those who take His word seriously. This blessing is found in verse 3 of this first chapter:

> Blessed is he who reads and those who hear the words of this prophecy, and keep those things which are written in it; for the time is near.

There is a message in this book that can make a difference in your life, if you will give attention to what it says and live your life in harmony with it. This book is not just pie in the sky. It is very practical, and gives us a proper perspective for living, including providing motivation for living a godly life. This book will bring blessing into your life. Note also that there is a sense of urgency here, "The time is at hand." We are nearing the time when the last pieces of the picture will be put in place, and God's plan and purpose will be complete. Don't miss it. We need to know what God is doing in our world and how it will end for the destiny of our eternal soul is at stake.

CHAPTER 11

Vision I

Sovereign Lord as Head of His Church
Revelation 1-3

THE MESSAGE THAT JOHN RECEIVED from the Lord was to be shared with those who were the followers of Jesus Christ (Revelation 1:1). In verse 4, John begins to write what was given to him and to send it to seven churches which were in the Roman province of Asia. These churches, located in what is now western Turkey, were experiencing pressure from external persecution and challenges to their faith from false doctrine that had crept into the church. Jesus declared in Matthew 16:18 that He would "build His church and the gates of hell would not prevail against it." This statement gives assurance that the Lord's church would ultimately triumph over Satan and all of his forces, but it also implies that there would be intense conflict.

The Book of Acts records some of the persecution that rose up against the Lord's church as Satan and Man's Kingdom were in opposition to what God was doing. In Acts 20:28-31 the Apostle Paul warned the elders from the church in Ephesus of dangers that they would face both external attacks and internal heresy:

> Therefore take heed to yourselves and to all the flock, among which the Holy Spirit has made you overseers, to shepherd the church of God which He purchased with His own blood. For I know this, that after my departure savage wolves will come in among you, not sparing the flock. Also from among yourselves men will rise up, speaking perverse things, to draw away the disciples after themselves. Therefore watch, and remember that for three years I did not cease to warn

everyone night and day with tears.

The message given to John for the Church of Christ is now recorded and sent to the seven churches in Asia, but it is for all who are within the Church throughout all the ages. At the end of what Christ says to each of these seven churches in Revelation 2 and 3 you will find a statement that applies the message to all who will listen. Again and again we find the words, "He that has an ear, let him hear what the Spirit says unto the churches." It is not just for this one church but for all of the Lord's people in His Church.

John begins his letter to the churches in verse 4, where he greets them with the confidence that God's grace and peace is enough to sustain them. He immediately turns their attention away from their earthly troubles to God's heavenly throne, and to the One who sits upon this throne. He is the Eternal God, the One who is, who was and who is to come. Our circumstances may change, but our God remains the same, and He sits upon the throne. Our Father is ruling, and with Him is the seven-fold Spirit, the Holy Spirit in all of His perfection. Seated upon that throne also is Jesus Christ, the resurrected, living Son of God.

This Jesus is the One who has revealed God to us, and reconciled us to God through His sacrifice on Calvary. We can rest confidently in the revelation that is about to be unveiled in this book because He is the Faithful witness. He is Truth. And this Jesus, to whom we belong, now rules as the Prince over all the rulers of earth. These earthly rulers may oppose, persecute and even kill God's people, but Christ is the One who will rule eternally, and He will right all wrongs. We can rest confidently in Him.

As John reflects on our Sovereign Lord, his heart bursts forth with praise and exaltation (verses 5-6). The praise is particularly directed to Jesus, the One who loves us with an eternal love. The love of Christ is beyond all human loves because it is unconditional and sacrificial. His love is demonstrated by washing us from our sins in His own blood. Having put away our sin, He has given us a glorious position with Him. We are a kingdom of priests, called of God to minister for Him in this present sinful world. In this book, we discover that we shall serve Him not only in this world, but forever in God's eternal kingdom.

John does not leave us in suspense as to the outcome, but instead assures us in this introduction (verses 7-8) that Christ is coming back in the clouds (often used to speak of God's glory). The world will finally see Him for who He is, and they will be judged by Him. Christ declares himself to be the "Alpha and Omega, the beginning and the ending." He is the One who began it all, as recorded in the Book of Genesis, and He will bring it all to a glorious conclusion. This Jesus is the eternal, almighty God, and He will triumph and bring God's plan for His creation to fulfillment. This is our source of comfort, and it provides the motivation needed to live in a world that is sinful and often hostile to God's people.

The purpose of this message is to reassure the hearts of those to whom John is writing. If the persecution they were facing should end with their death, their eternal future was bright, even glorious, because God and His people will triumph. Jesus is coming back again, and when He comes, He will execute justice and bring peace. This message from Christ to the churches applies to churches today, as well. What the past churches faced is the same as we currently face.

John writes to the seven churches in the Roman province of Asia to encourage them in a time of suffering and persecution (verse 9). He can relate to their persecution, since he has been exiled to the isle of Patmos. His confession of Christ as Savior and His ministry for Christ have brought him into disfavor with the Roman authorities. Patmos was a penal colony, and John's crime was "preaching Christ." It was the Lord's Day that is Sunday, the day that the church worshipped and celebrated the resurrection of Christ.

John was in the Spirit, worshipping, meditating and focusing on the Lord, when his attention was captured by a voice that sounded like a trumpet (verse 10). This voice has the sound of majesty and authority. It is a voice that immediately captures his attention, much like the trumpet-sounding voice that Moses heard at Mount Sinai (Exodus 19:16, 19).

In verse 11, the One who speaks again identifies Himself as "the

Alpha and Omega, the first and the last." This One who speaks truly is the beginning, the source of all that exists in this creation, and the last, the One who will bring all things to their consummation. John is given specific instruction to not only observe, but to write. The visions that he will soon witness are not for him alone. He is to carefully record them, and then send that record to the churches. Christ has a message for His church. What is contained in this book is the Lord's own message for His church, and He wants us to read His message.

The first vision that John sees is of Jesus Christ as the Sovereign Lord and the One who is the Head of His Church. Beginning in verse 12, John seeks to describe for his readers the glorious vision of one like the "Son of Man" in the midst of the seven churches where He is seen as the Lord of the Church. It is His church, and He declared in Matthew 16:18 that He would "build His church and the gates of hell would not prevail against it." God has exalted Him, and He is here seen as the Lord of the Church. In Ephesians 1:19-23 and in Colossians 1:15-19, we are told that God the Father has placed Jesus Christ in this position as Head of the Church.

John attempts to describe some of the details of His eternal glory, which has now been restored to Him. As on the Mount of Transfiguration, John finds this vision to be awesome and overwhelming. How can one describe that which is indescribable? How can one put into words something that is beyond human, finite comprehension? John uses symbolic language as he tries to help us, in some measure, grasp the awesome glory of the Son of God.

The first thing John saw, recorded in verse 12, was seven golden lampstands. In verse 20, these lampstands are interpreted for us as representing the seven churches to whom John was writing. Each church is set apart to shine as a light for Jesus Christ. This is the mission of every local church. The purpose of our existence as a local assembly is to shine as a light for Christ. These lamps appear to be arranged in circular fashion, and he notices that someone is standing in the midst of them.

This person who is in the midst of the lampstands is described as being like unto the Son of Man (verse 13). That term is used in Daniel 7:13-14 to speak of the Messiah. It was also the term that Jesus most often used to speak of Himself. He is in the position of authority, He is the central figure in these churches, and He is the Lord of the church. John tries to describe Jesus to his readers. John sees Jesus in all of His glory, so what he sees is beyond human comprehension. All John can do is to try to tell, in language that would convey some picture to us, how Jesus looked.

In verse 13, John first describes Jesus' garment as a robe that is long and flowing, one that speaks of dignity and honor. There is also a golden sash around His waist. His clothing gives an indication of a noble, royal position. This humble Son of Man is now crowned with glory and honor, and He is in the place of authority as Lord of the Church.

His hair is described as being pure white, as white as wool or as snow (verse 14). We find a similar description in Daniel 7:9 and 10:5. The picture given to us in this passage is one that speaks of mature wisdom and a sense of dignity. In England, and in the Colonial days of America, judges and dignitaries wore powdered wigs to convey this same idea.

John next describes His eyes as a flame of fire. Compare this with Daniel 10:6 and Revelation 19:12. Fiery eyes are those that penetrate, seeing into the very heart of things. He has complete and perfect discernment, and perception of all things. He is able to judge accurately and justly because He sees with complete insight. In Revelation 2 and 3, the Lord will evaluate each church with this perfect vision, passing judgment upon them or praising them.

His Feet are said to be like fine brass, glowing as it is heated in the furnace. Daniel 10:6 again gives us a similar description. In Scripture, brass often represents judgment and justice. The altar where sin was judged was made of brass (Exodus 38:1-2). The laver where the priests found cleansing from defilement also was made of brass (Exodus 38:8). The Lord's feet stand firm for justice and righteousness, and His feet stamp out all that is evil and unjust.

John describes the sound of many waters, as rushing water comes to mind as a way to describe the awesomeness of His voice (compare with Daniel 10:6). The idea here is of power and majesty, like that of a great cascade of water rushing over a mighty waterfall. If you have been to Niagara Falls, you have just a small glimpse of the mighty roar that John describes. The voice of Jesus is awesome, and when He speaks, it is with great authority. He is the Lord of the church, and we ought to stand in awe when He speaks.

Next we are told that His right hand held seven stars. In verse 20 of this chapter, we discover that these stars represent the messengers from each of these seven churches. The right hand is the hand of power, and these messengers are in His hand. There is security here, but there is also complete sovereign control.

We get a hint of what He is about to say to His Church, as John tells us that "out of His mouth goes a sharp sword." This double-edged sword is seen again in 2:12 and 16; 19:15 and 21. The word that proceeds out of His mouth is authoritative, piercing and powerful (Hebrews 4:12). The same Lord who created all things by His all-powerful word, now speaks as supreme in the midst of the churches. This is His church and His word is the final authority. As the righteous one, He must judge His church for what is out of harmony with His holy standard. He will reward faithfulness, but He also will judge those who have departed from His truth.

Finally John speaks of the countenance of Jesus, giving an overall impression of the glory of His being. He describes it as "the sun shines in its full radiance." In Matthew 17:2 John had a glimpse of this brilliance on the Mount of Transfiguration. Here, again, Jesus is seen in all of His glory. The Apostle Paul had a similar experience recorded in Acts 9:1-9, as he was overwhelmed by the brightness of the glory of Jesus on the road to Damascus.

The impact that this vision had on John is recorded in Revelation 1:17-18. He fell at the feet of the Lord, as one who was dead. He was able to rise to his feet only because the Lord lifted him up and spoke words of authoritative encouragement to him:

When I saw him, I fell at his feet as though dead. Then he

placed his right hand on me and said: "Do not be afraid. I
am the First and the Last. I am the Living One; I was dead,
and now look, I am alive for ever and ever! And I hold the
keys of death and Hades."

John's fear is comforted as the Lord reveals His full authority in this
statement. Jesus is the "First and the Last," the One who created all
things, brought all things into being, and who will bring all things to
the fulfillment of God's sovereign plan. No one can thwart the eternal
plan and purpose of God. What He began in Genesis, He will bring to
completion in Revelation – and He will do it in the person of His Son,
Jesus Christ. This is one of the keys that open the Book of Revelation
to us. The message of this book is that God will bring His eternal plan
into fulfillment.

The Lord reminds John that He has risen from the dead and has,
therefore, conquered the sin problem and all of its consequences. He
has fully paid the penalty of sin, and has therefore removed death as
sin's penalty. He is alive forevermore, and those who rest their faith in
Him will also share in everlasting life. He is the conquering Savior, and
the future is secure in His hands. To this He adds that He has the keys
of death and hell. Jesus spoke of this in John 14:6: "no one can come
to the Father except through me." No one can escape death and hell as
the penalty for sin, apart from faith in what Christ has done for us on
the cross. Death and hell are not in the future of those who rest their
faith in Jesus Christ.

The Sovereign Lord Evaluates His Church – Revelation 2 - 3

Jesus told His disciples that He would build His Church, and Scripture declares that He is the Head of the Church. He is the Sovereign Lord, and the Church is spoken of as His bride. Paul wrote in
2 Corinthians 5:10:

For we must all appear before the judgment seat of Christ,
that each one may receive the things done in the body, according to what he has done, whether good or bad.

This speaks of a time when the Lord will evaluate our lives and what we, as individuals, have done in serving our Lord, but it affirms the fact that those who belong to Christ are accountable to Him. It should not surprise us that the first thing that Christ will do in the list of "things which must shortly come to pass" (Revelation 1:1) is the evaluation of His Church and how faithfully it has served Him in this world.

As Jesus evaluates the seven churches in Revelation 2 and 3, we see this glorified Lord of the Church speaking with authority as He penetrates the heart of each of these groups. These seven churches were literal churches in the Roman province of Asia, which is now part of the country of Turkey. They were living in difficult days and were facing real persecution. John himself was in exile on the isle of Patmos (verse 9). From the human view, things looked pretty bleak for these believers. One purpose in these messages is to reassure their hearts. Even should they be put to death, their eternal future was great, because God and His people will triumph. Jesus is coming back again and, when He comes, He will execute justice and will bring peace.

In the evaluations of these seven churches, we find not only words of commendation, but also words of condemnation. Our Lord is fully aware of the true condition of each of these assemblies, and He challenges them with a call to repentance because some are in danger of losing their witness for Christ. As the Lord commended the seven churches for what they had done, He also spoke of things that were not pleasing to Him. There were various levels of compromise and departure in five of the seven churches.

It is important that the Lord of the Church evaluate and judge each of the assemblies that make up His church, but what we find in these two chapters sets the stage for what happens in the rest of the Book of Revelation. The evaluation of the churches also provides the reason why the judgments that come upon Satan and this world system are justified. While the Church of Christ is called to be a light for Him, the Scripture makes clear that Satan and his kingdom will seek to infiltrate the church with false doctrine and other forms of corruption that bring words of condemnation from our Lord. Jesus warned in the parable of the *Wheat and the Tares* in Matthew 13 that Satan would seek to infiltrate the Lord's church.

We gain a clearer understanding of this if we consider what Jesus said in the parable found in Matthew 13:24-30:

> Another parable He put forth to them, saying: "The kingdom of heaven is like a man who sowed good seed in his field; but while men slept, his enemy came and sowed tares among the wheat and went his way. But when the grain had sprouted and produced a crop, then the tares also appeared. So the servants of the owner came and said to him, 'Sir, did you not sow good seed in your field? How then does it have tares?' He said to them, 'An enemy has done this.' The servants said to him, 'Do you want us then to go and gather them up?' But he said, 'No, lest while you gather up the tares you also uproot the wheat with them. Let both grow together until the harvest, and at the time of harvest I will say to the reapers, "First gather together the tares and bind them in bundles to burn them, but gather the wheat into my barn."'"

The message of this parable is so important that Jesus interpreted it for His disciples in Matthew 13:36-43:

> Then Jesus sent the multitude away and went into the house. And His disciples came to Him, saying, "Explain to us the parable of the tares of the field." He answered and said to them, "He who sows the good seed is the Son of Man. The field is the world, the good seeds are the sons of the kingdom, but the tares are the sons of the wicked one. The enemy who sowed them is the devil, the harvest is the end of the age, and the reapers are the angels. Therefore as the tares are gathered and burned in the fire, so it will be at the end of this age. The Son of Man will send out His angels, and they will gather out of His kingdom all things that offend, and those who practice lawlessness, and will cast them into the furnace of fire. There will be wailing and gnashing of teeth. Then the righteous will shine forth as the sun in the kingdom of their Father. He who has ears to hear, let him hear!"

In this parable, we are told that Satan will infiltrate the Kingdom of God (presently seen in the Church). The world's system, with its philosophy and value system, will find its way into churches and it will become part of Satan's kingdom within the church. Some will teach false doctrine and introduce many ungodly ways into the church. Not only will people in the church be out of harmony with the Lord, but also leaders in the church are spoken of in 2 Corinthians 11:13-15 as ministers of Satan:

> For such are false apostles, deceitful workers, transforming themselves into apostles of Christ. And no wonder! For Satan himself transforms himself into an angel of light. Therefore it is no great thing if his ministers also transform themselves into ministers of righteousness, whose end will be according to their works.

The present condition of the church is seen in these seven churches of John's time and what is revealed is worthy of the Lord's condemnation and judgment upon those who are tares sown among the wheat. Jesus told His disciples that they should not try to separate the false from the true for they would surely err in their judgment, but that His discernment is absolutely true and He will separate true grain from the tares. This is what happens in what we read in the Book of Revelation.

The Lord first deals with His Church by preserving that which belongs to Him, and then bringing judgment upon Satan and the world system which has corrupted His Church. In the Old Testament, Satan sought to kill God's people on a number of occasions. When that attack was thwarted by God, Satan sought to corrupt the people of Israel with idolatry and other evil acts. The Lord's Church is under similar attack. If persecution is not effective in destroying the church, Satan will infiltrate the church, corrupting it and bringing the Lord's judgment upon it.

The pouring of God's wrath upon Satan and man's system is justified as we consider in chapters 2 and 3 what has been done to the Lord's Church. "The gates of hell will not prevail against the church," but they will cause the Lord's judgment to come upon His Church as all that is evil is rooted out. After the Lord has dealt with His Church and what they have allowed to creep into their assemblies, He will pour

His judgment on those who have infiltrated His Church. The Lord's evaluation and condemnation of the individual assemblies sets the stage for what happens in the rest of the book.

In the Lord's message to each church we discover things of which He approves and things of which He disapproves. Each message, while directed to a specific church, is intended for all of His churches and for all who have ears that are open to listen. When He finds things of which He disapproves He calls them to repentance. His desire is that His church might be pure and a true representative of all that He is. If Christ is the Head of the Church then His church as a shining light, should reflect His attributes.

As we look at each of these churches and the words of Christ, it is also important to note the characteristics that are taken from the vision of Christ found in chapter one. How the Lord is described is indicative of what He will say to that church.

Evaluation of the Church of Ephesus – Revelation 2:1-7

To the angel of the church of Ephesus write, "These things says He who holds the seven stars in His right hand, who walks in the midst of the seven golden lampstands: 'I know your works, your labor, your patience, and that you cannot bear those who are evil. And you have tested those who say they are apostles and are not, and have found them liars; and you have persevered and have patience, and have labored for My name's sake and have not become weary. Nevertheless I have this against you, that you have left your first love. Remember therefore from where you have fallen; repent and do the first works, or else I will come to you quickly and remove your lampstand from its place—unless you repent. But this you have, that you hate the deeds of the Nicolaitans, which I also hate.

He who has an ear, let him hear what the Spirit says to the churches. To him who overcomes I will give to eat from the tree of life, which is in the midst of the Paradise of God.'"

The first church, Ephesus, had the richest heritage and stands out as a model of success. It was founded by the Apostle Paul. It was the place where he stayed for the longest period. It was the "mother church" that reached out and spawned many of the other churches in this province. Timothy ministered in that church, and it was pastored by the last of the Apostles, John. It was the successful church, the most prominent church in all of Asia.

As the Lord assesses this great church, He is presented as the one who has the messenger of this church in His hand, and as the one who is in the midst of the churches. He speaks as the head of the church and, up to a point, they have been responsive to Him. However there is a word of warning in His message, and in it He challenges them.

He begins by taking note of all of their accomplishments. Their successes were many. He spoke of their works, accomplishments, and all that was worthy of praise. He speaks of their diligence and their labor or toil. There was a great amount of energy and effort expended in their work. This was a working church, and their labor was effective and very productive.

They were not only a working church, but they possessed patient endurance. There was persistence in their service as they faithfully served. They were committed to purity and exercised discipline, in regard to both moral purity and doctrinal purity. They maintained a strong Biblical stand, and were noted for faithfulness. They endured, labored, did not get weary, and continued to promote the cause of Christ.

This is a great, busy and successful church, yet it is not without fault. As the Lord of the Church evaluates this assembly, His commendation is now offset by words of censure. There is something wrong in this church, and it is at the very heart of what a church should be. Jesus had told His disciples that the central issue is, "Thou shall love the Lord your God with all your heart" (Matthew 22:37-38). The question Jesus asked Peter on the shore of the Sea of Galilee was, "Do you love me?" All these other things are good and worthy of praise, but the thing that really matters is, "Do you love me with all of your heart?"

The church at Ephesus might say that they did love Him, but the Lord saw into their hearts and knew that their love for Him had cooled. They had left their first love. When our love for Christ cools, the rest is just activity that will soon lose meaning. Where is this great church of Ephesus today? Our service may be significant, but the real value of that service comes when it comes out of a heart that is over-flowing with love.

Lovingly the Lord urges His people to turn around, to rekindle that first love and renew their devotion. If their love is not restored, the dynamic of their witness will soon be lost. Their light will soon be extinguished if their love is not rekindled. Above everything else, this relationship that we have with Christ is a love relationship. What we do for Him, we do out of love, or else it is mere activity. Even the church's commitment to orthodoxy becomes hollow without a love that motivates it all. This counsel is intended not just for them, it is for all who have ears to hear. The Spirit is not just speaking to this church, but to all the churches. Do we really love Him?

Evaluation of the Church of Smyrna – Revelation 2:8-11

> And to the angel of the church in Smyrna write, "These things says the First and the Last, who was dead, and came to life: 'I know your works, tribulation, and poverty (but you are rich); and I know the blasphemy of those who say they are Jews and are not, but are a synagogue of Satan. Do not fear any of those things which you are about to suffer. Indeed, the devil is about to throw some of you into prison, that you may be tested, and you will have tribulation ten days. Be faithful until death, and I will give you the crown of life.
>
> He who has an ear, let him hear what the Spirit says to the churches. He who overcomes shall not be hurt by the second death.'"

Not far away in the town of Smyrna there is another church. Its accomplishments cannot begin to measure up to all that Ephesus has done.

This is a church that may appear to be far less desirable, but it is one that is worthy of our consideration.

The church in Smyrna was in the very stronghold of Satan. The pressure of persecution was being applied to these believers. As a result of this pressure, they were not able to have some of the necessities of life. The Lord knew their need and spoke of the fact that they were in poverty. As far as the material goods of this world, they had very little. Likely the persecution had denied them opportunity to make a living and support their family.

It is important to note how the Lord referred to Himself as He spoke to them. He is the first and the last, the one who was dead and is alive. Being the first and the last means that He brought all things into being, and He will bring all things to completion. He is the Sovereign Lord of this Universe and they can rest in Him. Being the One who suffered death, He is able to understand what they are facing. Do not forget that He is the One who conquered death, and His victory is on our behalf. No persecutor can take away the life that He has given to us.

In verse 9 He says, "I know your works, your tribulation and your poverty." He knows with complete knowledge what this persecuted church is going through. He understands their need yet, as He evaluates their church, He proclaims them to be rich. It is interesting that He has no words of censure for this church. Ephesus is the successful church, while Smyrna is the one that the Lord declares to be rich spiritually.

The Lord encourages this church as they face persecution and even possible death. Note some of the things that He says. He says, "What you shall suffer." This is going to happen. As we live in this world, suffering is inevitable and in some places it will be severe. The Lord does not promise to keep us from suffering. This is the persecuted suffering church, and in our world today churches in various parts of the world suffer persecution. The words of Christ found here are applicable to all who suffer today for the cause of Christ.

The church of Smyrna is told that this suffering would continue for an extended period of time and it would even get worse. Some would be cast into prison in times of great trial. And for some it may result in physical death. But the Lord assures them of His presence and of His sustaining grace. He also assures them of the ultimate outcome. There is a glorious crown of life ahead for those who continue to be faithful in the face of persecution. Satan may inflict death upon God's people, but the Lord gives us a crown of life. All He asks is that we be faithful.

Again this message is not just for this church, but for all who will hear what the Spirit is saying. Physical death can only touch our bodies, but the second death is eternal separation from God in the Lake of Fire (Revelation 20:14). The greatest thing that you can have in this life is the assurance that you will spend eternity with the Lord forever. Many may have success and riches in this life, but having eternal life and enjoying the presence of God forever is true riches. The suffering church today can find true comfort in the words of Christ given to the church at Smyrna.

Evaluation of the Church of Pergamos – Revelation 2:12-17

> And to the angel of the church in Pergamos write, "These things says He who has the sharp two-edged sword: 'I know your works, and where you dwell, where Satan's throne is. And you hold fast to My name, and did not deny My faith even in the days in which Antipas was My faithful martyr, who was killed among you, where Satan dwells. But I have a few things against you, because you have there those who hold the doctrine of Balaam, who taught Balak to put a stumbling block before the children of Israel, to eat things sacrificed to idols, and to commit sexual immorality. Thus you also have those who hold the doctrine of the Nicolaitans, which thing I hate. Repent, or else I will come to you quickly and will fight against them with the sword of My mouth.
>
> He who has an ear, let him hear what the Spirit says to the churches. To him who overcomes I will give some of the hidden manna to eat. And I will give him a white stone, and on the stone a new name written which no one knows except him who receives it.'"

Pergamos was the capital of the province of Asia, and was a wealthy and beautiful city. It was also a center for pagan worship, with a number of temples dedicated to pagan gods. One of the chief gods was Asclepius, the god of healing, the serpent on the pole that symbolizes the medical profession today. Miraculous cures were attributed to this god. Being the capital of the Roman province, its people were also committed to worship of the emperor. The Lord recognized that this church was in the center of Satan's territory. He did praise them for the fact that they had not denied His name or the faith. They were in a place where persecution was a reality, and they had not turned away from the Lord. It is difficult to live under this kind of pressure, and the Lord commended them for standing true.

The Lord is pictured here as He addressed this church as the one who "has the sharp sword with two edges." This alerts us to the fact that there are some things in this church that warrant words of condemnation and the Lord's judgment. While He commended them for not denying the faith, He exposed some areas of compromise that caused Him great concern. He spoke of the *Doctrine of Balaam*, which recalls the prophet who was hired by the king of Moab to curse Israel. God did not allow Balaam to curse Israel, but Balaam did counsel Balak to use some young women to cause the men of Israel to compromise their sexual purity and to compromise with idolatry. Some 24,000 men of Israel died because of this compromise. Evidently there were some people in the church at Pergamos who were encouraging God's people to compromise with pagan practices.

The Lord also speaks of the *Doctrine of Nicolaitans*. The Bible does not tell us exactly what this group was teaching. Some believe it was a teaching that divides the church into clergy and laity. Others think it was a group that allowed liberty to become a license to sin. It is not important to know what the teaching was, but rather only that God hated this doctrine. This church was not opposing what God hated, in fact they tolerated it. They were allowing false teaching to get a foothold in the church. There was no discipline, and no censure of these false doctrines. Truth must not be compromised, because compromising truth soon leads to promoting error.

The Lord says that if the church did not turn around and deal with this false doctrine, He will use His sharp sword to deal with the problem. When we do not exercise discipline, the Lord will do it with His sword. He challenges them to listen carefully and respond positively. To those who do respond, there is promised blessing. It may be hard to deal with compromise in the church, but God blesses those who dare to obey His Word.

In verse 17, we are reminded that this message is for all who hear what The Lord says to this church, and for all those who have compromised God's truth. He extends His love and grace, offering an opportunity to repent. Along with the call to repentance, there is a promise that is worth pursuing. The Lord promises manna that will satisfy their soul, and also a new name written in a white stone that assures them of a glorious future in the Kingdom of God eternally.

Evaluation of the Church of Thyatira – Revelation 2:18-29

And to the angel of the church in Thyatira write, "These things says the Son of God, who has eyes like a flame of fire, and His feet like fine brass: 'I know your works, love, service, faith, and your patience; and as for your works, the last are more than the first. Nevertheless I have a few things against you, because you allow that woman Jezebel, who calls herself a prophetess, to teach and seduce My servants to commit sexual immorality and eat things sacrificed to idols. And I gave her time to repent of her sexual immorality, and she did not repent. Indeed I will cast her into a sickbed, and those who commit adultery with her into great tribulation, unless they repent of their deeds. I will kill her children with death, and all the churches shall know that I am He who searches the minds and hearts. And I will give to each one of you according to your works. Now to you I say, and to the rest in Thyatira, as many as do not have this doctrine, who have not known the depths of Satan, as they say, I will put on you no other burden. But hold fast what you have till I come. And he who overcomes, and keeps My works until the end, to him I will give power over the nations.

"He shall rule them with a rod of iron;
They shall be dashed to pieces like the potter's vessels"
as I also have received from My Father; and I will give him
the morning star.
He who has an ear, let him hear what the Spirit says to the
churches.'"

Thyatira was what might be called a blue-collar town, a place of industry and commerce. Lydia (a convert under Paul's ministry) was from this city and sold dyes produced there. As the Lord speaks to the church at Thyatira, He is described as one whose eyes are a flame of fire and His feet like fine brass. Flaming eyes speak of discernment and the ability to penetrate to the very heart. Feet of brass speak of judgment, and this metal is found in the Old Testament referring to the judgment of sin (as in the brazen altar where sacrifices for sin were made at the Temple). The Lord has words of condemnation for this church.

Before the words of condemnation, the Lord spoke, however, of the church's love, faithful service and works. This church seemed to be busy, and as time progressed, they were doing more, not less. However, lots of activity does not always mean that the Lord is pleased. We cannot deceive God with our activity, with our busy-ness. In spite of the good things the church was doing, there were some serious problems.

As there was compromise in tolerating false doctrine in Pergamos, the church at Thyatira was actually allowing false doctrine to be taught. It had worked its way into the church, and it was tolerated, now even allowing false teachers to be in a position of authority. The Lord says,

> Nevertheless I have a few things against you, because you allow that woman Jezebel, who calls herself a prophetess, to teach and seduce My servants to commit sexual immorality and eat things sacrificed to idols.

The name Jezebel goes back to some of the darkest days, spiritually, in Israel. Jezebel was the wife of King Ahab. She brought the worship of Baal into prominence in Israel and was in conflict with God's prophet, Elijah. Her name speaks of false worship and the corruption of God's people. Her name and reputation is now used by the Lord to speak of one who was teaching in this church. Her teaching was actually encouraging immorality and idolatry.

The Lord was patient and gave time for repentance, but it was not forthcoming. There is no alternative but to judge this corruption that has become a part of the church. The Lord is surely going to judge this church because of their apostasy, because they have departed from the truth. The Lord warns them that they will incur the judgment of the Great Tribulation unless they repent. What He says to this church is a warning to all churches: God will not tolerate evil in the church, and He will surely judge false doctrine and those who depart from His truth. We can certainly see this today, how false doctrine has crept into the church. It was tolerated at first, and now the church has become corrupt with error.

There are, however, some people even in this corrupt church who have not embraced the false doctrine, and are standing true to the Lord and His truth. The Lord encourages them to hold fast and remain true, and He will put no other burden on them. This battle for truth is a priority, and they need to stay focused on this one thing. Never surrender the truth of God; hold fast. Again there is great reward for those who remain true to God and to His Holy Word. God has a glorious future ahead for His faithful servants. They may suffer now as error seems to be winning, but God's truth will ultimately triumph, and His true servants will reap the benefits.

There is a choice that needs to be made, and those who reject false doctrine and hold to God's truth will rule with Christ in His kingdom. He is coming again and their faithfulness will be rewarded in eternity. The "morning star" calls us to focus on a new day, a day when God will restore His creation and remove all that is evil. Again it is for all who will hear.

Evaluation of the Church of Sardis – Revelation 3:1-6

And to the angel of the church in Sardis write, "These things says He who has the seven Spirits of God and the seven stars:

'I know your works, that you have a name that you are alive, but you are dead. Be watchful, and strengthen the things which remain, that are ready to die, for I have not found your works perfect before God. Remember therefore how you have received and heard; hold fast and repent. Therefore if you will not watch, I will come upon you as a thief, and you will not know what hour I will come upon you. You have a few names even in Sardis who have not defiled their garments; and they shall walk with Me in white, for they are worthy. He who overcomes shall be clothed in white garments, and I will not blot out his name from the Book of Life; but I will confess his name before My Father and before His angels.

He who has an ear, let him hear what the Spirit says to the churches.'"

As we look at the next church, we realize that sometimes it is difficult as we look from the outside to tell whether a church is dead or alive. We cannot always tell at first glance whether a church is dead or alive, but the Lord Jesus is the Lord of the Church, and He knows the true state of each church. It is His evaluation that really counts, and we need to listen to what He says about this church.

As the Sovereign Head of the Church, Jesus said, "I know your works, that you have a name that you are alive, but you are dead." Here is a church that has a reputation for being alive, but as the Lord penetrates into what is true, He finds that they are spiritually dead. The description of the Lord is that of one who has the sevenfold Spirit of God and who holds the seven stars in His hand. He is all-wise, with complete and perfect discernment. He sees things as they really are, and the messengers of each of these churches are in His hand. He is sovereign. He is the Lord of the Church, and He will evaluate every local assembly.

Sardis was a proud city noted for its Acropolis, 800 to 1500 feet high, with almost vertical rocky cliffs, making it virtually impregnable. With its lofty position, the city was easily defended, giving rise to a spirit of complacency. Sadly, this same spirit seemed to permeate the church in that city. What the Lord has to say in evaluation of this church is rather brief. There are no words of commendation as with other churches.

All that He had to say was, "You have a name that you are alive, but you are dead."

The image that was projected in this church was very positive. Their reputation was good, and they appeared to be alive. The fact was, as the Lord saw them, they were spiritually dead. The reality was missing, the power was gone. Many churches fall into this category today. They may at one time have been a strong church, and they may have a good reputation, but now they are empty and dead. Oh, they still go through the motions. There are still activities, but no life, no power, no effective ministry. The Lord sees the inner reality, He sees the heart. His verdict was that this church was dead.

It is important for us to note, however, that the Lord does not give up on this church. It is still His concern, and He has a challenge for them. He says, "Be watchful," meaning be alert and wake up. They needed to shake off their apathy and realize the gravity of their condition. "Strengthen things that remain," states that there is still some hope, but they must wake up and take action or they were in danger of dying. Their works were not perfect before God. God really was not pleased with this church, but there was still some hope.

There was a time when this Church was responsive to the Lord and His Word, but those days were past. The Lord calls upon them to look back and remember those days, and turn around and renew their commitment. Revival is new obedience to old truth. Start doing what you know you should do. If you do not take corrective action then, in an unexpected time, the Lord will come to judge this church.

The Lord speaks of judgment, but He recognizes that even in this dead church, there are a few who are still true to the Lord. They have not defiled their garments. Their heart is still right before the Lord. The Lord knows those who are truly His, and He will richly reward them for their faithfulness in the midst of deadness. He encourages these faithful ones that they will be clothed in white garments (His righteousness) and He will not blot their names out of the book of life. Rather He will confess them, as His followers, before God the Father and before the angels of Heaven. As with the other churches, the message is intended for all who will listen.

Evaluation of the Church of Philadelphia – Revelation 3:7-13

> And to the angel of the church in Philadelphia write, "These
> things says He who is holy, He who is true, He who has the
> key of David, He who opens and no one shuts, and shuts
> and no one opens: 'I know your works. See, I have set before
> you an open door, and no one can shut it; for you have a little
> strength, have kept My word, and have not denied My name.
> Indeed I will make those of the synagogue of Satan, who say
> they are Jews and are not, but lie—indeed I will make them
> come and worship before your feet, and to know that I have
> loved you. Because you have kept My command to perse-
> vere, I also will keep you from the hour of trial which shall
> come upon the whole world, to test those who dwell on the
> earth. Behold, I am coming quickly! Hold fast what you
> have, that no one may take your crown. He who overcomes,
> I will make him a pillar in the temple of My God, and he shall
> go out no more. I will write on him the name of My God and
> the name of the city of My God, the New Jerusalem, which
> comes down out of heaven from My God. And I will write
> on him My new name.
> He who has an ear, let him hear what the Spirit says to the
> churches.'"

The Philadelphia church appears to be small and struggling, yet very
much alive. In addressing this church, the Lord spoke as the One who
is Holy and true, and as the One who has the key of David, the key to
the kingdom. When He opens a door, no one can shut it, and when He
shuts a door, no one can open it. The Lord wants to assure this small
and struggling church that He is in authority, and that they can take
comfort in what He is doing. They may be small in numbers, but the
Lord commends them for their faithfulness. They had not denied His
name, and they were faithful to His Word – meaning that they not only
proclaimed it, but they lived it on a daily basis. The Lord's standard for
those who are His people is that they be faithful.

They may think that they are small or weak and do not have much impact, but the Lord says that He will set before them an open door that no one can shut. When God opens a door, we can expect Him to work in a special way. This faithful band of believers can rely on the Lord to meet their needs and to bless their ministry. You may feel overwhelmed and weak before your enemies, but one day they will bow before you and acknowledge that they were wrong. The Lord will fight for His people, and there will be ultimate victory. Our responsibility is to be faithful. The Lord will deal with our enemies and those who lie about us.

The challenge is for this church to patiently endure and continue to be faithful. The Hour of Trial is said to come upon the whole world. It is undoubtedly the time when God's judgment will be poured upon the earth in the period called the Great Tribulation. As in Egypt when God's wrath was poured upon the Pharaoh and the Egyptians, the Lord's people were spared. God's judgment has been executed on Christ as He bore our sins to the cross of Calvary and there died in our place and for those who will choose to believe there is no more condemnation (Romans 8:1). God's people may suffer now from the hand of the enemy, but they will be spared when God's wrath is poured upon this world and those in it.

The motivation for both this church and for us is to be faithful in believing that our Lord is coming back and will reward His servants. Crowns are promised to those who remain true and faithful. As we live today, we are really living for eternity. A pillar in the temple speaks of stability, and there are words here that also speak of security. To have a place in God's Kingdom, to be a part of the New Jerusalem, this is what really matters. The Lord's name is inscribed on His people. We belong to Him and that will never change.

Evaluation of the Church of Laodicea – Revelation 3:14-19

And to the angel of the church of the Laodiceans write, "These things says the Amen, the Faithful and True Witness, the Beginning of the creation of God: 'I know your works, that you are neither cold nor hot. I could wish you were cold or hot. So then, because you are lukewarm, and neither cold nor hot, I will vomit you out of My mouth. Because you say, "I am rich, have become wealthy, and have need of nothing"—and do not know that you are wretched, miserable, poor, blind, and naked— I counsel you to buy from Me gold refined in the fire, that you may be rich; and white garments, that you may be clothed, that the shame of your nakedness may not be revealed; and anoint your eyes with eye salve, that you may see. As many as I love, I rebuke and chasten. Therefore be zealous and repent.'"

The final church in this group being evaluated by Christ is Laodicea, and there is little to commend them because a serious condition existed in that church. This church again demonstrates how Satan and the world have impacted the church. The Church of Laodicea was self-sufficient and had no sense of need. Their own assessment was that, "they were rich, increased with goods, and have need of nothing." Many churches today can fit pretty well with this evaluation. There are beautiful buildings, ample resources, and all kinds of programs and activities, but where is the power of God? Laodicea was satisfied that they had it all together and their needs were few. The Lord saw something very different. The reality was that this church was wretched, miserable, poor, blind and naked. Their needs were much greater than they realized. They were blinded by pride, believing that they were rich and needing nothing. This is the tragedy of the complacent church. Not only are they in desperate need, but sadly they do not know it.

The Lord is grieved with this church. He is ready to spew them out of His mouth. They are nauseating, and yet He still pleads with them. We see His grace and patience. Instead of giving up on them, He lovingly urges them to stop and take inventory. He urges them to humbly acknowledge their need, and recognize that He is able to completely meet their need. True riches are not found in material things. Eternal riches and true gold are found only in Christ. This gold is purified and has eternal worth. He has white raiment to give us to not only cover our nakedness, but to beautifully adorn us. As we come to Him, we can be clothed in His righteousness. This is the only adequate covering for our nakedness. The Lord has a special eye salve that can bring healing and sight to our blind eyes. Every need of this church can be completely met in Jesus Christ. His words to them were words of rebuke, but His rebuke came from His love. He truly cared for them.

In this context, we find one of the greatest invitations ever offered. The Lord does not just reject the whole church, even though He might have done so. In love and grace, He reaches out to those within this church, or within any of the other churches. Even when the church has grown cold or apostatized, the Lord still is reaching out to individuals who are willing to respond to His invitation. The picture is painted here of One who stands at the door seeking admission into our lives. He wants to have a relationship with us. He wants to fellowship with us. He wants to share His riches. He wants us to eat at His table, to share the feast that He has prepared.

The Sovereign Lord of the Church is now seen knocking at the door, seeking entrance into the assemblies that have shut Him out, but He also speaks to individuals within these churches who desire a personal relationship with Him. There must be a response to this knocking and to this invitation. He will not force His way in. You must hear His voice, listen to the invitation and open the door. It is the responsibility of each one who hears the invitation to respond to it. This invitation has eternal implications. There is an offer here that you need to consider. He will not only give you a place in His kingdom, when He returns to rule as King of kings and Lord of lords, but He will give us the privilege to sit with Him upon His throne. What a glorious prospect, to sit with the King on His throne, and to rule and reign with Him. Nothing that this world could ever offer us can compare with this invitation. He closes this message to this church as He closes all of the other messages. If you have an ear, listen, pay close attention to what is being said. We are responsible for what we hear. We have been given ears and we need to use them. We have heard with our ears what the Lord has said. God's

Spirit has given us a special opportunity and we need to respond to His invitation.

While these seven churches were existing in the time when John wrote, they also provide a picture of churches throughout the ages. Some are faithful and true like Smyrna and Philadelphia, but there are others that have been corrupted by Satan and the influence of this world, or that have either cooled in their love for Christ or are unaware of their true spiritual poverty. What Jesus said in Matthew 13 is seen here in Revelation as Jesus evaluates the church. With all that Satan has done to diminish the impact of the church, and even to bring the judgment of Christ on some in it, we need to know that the words of Jesus in Matthew 16:18 are still true, "the gates of hell shall not prevail against it" (His Church).

The Lord will separate the tares from the wheat so that the false will be removed into judgment, but the true followers of Christ will prevail in the end. Those who are faithful and true in their faith in Christ will enter into His kingdom and the Lord will bring judgment upon this world and upon Satan for what has been done to the people of God. Our Lord has said vengeance is His, and He will bring justice to those who have suffered at the hands of Satan and the forces of this world system. This is what is presented to us in the Book of Revelation. The Lord brings judgment upon Satan and man's system that has persecuted and corrupted a portion of the Lord's church. His church is seen as ultimately triumphant in God's plan.

As we consider this first vision of Christ as the Lord of the Church, and as we consider what He says about the condition of His church, we find things that are very disturbing. How did the Lord's Church get in such an unholy condition where it is infiltrated with false doctrine, idolatry and immoral activity? If it is His church, what has happened to bring it to the place where it is found worthy of His judgment? The truth is that the Kingdom of man, empowered by Satan, has infiltrated the church and has corrupted it to the point that judgment is merited. This fact also provides the context for what is about to unfold in this book. Our Lord must not only judge what is false in His church, but He also must judge the kingdom of man and Satan, who are responsible for what they have done to His church. The Lord will avenge His people and His church. The outpouring of God's wrath on this world and on Satan's kingdom is justified when we understand the reality of this great conflict.

Vision II

Sacrificial Lamb Declared Worthy to Reign
Revelation 4 - 5

THE FIRST VISION OF THE EXALTED CHRIST, seen by John as he was in exile on the isle of Patmos, presented Jesus Christ as Lord over the church on earth, the visible representation of Christ's church on earth. As we look now at the second vision, we see John transported, in spirit, into heaven where he is in the presence of God who is seated upon His throne. John's attention is directed to the one who is seated upon the throne, and he describes a vision of the sovereign God. In this vision, we see Jesus Christ as He is viewed from the Throne Room of God in Heaven.

Here we see what might be described as the command center for the entire universe as John is ushered into the Throne Room of God, where all that goes on in this creation is under His control. All creation came into being by the power of God's sovereign command, and this universe is sustained by the power of His Throne. God is sovereign and has an eternal plan for all that He has created. Satan and humans have rebelled against God and sin has entered into this universe, but God is not thwarted. At times it may appear that things are out of control, but God is still moving toward the purpose that He has established.

At times people may ask, "Why doesn't God do something?" It may appear that God is silent and that He does not care about what is happening in our world. The reality is that God is long-suffering and He will allow humans to continue in their rebellion, but only to a point. God will intervene; He will speak and exercise judgment over this world.

God's eternal purpose is about to be unfolded and Christ is the one who will open the sealed scroll. As we are ushered into God's Throne Room, we see Him as the awesome God who is worthy of our worship. These two chapters are really the heart and soul of this book. Everything in the rest of this book emanates from the Throne of God.

Jesus taught us to pray, "Thy kingdom come, your will be done on earth as it is in heaven." That prayer soon will be answered. God will intervene and gloriously triumph over the evil of this world. All those who know and love Him will bow before His Throne in jubilant worship. This Book of Revelation is really all about this glorious triumph, and it is filled with jubilant worship. Twenty-four times in these 22 chapters, we find the word "worship." Some of the greatest worship scenes found in Scripture are in this book. Let's look now into the Throne Room of God, and bow with those who worship before Him.

The radiant glory of God is compared to brilliant gem stones and the multicolored rainbow (Revelation 4:3). Ezekiel had a similar vision of God's throne. God is light, and when light is refracted, we see all the various colors of the rainbow. God's glory has many facets, and there is no way to adequately describe it in human language. John tries to give us a glimpse of the awesome power and authority of God that proceeds from His throne. He can only describe it as "lightning, thunder and voices" (verse 5). There is sovereign authority and power when God speaks, and God is about to speak. The sevenfold Spirit of God, God's Spirit in all of His perfection, proceeds from the throne like burning lamps of fire.

As John is overwhelmed by the One who sits upon the throne, he becomes aware that there are other created beings also present. They are all gathered around the throne in circular fashion, facing the One who is seated there. It seems there are two groups of beings that John sees. First he sees 24 elders seated on seats (verse 4). There are three things about these beings that captured John's attention. First, they are seated on seats, actually thrones. Secondly, they are clothed in white robes and, thirdly, they had gold crowns on their heads. I believe that these three descriptions help us identify these elders. First we might note that elders in Scripture usually are representatives of God's people. Then as we look at the three things said to be true of them, we realize that each of these three things is promised to God's people as Christ evaluates His Church. They are to be seated on thrones (3:21). They are to be clothed in white raiment (3:5), and they are to be given gold crowns for faithful service (2:10; 3:11). The Greek word for crown used in this passage is not the word "diadem," referring to one who rules, but it is "stephanos," a word which spoke of victor's crowns. This is the word that was used to crown athletes for their accomplishments, and these crowns are given to the followers of Christ as a reward for faithful service.

Next, John records that there also are four living creatures around the throne of God. These beings, also created by God, are unlike anything in our human world. The Book of Ezekiel is of great help to us because the prophet Ezekiel saw the same thing when he was ushered into the Throne Room of God (Ezekiel 1:5-28). In a similar fashion, John seeks to describe these living creatures for his readers. He tells us that they were "full of eyes before and behind" (Revelation 4:6). By this John tells us that they could see more fully in every direction with great discernment, understanding what God is about to do.

In verse 7 John seeks to describe how they appeared to him. They had faces that John could only try to describe by using some of the attributes of other things in this created world. He sees in their faces some of the qualities of a lion, some of a calf, some human-like and also the qualities of a flying eagle. Each of these beings also possessed six wings (verse 8) and their mission was to extol the Holy God. Isaiah had a similar vision in Isaiah 6. In Ezekiel 10:15, 20-22, these living creatures are identified as cherubim. When God instructed Moses to build the Tabernacle, the inner room was to represent the Throne Room of God. In addition, on the ark there were cherubim as the angelic beings that continually celebrate the glory of God's holiness.

In verses 9-11, we see that the worship of these cherubim produces a similar ascription of praise that comes from the 24 elders. All created beings, whether heavenly or earthly beings, are seen as they join together in worship before the throne of God. He alone is worthy of worship, and what God is about to do will elicit a celebration of praise. As these elders worship the One who sits upon the throne, they cast their crowns before the throne. There is clear recognition here that all honor and glory belongs to the Lord. Any crown of reward that we might receive for something done here on earth is really not of our doing. First we were incapable of doing anything for God until He saved us by His grace, renewing us in Christ. Having been saved, we are then empowered by God's Holy Spirit and anything we may accomplish is really done by Him. This scene may suggest to us that the rewards we receive for faithful service may in some way increase our capacity to worship and glorify the Lord.

As we look at this Book of Revelation, we should try not to allow ourselves to get so occupied with all of the details of the Tribulation, and of this man we call the Antichrist, that we miss the real message. God is on His Throne. He is working out His sovereign plan. He will speak in judgment, and He will establish His kingdom of righteousness. As we work our way through this book, let us not lose sight of the perspective that we get here from the Throne Room of God. As God accomplishes His glorious will and purpose, let us bow before His throne, attributing all glory and honor unto Him. This scene at the Throne of God prepares the way for all that is to follow, so that as we watch God's plan unfold, we are moved to worship and exalt His glorious name.

As God sits upon His throne, there is a scroll in His hand (Revelation 5:1). This scroll is sealed with seven seals. With the opening of this scroll, God's eternal plan will be brought to completion. God's design in creation was to create the earth, and the heavens above it, as a dwelling place for humans. His design in making humans after His own image and likeness was to live in fellowship with this man that He had created. At creation, God also gave this man authority to rule over this earthly creation and all of the other created things in it. With the entrance of sin, there was a breach in this fellowship and an attempt to thwart the plan of God. The rule of humans over God's creation has been restricted by sin and by the curse upon creation that came as a result of sin.

John's attention is captured by the loud voice of an angel who shouts a challenge from God's throne. The challenge is, "Who is worthy to open the book, and to loose the seals on it?" The opening of this scroll is the fulfilling of God's eternal plan and purpose for His creation and for humans. Is there no one who can meet this challenge and bring God's plan to fulfillment? With the sin and rebellion of humans, the challenge now requires some provision for redemption and for reconciliation between God and man. Who is able to put away the sin problem and establish God's righteous kingdom on earth? The kingdoms of this world must be subdued, and they must become the Kingdom of our Lord and of His Christ. Satan and his forces must be defeated.

As this challenge is issued, there is no response. There is no man in heaven, on earth or even under the earth able to meet this challenge. There was no one to step up to be man's champion. In verse 3, we are specifically told that there was no human who was able. Some might consider it, but the fact is that no one is able. We are all sinners. How could we meet this challenge? It was not a matter of reluctance; it was a matter of inability. No one was worthy, no one was able, and no one could do what needed to be done. John was so dismayed and grieved by this that he wept much. The question is "Shall God's plan remain unfulfilled?" What a tragedy. John wept much because of this.

As John weeps, one of the elders comforts him and points his attention to the Lion of the tribe of Judah, the Root of David. There is a champion, one who is able to meet the challenge and accomplish God's plan. God promised David that one of his descendants would sit upon the throne forever. The Lion of the tribe of Judah refers to the Messiah, and Old Testament prophets spoke again and again of His coming. (Genesis 49:9-10; Isaiah 11:1, 10; Jeremiah 23:5, 33:15). This Lion has prevailed, triumphed, and conquered the enemy. He has prevailed to bring God's eternal plan to completion. The finished work of redemption has triumphed over sin, death and hell, reconciling us to God through the sacrifice of the Lamb.

As John looked to see this Lion, what he saw was a Lamb. The Lamb gave evidence that it had been slain. The Lion and the Lamb come together in the person of Jesus Christ. This was a puzzle for many people in the day of Jesus. The Lion speaks of one who rules, and the slain lamb speaks of one who suffers and is offered as a sacrifice. The problem for many people, in the day of Jesus, was how could these two be one person, one Messiah? John in this passage sees them as one. The Lamb who was slain is the Lion who shall rule. As our champion, He has defeated sin, death and hell. He has conquered Satan. Salvation is now offered to us as a free gift. He has met the challenge, and has brought to completion the eternal plan of God.

Note that this Lamb is now in the midst of the Throne, in the midst of the elders. He is the pre-eminent One, He is worthy of all glory, honor and praise. As John looks closely at this Lamb, he sees seven horns and seven eyes. The horns speak of authority and power and the number seven indicates that His authority is full, and His power is complete. In Matthew 28:18, Jesus told His followers that all authority has been given unto Him. We also are told that the seven eyes are the seven Spirits of God, or the Spirit of God in all of His fullness and power (John 3:34).

As John looks in awe, the Lamb comes and takes the scroll from the hand of the One who sits upon the Throne. He is able to bring to completion God's plan. What John is about to see unfold before his eyes is the eternal plan of God. God will judge sin, He will destroy man's kingdom, and the righteous, eternal kingdom of God is about to be established. And Jesus Christ is the one who will bring all of this to pass. He is the champion, and His death has provided for the restoration of all things. As He takes the scroll, He assumes all authority to bring to completion the eternal plan of God.

What we see described by John is also presented to us in Hebrews 2. In that passage, the writer of the Book of Hebrews quotes from Psalm 8 as he is contemplating the high position that God has given to man. Man is made a little lower than the angels, but he has been given dominion over all of the created things on earth. The writer goes on to say that there is nothing that is excluded from man's earthly authority, however, he also adds that this dominion is not a reality at this time. Man is not in control over this creation, but there is one who has become man for us. We see Jesus, who became a man in order that He might redeem us and reconcile us to God. In doing so, He now brings many sons of God with Him into eternal glory. This is what we see in this scene in heaven.

As the Lamb steps forward to take the scroll, all heaven breaks forth in waves of praise and songs of acclamation. Although many events will yet unfold on earth, the result is assured. The Lamb has prevailed, and the Lion will rule. There will be other times in this book when heaven will resound with praise and acclamation, but it all begins here. This praise seems to come in three movements, with one flowing into the next.

First, in verses 8-10, the elders and the cherubim fall down and worship the Lamb as one who is worthy. The song they sing is one of redemption. They praise the Lamb because He has redeemed us to God, by His own blood. They have come from every nation on earth, and are now in the family of God. They glorify the Lamb for His work of redemption. With harps and singing, they celebrate the Lamb. Note what is said about the prayers of the saints, for now all of those prayers are about to be answered. How long they have prayed, "Thy Kingdom come." How long they have prayed that God would right all wrongs, and that God would deal with evil. Long they have prayed for Satan to be defeated, and for God's truth to prevail. All of these prayers are about to be answered, as the seals are broken and this scroll is unfolded.

They praise the Lamb because He has delivered them from sin, re-deeming them unto God. There is more: He also has made those who follow Christ to be a kingdom of priests before God. We can enter His presence, and offer both prayer and praise. And His redemptive work has provided a glorious prospect. We shall reign on earth with Him. It was God's purpose and plan that humans have dominion over God's earthly creation (Genesis 1:26). Our champion has won the right for humans to reign with Him (Hebrews 2:5-9).

Secondly, as the cherubim and elders worship before the Lamb, they are joined by the whole host of angelic beings (verses 11, 12). The number was beyond John's ability to count, as all the hosts of heaven join in giving praise unto the Lamb. This Lamb that was slain is worthy to receive power, riches, wisdom, strength, honor, glory and blessing. It seems that there are not enough words, and not enough ways, to give Him the honor He really deserves. He is worthy of all acclamation. All praise belongs to Him.

The final wave of praise and adoration comes from every being God has ever created. Note who is included in this group: every being in heaven, on earth, under the earth, in the sea, and all that are contained within them. All bow to acknowledge that He is worthy. They worship the One who sits on the throne, and they worship the Lamb. What we see here is what we read in Philippians 2:10-11. God has declared that "every knee shall bow and every tongue shall confess that Jesus Christ is Lord." Not only those who follow Christ, but ultimately every being (human or angelic) will bow in acknowledging that Jesus Christ is the Lord of all creation. He is worthy to be praised. This does not mean that everyone who bows before Christ is now one of His own. It is the bow of the conquered one before the victor that is seen here.

This glorious worship scene ends with the cherubim adding their "amen," and with the elders prostrate before Him in worship. If we are going to understand the rest of the Book of Revelation we must see it in the light of this scene as Christ is bringing God's plan to completion. Heaven has declared Him worthy, and He will begin to exercise judgment on the Kingdom of Man as He opens the seals that reveal the fulfillment of God's eternal plan.

Vision III

Righteous Judge Over All the Earth
Revelation 6-18

$\mathbf{T}$HE NEXT VISION RECORDED BY JOHN opens another view of the exaltation of Jesus Christ. This vision covers a large portion of the book, and pictures the Lamb opening the seals – resulting in judgment upon this world system and those who have rebelled against God. In John 5:22-27, Jesus declared that God the Father has committed all judgment unto the Son. The Father has given the Son all authority to execute judgment. This is what John sees in the Book of Revelation, as He sees the Lamb of God opening the seals and executing God's righteous judgment on this world.

Before we go any further in the study of Revelation, we need to make sure that we do not miss the big picture. We need to stand back and see the overview of what is happening. In Revelation 5, we saw the Lamb step forward as the champion of man, as the only hope for our sinful race. This Lamb is the Son of God and He is acclaimed as the One who is worthy to open the seals of this scroll and bring the plan of God to a glorious end. The thing that we saw about this Lamb is that He has been slain. In the conflict with Satan and human sin, He suffered death for us, yet He triumphed over death as He rose again from the grave. All of heaven sang His praises, because He triumphed over Satan and all of His forces. He won a glorious victory over sin, death and hell.

So as we come to Revelation 6, we see the Lamb opening the seals of God's plan for dealing with the kingdom of this world and the establishment of His kingdom. In a military conflict, the plans of battle are kept sealed and hidden from the enemy. The difference here is that Christ has been established as the victor, and the outcome is no longer in doubt. While there are still some skirmishes with the enemy, the victory has been assured. The Lamb has triumphed over Satan, and we can rejoice in Him, and worship at His feet. God's Word tells us clearly that Christ is the Triumphant One who has defeated the enemy (John 16:11; Colossians 2:15; Hebrews 2:14-15).

In Revelation 5:9-10, the saints worship and praise Him because He has "redeemed us to God and has made us a kingdom of priests before God and we shall reign upon the earth." The question is resolved, the victory is won, and the outcome of the conflict is certain. The issue has been decided, for the slain lamb has triumphed and is acclaimed as victor. He is worthy to exercise all authority. He is worthy to rule and reign over God's creation (Revelation 5:11-14). It is with this perspective that we proceed to look at the remainder of what is revealed in Revelation. What we see unfold from this point in the book is the consequences of the victory He has won. As the One who is declared worthy to rule, He provides details of how His victory will unfold, and how this victory will impact both the kingdom of Satan and the kingdom of man.

These seals are opened by the Lamb, so that His people might be comforted and encouraged, knowing that the outcome is assured. The victory has been won, and the enemy is powerless to change the outcome. Oh, we continue to wrestle with the enemy in the strength of our Lord, but the issue has been decided. It is decided not by our wrestling, but by His death and resurrection. Before we look at these seals and all of the details that unfold, it is important that we focus on the big picture and see the flow of what is really happening here.

It is the unveiling of Jesus Christ, and now He is seen as the Lord of all the earth, the One who will judge and destroy all that is evil. What unfolds before us is the glorious result of His redemptive work, the battle that He has won for us on Calvary.

There are several things that we must see if we are going to understand what is about to unfold. First, we need to understand that this slain Lamb is the Sovereign Lord over heaven and earth, He is the Lion of the tribe of Judah (Revelation 5:5). It is also important that we see that the events that follow are not just random events. As each seal is opened, it is the Lamb who opens them (Revelation 6:1, 3, 5, 7, 9, 12; 8:1). As victor, all authority has been given to Him. He is in control, and as Sovereign Lord He begins to unfold the plan of God that will lead to the establishment of God's Kingdom upon this earth. Yet for God's kingdom to become a reality, all pockets of rebellion must be destroyed. All evil must be judged. Justice and peace cannot prevail until evil is stamped out and all resistance has been crushed.

It is important that we do not lose sight of this as we continue through our study of Revelation. The Lamb is Sovereign and sits upon the throne. He is the One who opens the seals that will bring judgment upon the wickedness of both man and Satan. The movements of this book are not under Satan's control, but are under the Sovereign hand of the Lord. This message is to bring encouragement and hope to God's people who are suffering under attacks of the evil one.

The opening of these seven seals will bring the culmination of the struggle with evil. The plan and purpose of God is about to unfold with the opening of these seals. In reality, these seven seals occupy a major portion of the Book of Revelation (Chapters 6-18). When they are all opened, God's judgment of earth and its kingdoms will be complete. With the opening of these seals, we are ready for the triumphal return of Christ to earth, and establishment of His kingdom.

There are six seals opened in Revelation 6. The seventh and final seal is seen in Revelation 8:1. The opening of the seventh seal brings forth seven angels who sound their trumpets, announcing God's judgment upon the wickedness of humans. When that seventh trumpet sounds, all rebellion will have been judged and all resistance will have been crushed. In Revelation 11:15-19, we see the sounding of this seventh trumpet and the glorious outcome that results. Note that this is a scene of worship, as the kingdoms of this world become the Kingdoms of our Lord and of His Christ. As all heaven rejoices, there is anger on earth as human rebellion is finally destroyed. The sounding of this seventh trumpet brings us to a glorious conclusion.

To understand the flow of Revelation, we also must understand that as the seventh seal contains these seven trumpets, so the seventh trumpet also contains the seven bowls of God's wrath. These bowls contain plagues very similar to those of Egypt in the days of Moses. As God judged Pharaoh and his people, He also will pour His judgment upon this rebellious world and man's kingdom. As these seven seals are opened, all rebellion is destroyed, God's people are vindicated, the blood of martyrs is avenged (6:9-11), prayers are answered and true justice prevails on earth.

In Revelation 6:1, we see the Lamb opening the seals, accompanied by a noise like thunder. When God spoke from Mt. Sinai, the sound was awesome. God is going to speak again, and when He does, He will speak in judgment. All rebellion will be crushed, and the way will be prepared to establish His kingdom of righteousness and peace. Revelation 15 helps us get the proper perspective for the judgment of God. Before the bowls are poured on earth, we see a celebration scene in heaven.

In Revelation 15:3, we are told that they sing the song of Moses. The Song of Moses comes out of Exodus 15, as God's people celebrate His triumph over Pharaoh. God has judged the Egyptian army, and they are destroyed in the Red Sea. For Israel, there is deliverance, a great time of celebration and worship. God's wrath had been poured out in the ten plagues, and it is brought to a conclusion with the destruction of Pharaoh's army in the Red Sea. What we have in Revelation is parallel to what happened in Egypt, but on a much larger scale, and it is worldwide. This is what happens when the Lamb opens the seals. God's people have long prayed for evil to be defeated, and for God's kingdom to come. These prayers are answered when the Lamb opens the seven seals. Psalm 2 also speaks of this, as the nations have rejected God and His Son, Jesus Christ, but God will speak again. He will have the last word. In this psalm we are urged to bow in submission, to kiss the Son and acknowledge His Lordship.

The outpouring of God's wrath does not come until we get to the seventh seal, and all that is contained in it. In that seventh seal are the seven trumpets and the seven bowls of wrath. Before God pours out His wrath on earth, He allows things to come as warnings of what is ahead. The six seals that we find here in Revelation 6 can best be understood if we put them alongside of what Jesus said to His disciples in what we call the Olivet Discourse. In Matthew 24, Jesus answers the disciples' questions concerning His return and the end of the age. In Matthew 24:4-14, Jesus told them what to expect before the outpouring of God's wrath, as the earth is judged. He describes these things as the beginning of sorrows; which awaken the people of earth to the fact that they are accountable to God, and that the Day of Judgment may not be far away.

What Jesus listed in Matthew, we now see here in Revelation. Jesus said that many will arise as false Messiahs (Matthew 24:5), there will be wars and rumors of war (24:6-7), there will be times of famine (24:7), pestilence in many places (24:7), and persecution and martyrdom for God's people (24:9). Beginning in Matthew 24:15, Jesus spoke of the Great Tribulation that would bring man's day to an end as God judged this world and Christ returned to establish His kingdom. When we take this outline that Jesus gave us and compare it to what is unveiled in Revelation, it all begins to come together.

The Lamb Opens the First Six Seals – Revelation 6

When the first seal is opened in Revelation 6:1-2, John sees a rider on a white horse who comes with a bow to conquer, as a crown is given to him. Since Christ comes on a white horse in Revelation 19, some may want to follow that interpretation here, but Christ's appearance on a white horse must wait until this Tribulation time is over (Matthew 24:27-30). Instead, as we compare this description with what Jesus said in Matthew 24, it appears that this rider on a white house is an imitator, a false Messiah. Jesus said many of them would come. They come as though they are champions, offering hope and solutions to human problems. They actually are deceivers, bringing false hope to the people of this world, and turning their attention away from the only one who can truly meet our needs. God will allow men like this to arise, and the Antichrist will certainly be a conqueror like that who will be looked upon as a savior.

In Revelation 6:2, the white horse indicates that he comes offering peace to Israel, but this rider also has a bow. He is a deceiver and he is intent on conquering. Conquering is the purpose stated in this passage. We note also that a "crown was given to him," indicating that God will allow this deceiver to come to power. God will allow evil to come to a head in the person of this Antichrist.

In Daniel 9:26-27, this final ruler is referred as "the prince who shall come." This prince will come with a plan for peace, offering a covenant to Israel. This covenant offers Israel some concessions that entice them to accept this covenant and, with it, the hope of peace. While we are not told what is contained in this covenant, it may be a plan that offers a solution to the Middle East crisis. This covenant may also contain a proposal that would permit the rebuilding of the Temple, because both the passage in Daniel 9 and in Matthew 24 speak of the Temple.

Daniel tells us that this prince will break his covenant in the middle of that seven-year period and open the way to the Great Tribulation. He will violate the covenant in such a way that it is called the "abomination of desolation." Jesus told His followers in Matthew 24:15 that this would be the time for the people to flee from Jerusalem and Israel, because this prince would turn on them and war against them. What appeared to be a solution for Israel turns out to be a covenant with death and hell, as stated in Isaiah 28:14-29. Isaiah goes on in this passage to predict how God will overturn this covenant and bring deliverance to His people.

The opening of the second seal in Revelation 6:3-4 introduces the red horse that speaks of war. Our world has been plagued with wars of many types. Very few generations have ever lived without war, or at least the threat of war. God may allow war to come as an instrument of judgment upon a nation, or He may use it to awaken people out of their apathy or bring them to their knees. The peace plan of this prince will not last long, and the world will again be engaged in war with great loss of life. James 4:1-3 identifies the cause of warfare, both in the lives of individuals and with nations. The cause is greed and a desire to have what belongs to someone else. Human leaders have become drunk with the desire for power. No human leader can ever bring true peace, because he cannot deal with the sin problem.

The third horse revealed in the opening of the third seal (6:5-6) is black and represents famine and economic disaster. The situation described here is not only a shortage of the staples of life, but inflation that leaves people unable to purchase the basics. A measure of wheat was what was needed to feed one person and that will require a full day's wage for the working person. If a person will take lesser quality food, he could get three measures to feed his family. In our world today, there is hunger and famine, as this horse has appeared many times. In spite of these awful things, humans still do not turn to God, the One who can supply all of their needs. Those who will not respond to these warnings will suffer even greater judgment that is yet to come. God uses these things to awaken men and to call them to seek His face.

The opening of the fourth seal in 6:7-8 ushers in the pale horse that appears as yellowish- green in color. It is the color of sickness and death. Note that it is followed by Hades. Death captures the body, and Hades captures the soul. Again, Jesus spoke about pestilence, and we have the same thing here. Many times God has allowed plagues of disease and sickness to strike the people of this world. He did that with the people of Israel in the Old Testament when judgment was necessary. Some of the plagues that have come upon our world have been things like, cholera, bubonic plague, great flu epidemic, and HIV/AIDS. It seems as though when we conquer one disease, another one crops up. Human life is fragile, and we are all accountable to God. We need to repent and submit to God's authority in our lives. The Day of Judgment is coming, and these events are meant to call people to attention. These four things are not the end, but they solemnly remind the people of this world that the end is coming, and each person needs to be prepared. Tragically, many ignore these warnings and keep on living in sin.

The fifth seal (6:9-11) provides another reason for the judgment that is about to be poured upon the earth. As this seal is opened, John sees the souls of those who have been slain for the cause of Christ. God's people throughout the ages have suffered persecution, and even death, because of the world's hatred of them. Jesus warned His disciples that the world would hate and persecute them. Those who follow Christ can expect to suffer persecution, and many will lose their lives as martyrs for the cause of Christ. The kingdom of Satan and Man's kingdom is in conflict with the Kingdom of God.

As this seal is opened, we see many of these martyrs under the altar of God. They are in the Lord's presence, but there is a cry for justice. God must avenge the death of these who innocently suffered for their faith. God is just, and He must bring justice to this earth, its kingdoms, and the people within. These martyred people are encouraged to wait a little while longer because there are more who will join their ranks before it is all over. God's Word encourages us not to avenge ourselves, but to trust God to bring justice in His own time (Romans 12:19). One of the reasons why God's wrath must fall upon this world is to avenge those who have suffered and even died because of their faith. In Revelation 19:1-6, we see the people of God in heaven praising God because He has avenged His people.

These five seals give us reason for what is to follow as God's wrath is poured out. God has again and again sought to get the attention of those who live on this earth, but they have ignored His Word and have even failed to respond to His warnings. Instead of repenting, they have turned in anger and hostility against His people. God must act. Even when the wrath of God is poured upon the earth, many refuse to repent. Revelation 16:8-11 tells us that they will blaspheme God and refuse to repent. When Christ descends from heaven to establish His kingdom, the armies of earth gather together to war against Him (Revelation 19:19).

When the sixth seal is opened by the Lamb, there is a description of some of the cataclysmic events of which Jesus spoke in His Olivet Discourse in Matthew 24. Prior to His return, He speaks of cataclysmic upheaval in the heavens and on the earth. It is obvious that God is shaking the entire universe, as He is about to release His wrath upon His creation. In Revelation 6:12-14, we see a description of that shaking with a great earthquake on earth. There have been many earthquakes over the years, and some of them were devastating or what we might call great, but this one is what God calls "great." It may be one that will be felt around the world. It will be a shaking that will bring terror to the hearts of those who dwell on the earth.

One of the most stable things in our creation is the heavens and all the objects that are there. There is such stability that scientists can tell us exactly where the stars will be on a given night, tracking the various phases of the moon, and even predicting the next time that a comet will appear. Here we are told, however, that this will all change. The sun will be turned dark, the moon will become like blood, and the stars will be shaken so that they will appear to be falling from their fixed position. Meteors will fall on the earth, and the heavens will appear to be rolled up like a scroll. Nothing like this has ever happened. This will truly be a cataclysmic event.

At the same time, the stability of the mountains will be shaken and islands will be moved from their moorings. When God spoke at Mt. Sinai, the mountain shook, and the people knew that God was there. God will shake this universe in such a way that everyone on earth will know that God is there. There will be no atheists or agnostics on that day. There will be a true sense that the end of the world has come. In the prophetic Scriptures, God spoke through the prophets to warn of the coming of the Day of the Lord when God would move in judgment, holding humans accountable for their deeds (Isaiah 13:9-11, 34:1-8; Joel 2:1, 2, 10, 11, 30, 31; Zephaniah 1:14-18; 1Thessalonians 5:1-3; 2 Peter 3:10).

In Revelation 6:15-17, we see how the people of earth will react to what God is doing. There is confusion and terror as people try to escape the coming destruction, but there is not a place on earth that will not be affected by this great shaking. There will not be a person on earth who will not be impacted. This includes kings and political leaders, people with power and held in high esteem, rich, affluent members of our society, chief captains and great warriors, people who have gained fame or notoriety, and common people, both free and in bondage. As we look at this list, it is obvious that there are no exceptions. People of every class and status will be impacted when God begins to move in judgment.

The people will have a desire to flee, looking for a place to hide. Fear and terror will grip their hearts, with their only desire to find a hiding place. They flee to the mountains, looking for some kind of refuge: a cave, a den or a place among the rocks where they might be safe. It is clear that they know what is happening. The end is coming; judgment day has come and they do not want to meet God. Their cry is that the mountains might hide them, or even that the mountains might fall and crush them. Anything would be better than facing a Holy God. Anything would be better than facing the wrath of the Lamb. They know that they have rejected God and His Son, Jesus Christ. They know that they are guilty before Him, and now they just want to hide.

Isaiah 2:10-22 describes this scene. Psalm 1:5 tells us that sinners will not be able to stand in the Day of Judgment. Adam and Eve tried to hide from God when they knew that they had sinned, but there is no place to hide from the Omniscient and Omnipresent God. There is no escape when God begins to pour His wrath upon the people of this earth who have rejected Him and His Son. The rest of the Book of Revelation will fill in the details, as the Holy God holds sinful humans accountable before His face. Hebrews 10:31 tells us that "it is a fearful thing to fall into the hands of the Living God." Note here that it speaks of the "wrath of the Lamb," the same One who said, "Come unto me all you that labor and are heavy laden and I will give you rest" (Matthew 11:28). Those who reject this gracious offer of the Lamb, refusing the salvation that He provides, will face His wrath.

There is only one hiding place that can protect you from God's wrath, and that is the refuge that God has provided in His Son, Jesus Christ. He has endured God's wrath for us and those who rest their faith in Him, and in His finished work of redemption, are completely secure. In the very next chapter (Revelation 7), we see God's people standing before His Throne, protected from His wrath. As in Egypt, the wrath of God comes only upon those who reject Him. So when the Day of the Lord comes in this time of Tribulation, God will provide protection for those who have rested their faith in Jesus Christ and what He has for all who believe in Him.

The seventh seal is recorded in Revelation 8:1, and the opening of that seal introduces seven angels who announce God's judgment with the sounding of a trumpet. As each trumpet sounds, humans are called to attention as God is speaking in judgment. When the seventh angel sounds his trumpet, it is to announce the outpouring of God's wrath, as final plagues are brought upon those who have embraced human rebellion against God's coming Kingdom. The plagues are similar to what happen in Egypt when the Pharaoh refused to submit to God's authority.

Before these final judgments come upon earth with the opening of the seventh seal, there is a pause in the record to provide an opportunity for the Lord to assure His people that He will protect them from this awful judgment that is about to come upon the earth and the people of earth. When God's judgment was poured upon Egypt in the Book of Exodus, God provided protection for His people. There is comfort found in a similar assurance for God's people in Revelation 7.

The Lord's Protection for His People – Revelation 7

Before God will allow the winds of wrath to blow upon the earth, He sends His angelic messengers to restrain those winds of judgment. Before those winds blow, God will provide protection for His people, so that they might escape God's wrath or be kept safe. There are two groups of people recorded in this chapter. God provides protection for both groups, yet He deals differently with them.

The first group under God's protective care comes from the nation of Israel. The Scriptures assure us that God will faithfully fulfill the promises made to His covenant people. As He protected them in Egypt, He will again protect them in this time of tribulation. Before He will allow the winds of wrath to blow on the earth, another angel is sent with the seal of God in his hand (Revelation 7:2-3). God will place a protective seal on the foreheads of some of His people. They will be upon the earth when the winds of wrath blow, but they will be spared and protected by God's seal.

It is clear that these servants of God are all from Israel, as they are numbered from their particular tribe. There are 12 tribes in Israel, and there are 12,000 sealed in each tribe, giving a total number of 144,000. What is about to happen in this time of Tribulation is very similar to what God did in Egypt in the days of Moses. Some of the same kinds of plagues will come, only on a much wider scale. As God spared His people in Egypt so that these judgments did not touch them (the plagues that came upon the Egyptians did not come upon the Hebrews), so He will do again.

Revelation 9:4 makes a clear distinction between those who are sealed by God and those who are not. Later in Revelation, we will see another mark on the foreheads of those who live on earth. This is the mark of the beast, and God's wrath will be poured upon those with that mark. Different groups of people have tried to lay claim to this passage, but it is very clear that all those who are sealed by God are from the tribes of Israel.

This seven-year period of Tribulation is a time that God will bring to completion the restoration of His people in Israel. In Daniel 9:24, we see God's purpose set forth:

> Seventy weeks are determined
> For your people and for your holy city,
> To finish the transgression,
> To make an end of sins,
> To make reconciliation for iniquity,
> To bring in everlasting righteousness,
> To seal up vision and prophecy,
> And to anoint the Most Holy.

God has a specific plan for Israel, and He will use this seventieth seven (7 years of Tribulation) to bring to completion His restoration of Israel.

While this period of time will bring judgment upon the nations of the earth, it will bring salvation to many in Israel.

The Apostle Paul writes of this in Romans 9-11, concluding with the following statement in Romans 11:25-29:

> For I do not desire, brethren, that you should be ignorant of this mystery, lest you should be wise in your own opinion, that blindness in part has happened to Israel until the fullness of the Gentiles has come in. And so all Israel will be saved, as it is written:
> "The Deliverer will come out of Zion,
> And He will turn away ungodliness from Jacob;
> For this is My covenant with them,
> When I take away their sins."
> Concerning the gospel they are enemies for your sake, but concerning the election they are beloved for the sake of the fathers. For the gifts and the calling of God are irrevocable.

The prophet Zechariah spoke of God's restoration of Israel when their people recognize that Jesus Christ is their true Messiah, and they turn to Him. Zechariah 12:10 records this for us:

> And I will pour on the house of David and on the inhabitants of Jerusalem the Spirit of grace and supplication; then they will look on Me whom they pierced. Yes, they will mourn for Him as one mourns for his only son, and grieve for Him as one grieves for a firstborn.

This restoration may come through the ministry of two prophets that God will send in the power and spirit of Moses and Elijah, as recorded in Revelation 11:3-6. They will minister for God in the city of Jerusalem for three and one-half years.

This group of 144,000 Israelis, seen again in Revelation 14:1-5, is standing on Mt. Zion with the Lamb of God. God will preserve His people on this earth, and they will dwell with Him for all eternity. God's covenant promises to Israel's patriarchs will be fulfilled, but it will be completed in this awful time of Tribulation. They are seen on Mt. Zion as "redeemed ones," and God will fulfill His promises to them.

There is a second group in Revelation 7:9-17, whom God protects as the winds of wrath blow upon this earth. While some are divinely protected as they live through this period of wrath, others escape the wrath in another way. This group is seen in heaven before the throne of God. They are a great multitude, an innumerable group coming from every nation, tongue and people. While the first group is from the tribes of Israel, the second group comes from the other nations of the earth. They are clothed with white robes and have palms in their hands. They are celebrating God's wonderful salvation. There is worship and rejoicing that is directed to God and to the Lamb. These people are obviously believers.

When John is questioned about who they are, he confesses that he needs help in this area. One of the elders provides the answer for him, telling him that this group has come out of great tribulation. They have been washed in the blood of Christ. They are God's righteous ones, made so by the sacrifice of Christ. We are not told whether these believers come out of tribulation by rapture or by death. The Bible teaches that the Lord will take His people out of this world before this time of wrath begins, but others will be saved during this time, and some of them will suffer death for Christ. In 6:9-11, we saw that more believers were yet to be added to the number of those who are martyred. Revelation 13:7, 15 describes believers who are put to death because they refuse to worship the beast. This great number that John sees in heaven is those believers whom God has taken from this time of wrath. Before we move on to the record of God's judgment which is to come, there are some great truths to be discussed.

First, God will protect and preserve His people (Israel) when the Day of Wrath comes upon the earth (7:1-8). Secondly, God also will snatch His people from the earth, before the winds of wrath blow. This rapture is mentioned in 1 Thessalonians 4:17. Thirdly, some who come to faith in Christ during the Tribulation will suffer and die, but God will bring His own out of this time of Tribulation into glorious victory. God's people are not consumed. Christ has borne the wrath of God for us. Whether protected in it or delivered out of it, God's people are secure in His hand.

We need to see the sufferings of this present world in the light of the glorious future that God has for His people. As Paul wrote about his impending death in Philippians 1, he said that he did not know what to choose. He knew that God could deliver him from the Romans and spare his life, but he also knew that he could be put to death. Both prospects had their advantages, although he said that to be with Christ would be far better. Here in Revelation 7, we see a more detailed description of what God has ahead for those who are His own, whether they are spared or come out of trial by way of death. Here they are celebrating before the throne of God in their white robes, having been washed in the blood of Christ. There is no greater joy, no greater privilege, than to be in the presence of the Lord, standing before His throne, accepted in His Son.

God's people are not only to be in His presence before His throne, but to have the privilege of serving Him in His Temple. To serve the king is a high honor. To serve in His Temple involves worship as God's people bring glory and honor to His name. And this service is perpetual, day and night. In this life on earth we are restricted by time and limitations of our physical body, such as weariness. This limitation is no longer a factor. The One who sits upon the throne shall dwell among them. The term used here is to pitch one's tent or to tabernacle. The glory ahead for us in heaven is not just a perfect environment, but also the enjoyment of continual fellowship with the Lord. This is the purpose for which we were created.

The sufferings that we experience here on earth are all the consequence of human sin. God created a perfect earth. There was no lack in God's provision for His creatures, but with the curse came many problems and much suffering. This is all ended when we are in the presence of the Lord. There will be no more hunger and no more thirst. God will provide all that we need. The suffering that comes from extreme weather conditions also will be in the past. All painful experiences from this sin-cursed earth will be gone.

In Revelation 7:17 we find an interesting concept, as the Lamb is the one who is shepherding His sheep. He became one of the flock in order that He, as man, might die for our sin. Now one of the flock is exalted as the shepherd. As our shepherd, His provision is sufficient to meet our every need. He shall feed them, and lead them to the living fountains of waters. We are under His care, and He will provide for our every need.

As God's people have suffered much under the curse of sin, and been hated by the world, so they are now comforted as all suffering is in the past. Tears are a part of living in this sin-cursed world, and God never tells His people that they should not cry. The Lord Himself wept over what He saw in this wicked world (Luke 19:41). What He does say is that God will wipe away all of these tears. His people come out of the tribulations of life into the glories of His presence. Before we ever see the awful suffering of tribulation, we are assured of His comfort.

Judgment Resumes – Revelation 8 - 9

Having protected His people from the winds of God's wrath, the Lamb now resumes with the opening of the seventh seal. This is the final seal, and it announces the completion of God's judgment upon the kingdom of this world, and those who have rejected God's rule. This is a very solemn moment in human history, and John takes note of that fact as he says in 8:1: "there was silence in heaven about the space of half an hour." God is a gracious and merciful God, and He takes no delight in the death of the wicked. God calls men to repentance but when His grace is rejected, judgment is the only alternative.

As this seventh seal is opened, John sees seven angels with trumpets, ready to announce the judgment of God upon this sinful world. We will discover later that when the seventh trumpet sounds, there are seven angels ready to pour God's wrath, bowls of plagues, upon the people of earth. As in Egypt, the plagues increase in intensity as humans refuse to repent and continue to blaspheme God. As Pharaoh and his men hardened their hearts against God, so will the Antichrist and all those who follow him.

Before the angels sound their trumpets and John describes the judgments, there is another angel who appears on the scene. In verses 2-6, this angel approaches the altar with a golden censer filled with incense. This is very significant and helps us to see the judgments from heaven's perspective. As in 5:8, we are told that this incense offered up at the Throne of God is related to the prayers of God's people. The prayers of the saints are seen ascending before God. Having offered the incense with the prayers of the saints, the angel proceeds to fill that same censer with coals of fire from the altar, and then casts those hot coals upon the earth.

There is little doubt as to the significance of this. The message seems to be clear that the fiery judgments that are to fall upon the earth come in response to the prayers of God's people. The same censer is used both to bring the prayers of the saints up to God, and to send the coals of fire down upon the earth. It is important that we do not miss this perspective. God is responding to the cries of His people. The plagues that follow are very similar to those that fell upon Egypt in the time of Moses. In Exodus 3:7-9 God tells Moses that what He is about to do in Egypt is in response to the cries He has heard from His people. There are times we might feel that God does not respond to our cries. When the saints are oppressed and cry out to God, it may seem as though God is not responding. He does hear, and He surely will respond. We just have to wait.

In Luke 18, Jesus told the parable of the unjust judge, concluding in verses 7-8 that God is just and hears the cry of His own. He will surely avenge them. He will right all wrongs. We are taught in Scripture that we are not to take vengeance into our own hands, because that belongs to God, and He will surely bring justice. In Revelation 6:9-11, we heard the cries of those who were martyred. These cries will bring a response from God's throne. Throughout the ages, God's people have cried to Him about evil and injustice in this world, and they have also prayed, "Thy kingdom come, Thy will be done on earth as it is in heaven." If God's kingdom of righteousness and peace is to become a reality, God must put down all rebellion against His kingdom. If His will is to be done on earth as it is in heaven, He must judge sin.

These judgments represent the wrath of God against all of the evil and injustice that has been allowed to go unpunished. Justice must prevail if there is a God and He is to reign. In James 5:1-6, we are assured that God will avenge those who have been oppressed and treated unjustly. In Revelation 8:5, we see that with the outpouring of these coals, there are voices, thunder, lightning and an earthquake. As at Mt. Sinai, these indicate the presence of God, and the fact that He is about to speak. The silence is broken and the trumpets are about to sound. The plagues that will come upon the earth must be seen from this perspective. God is responding to the prayers of His saints, and He is going to bring justice upon the earth. Listen as God speaks.

When we come to the end of God's judgment in Revelation 18 and 19, we again read that these judgments are to avenge the wrongs that have been done to God's people. The saints are called upon to rejoice because God has heard their prayers and avenged them for the suffering they have experienced at the hands of the world's people. Note what is said in Revelation 18:20: "Rejoice over her, O heaven, and you holy apostles and prophets, for God has avenged you on her!" We find a similar statement in chapter 19, verses 1-2,

> After these things I heard a loud voice of a great multitude in heaven, saying, "Alleluia! Salvation and glory and honor and power belong to the Lord our God! For true and righteous are His judgments, because He has judged the great harlot who corrupted the earth with her fornication; and He has avenged on her the blood of His servants shed by her."

In Revelation 8:7-13, we hear the first four trumpets sound, announcing God's judgments. These plagues are very similar to what happened in Egypt in the days of Moses, only now they are on a worldwide scale. In these first four plagues, the judgment of God strikes humans indirectly, as it touches the environment. Later there will be plagues that touch man's person, but at first it just strikes the world around him. We also note that these first four plagues are limited in scope, affecting only one-third of the vegetation, one-third of the oceans, one-third of the fresh water and one-third of the heavenly lights. As the remaining plagues come, they will increase in intensity, and strike humans more closely. It is apparent that even as God moves in judgment, He moves slowly in stages, giving humans opportunity to repent. God is gracious and merciful and His desire is that humans might come to repentance.

The sounding of the first trumpet in verse 7 brings the announcement of a great hail storm. Similar to what God did in Egypt, He will again send a storm that brings hail and fire (probably lightning) on the earth, resulting in the destruction of one-third of the vegetation. Certainly that would have a devastating effect upon the human food supply, along with other attending consequences.

With the second trumpet recorded in verses 8 and 9, we are again reminded of the plagues in Egypt, as water is turned into blood. Since this judgment is now worldwide, it affects the seas and not just a river as in Egypt. In this plague, one-third of the oceans are polluted, which certainly affects the fish and other seafood, again touching the food supply. It also was responsible for destroying one-third of the ships traveling on the seas.

In the judgment that comes with the sounding of the third trumpet (verses 10-11), we see that one-third of the fresh water supply is polluted, having a more direct effect upon humans. It does not say that these waters are turned to blood, but they are polluted so that those who drink them will become ill and die.

The next plague that comes with the sounding of the fourth trumpet, recorded in verse 12, has an impact upon the heavenly lights that God created to provide light and heat for men on earth. In this plague, one-third of the sun, moon and stars are affected. It appears that there would be a loss of light, heat and energy. We can only imagine how such a loss will impact human life at that time.

In these four judgments, we see some of the basic things of life affected. God has graciously provided food, water, light, heat and energy for all humans, both righteous and unrighteous. Humans live as though they were not dependent upon God, and they fail to give thanks. As God touches some of the very basics of life, in a large enough proportion to have an impact, humans still do not repent. In verse 13, we understand that the next three judgments will be much more intense. Before these trumpets blow, there is a warning given to the people of this world. The angel pronounces woe upon those who would suffer under these plagues. God is gracious and continues to give humans opportunity to repent before it gets worse.

The trumpet judgments continue in Revelation 9, where we hear the fifth and sixth angels sound their trumpets, announcing God's judgment upon those who are experiencing God's wrath. These two judgments are called "woes" because of the intensity of their nature. The Bible makes it very clear that God is loving, gracious and merciful, but He also is just, holy and righteous. He takes no pleasure in judgment or in the death of the wicked, but when humans refuse His grace and rebuff His pardon, there is nothing He can do but let them experience the consequences of their choice.

In the first four trumpets, God sought to show humans how much they were dependent upon His gracious provision, allowing them to lose some of the basics of life, food, water, light, heat and energy. There was little or no response to these judgments. Therefore when the next two trumpets sound (those described as "woes"), God allows humans to suffer the consequences of their sin in a more personal manner. In these woes, God allows humans to experience some of the torment of hell, and the penalty of sin (death). Since there was no response to the earlier judgments of the first six seals, and no response to the first four trumpets, so now God pulls back the curtain and lets humans experience hell on earth.

In this first woe, the key to the bottomless pit is used to open its gates and unleash a great horde. When the pit is opened, there is a great amount of smoke, as if coming from a huge furnace. Coming out of the smoke is an invading force that is like a great horde of locusts. When the plague of locusts came upon Egypt in the time of Moses, they swarmed over everything, devouring every green plant that was in the land. This locust-like invasion, however, is different. We are told specifically that they did not touch any of the vegetation, but instead attacked the people who were not marked with God's seal.

It seems very clear that these attackers are not literal locusts. Rather they appear to be demonic-spirit beings that come out of the pit. Their identification is clear when we consider the following statements. First they come from the pit, the abyss. This is the place where some demonic-spirit fallen angels have been held in chains according to 2 Peter 2:4 and Jude 6. This is also where Satan will be bound, according to Revelation 20:1.

Secondly, this passage tells us that they have power to torment (verses 3, 5). From Scripture we learn much about demonic attacks and how they torment those who are under attack. In verse 4, it is specifically noted that they attack only humans. Physical locusts normally attack green plants, but they are commanded not to hurt the green plants and attack only people who are not under God's protective seal.

Next, when we consider the description of this horde, verses 7-10, we realize that they are unlike any locust that is known to mankind. In verse 11, we discover that this horde has a leader, a king. He is an angelic being, actually a fallen angel, and the abyss is the place made for him. This certainly identifies this leader as Satan. Humans have chosen to follow Satan and his kingdom, rather than submit to the authority of God. In paganism, Satan and demons are worshipped and served. It is significant that we speak of our own time as Post-Christian and Neo-Pagan. With all that is connected with Spiritism and New Age philosophy, the people of our world have aligned themselves with the kingdom of Satan. They have sought to get in touch with supernatural power and supernatural knowledge, without submitting to what God has revealed in His Word.

When humans choose Satan and his kingdom rather than God and His kingdom, God will allow the opportunity to experience the consequence of this choice. It will be like hell on earth, only God will graciously limit this invasion to just five months, according to verses 5 and 10. Before the final judgment comes, God gives humans a brief glimpse of the torment that results from rejecting Him. Note also in verse 6 that the torment is so severe that they would like to die, but death will not be allowed as an escape from this experience.

As the sixth trumpet sounds (verse 13-19), a directive comes from the golden altar before God. That is the altar of incense that ascends to God, linked in the book of Revelation with the prayers of the saints. Again we are reminded that God is responding in justice to those who have cried to Him. The directive is to set free four angels that had been restrained until this special mission. These angels have been held bound in the river Euphrates. This river is associated with Babylon, which we will see again in this book. Babylon is the very heart of Satan's kingdom and it must be destroyed before God's kingdom can be established.

As the death angel went through Egypt, these four angels go out over the earth with the mission of killing one-third of earth's population. With these four angels, there is a massive army used to deploy the mission. The number is given as "two hundred thousand thousand," which would be two hundred million. Note that the horses in this scene breathe out fire and brimstone, which Scripture has used in describing Hell. It is not just torment, but death. Again humans are given a preview of hell, not only as a place of torment, but as a place of death.

As God was gracious in limiting the torment to five months, here He again limits the number of humans that may be killed to one-third. Our God is longsuffering, and even in these woeful judgments He is still seeking to show men the consequences of their evil choices, and seeking to bring them to repentance. Before the Great White Throne judgment, when all unrepentant sinners will be cast into the Lake of Fire, God wants humans to see where the path they have chosen really leads. If people continue to reject God's love and the gracious provision and pardon that He has provided through the sacrifice of His own Son, the only alternative that awaits them is torment and death. God takes no delight in either of these, and would like to turn the hearts of humans away from sin.

The last two verses of this chapter (20-21) are some of the most significant in this book. Here is where we find the reason for the awful judgments that are described here, and it is here that we see the necessity of eternal punishment in the Lake of Fire. Humans are permitted a preview of hell. They experience torment and they see death strike one-third of their fellow human beings, yet it has no impact on the choices they continue to make. They are incorrigible, determined to rebel against God's grace.

Regardless of what they have experienced, they still refuse to acknowledge or worship God. They continue to worship demons and idols. The real issue is: what is the true condition of their hearts? We worship what we love, and these men continue to reject God and cling to the lies of Satan, loving and worshiping gods that have no reality at all. God alone is worthy of our worship, yet many choose to worship something that they themselves have made. Satan doesn't care what we worship, as long as we don't worship God. 1 Corinthians 10:20 makes it clear that when people worship idols, they are really worshipping Satan and demons.

The second charge against these humans has to do with their persistence in sinful behavior. In spite of the fact that God allows them to have a taste of the torment of hell, they refuse to repent and continue in their sinful behavior. When God is not at the center of the human heart, sin will reign. When humans refuse to worship God, they will not hold sacred that which God holds sacred. They will continue to violate those things that God says are sacred. Note the specific sins that are mentioned here.

Murder violates the sanctity of human life. God is the Creator, the author of human life, and He has made man in His own image. Murder violates that image, holds it in contempt and destroys what God calls sacred. Sorcery, the word used here is "pharmakia," the Greek word from which we get our English word pharmacy. It is speaking of the use of drugs to produce spells, trances and out-of-body experiences. This violates the sanctity of the human body.

The next word in this list is fornication, a word that speaks of all kinds of illicit sexual activity. This is worthy of God's judgment because it violates the sanctity of marriage, as established by God. The final word in this list is thefts. We might think that this is not as great a sin as the others in this list, but God's Word places a high value on the right of personal property, the sanctity of personal property. God's law protects ownership and condemns those who violate His law. God must judge when humans persist in violating what He holds sacred.

The Comfort of God's Reassurance – Revelation 10

In times when we feel overwhelmed or surrounded with difficulty, it is good to be reassured that our God is there and will take care of His own. As we study the Book of Revelation, we find that this is a recurring theme. As the trials of life come, and even as the Tribulation unfolds with all of its judgments, God is there and will protect and provide for His own. God will bring His purpose to completion, and He will shelter those who are His.

We saw in Revelation 7 that there was a reassuring message of comfort between the opening of the first six seals and the final one. Now again in Revelation 10, after the first six trumpets have sounded, there is a message to comfort and reassure God's people before the final trumpet sounds. Before the bowls of God's wrath are poured upon the earth, there is a note of reassurance. This message of reassurance focuses on several facts that bring comfort, even in times of stress.

The first fact that brings comfort is that God is present with His people as they go through the trials of life, and even the experiences of the tribulation. This is seen in verse 1 of this chapter, as John sees another mighty angel come from heaven. This angel is not identified, but the description that is given makes it clear that he is sent by God and he is a representative of God. Note the following things: The angel descends from heaven, clothed with a cloud, often found in Scripture as representing God's presence. There is a rainbow upon his head (in 4:3 we saw the bow around the Throne of God); his face is as the sun (speaks of the radiance of God's glory, note Matthew 17:2); and his feet are as pillars of fire (similar to what we find in Revelation1:15 where it is used in the description of Christ).

Because of these descriptions, some biblical scholars have concluded that this angel is Jesus. I am not convinced that we need to come to this conclusion, but this description does illustrate the presence of God. God is present in all of His glory and majesty. In the midst of all the tribulation, and in the midst of all that is going on in earth, God's people need to know that God is present. He has not abandoned His people, and we are comforted in that knowledge.

The second comforting fact is found in verse 2, where we are reminded that God is in control. We need to know that when everything seems to be coming apart, God is in control. It is important to note that the scroll is in His hand, and it is open. Whether this is the same scroll as before, we cannot say for certain, but it is open and that means that God's plan is going forward. God is doing what He purposed; He is in control. We also see that this angel has his feet firmly planted, with one foot upon the sea and the other upon the earth. This seems to communicate the fact that heaven rules over both the earth and sea, and God is bringing to completion all He planned to do. He is in control.

The next thing that we need to note comes out of verses 3 and 4, where we discover that God is about to speak. Although it may appear at times that God is silent, He is not. And when He does speak, it is an awesome experience. As when the lion roars, people pay attention. The roar of the lion is not to be ignored. And when God's roaring voice is heard, it is accompanied by seven thunders. It is awesome when God speaks from heaven, and what He has to say here is so solemn that John is not permitted to record what he heard. In this book God is unveiling things for us, but here He chooses not to permit John to record what is said. It is important just that we know that God is not silent. Just because He does not always respond when we think that He should, that does not mean that He is silent. He will speak, and when He does it is awesome.

In verses 5-7, it is reassuring that God will not delay any longer. While John does not record the words of the thundering voice, he does tell us what the angel has to say. This is what we need to know. What he has to say is backed with a solemn oath. By this, we know that his message is absolutely certain. The oath is taken in the name of the One who created all things. God's honor and reputation is put on the line to back up the truthfulness of this message. What he says is, "No more delay." In 6:10-11, those souls under the altar who cry out for justice are told to wait a little longer. God's time has not yet expired. He is patient and longsuffering, giving people opportunity to repent. Now the time has come, and God will bring this time of trouble to a swift end.

Peter warns in 2 Peter 3:3-9 that we must not misinterpret the patience of God. God's delay is not a lack of action with the fulfillment of His promises. "God is not slack"; He will act. He is gracious, and is giving more opportunity for repentance. Here He says, be assured that when this seventh angel sounds and the bowls of wrath are poured out, this will signal the end. God is bringing it all to completion, and will move swiftly.

With the sounding of this seventh trumpet, the bowls of wrath will be poured upon the earth. The kingdom of man will be destroyed, and God's eternal plan will be brought to completion. When man's kingdom is destroyed, the righteous Kingdom of God can be established. God has spoken many times through His prophets about this kingdom, and He will keep His word. Verse 7 reassures that God will act and accomplish His purpose. Man's kingdom will be destroyed, and God's kingdom will be established.

Man has not been faithful in his stewardship, and he is responsible to God for his rule over this created world. The Creator will hold humans accountable, and will judge their unfaithfulness. He will then place this stewardship in the hands of His Son, who has won the right to rule and reign in the Kingdom of God. No matter how bad things may get, no matter what happens, God is in control and He is bringing His plan to conclusion. We can rest secure, knowing these truths.

John is told in verses 8-11 to go to the angel and take the scroll out of his hand and eat it, assimilating its contents into his being. He also is told that although it will taste sweet in his mouth, it will become bitter when it gets into his stomach. In 10:11 he is told that he must declare this message again to the inhabitants of earth, "people, tongues nations and kings." That is the challenge given to John: to declare God's message. If this message is to be declared, it must first be assimilated.

God's message must become a part of us before we can ever effectively communicate it to others. And if it is to be assimilated, there is both sweetness and bitterness, joy and sorrow, in its content. The fact is that there is still some sorrow ahead for God's people; but it will soon be over and God's kingdom will prevail. God's message is full of grace and sweetness, but there is also a bitter side that needs to be proclaimed. There is a danger when only the sweetness of God's message is proclaimed. When people are told only of God's love and grace, they may come to the conclusion that God is so loving and gracious that He will never judge sin. This is not true. God is love, but He is also holy, just and righteous.

As the Righteous God, He must judge sin, and there will be no second chance. God wants you to respond to His love, but if you will not respond to His message of grace, you will hear Him speak in judgment. God is patient and longsuffering, but the Day of Judgment will surely come. This is the message of this chapter. God wants to reassure our hearts. He is present and in control. He is not silent, but will speak, and when He does, it will be with an awesome voice. Do not misinterpret God's longsuffering as a delay or as an indication that He will not judge. God will complete His plan and purpose, including judgment upon the people of this earth and the kingdoms man has established. The one who knows and believes these truths will continue to faithfully deliver God's message.

Rejecting God's Message – Revelation 11

God often spoke through the prophets of a very special time in Israel's history, when God would send the Messiah to deliver Israel and establish God's kingdom. That long-awaited day arrived when the king was born in Bethlehem, as God said. For centuries, the people of Israel had heard about this king and had looked forward to His coming. With His coming, they anticipated deliverance from their enemies and the beginning of a new and glorious age. The Messiah would come, and He would champion His people and lead them into greatness and glory. When the day finally arrived, and the king rode into their city, however, it was not what they had expected. This One who was being proclaimed as their king had grown up in Nazareth, in the home of a humble carpenter. The deliverance of which He spoke was a spiritual deliverance, freedom from sin and all of its consequences. He spoke of truth and righteousness. There were unexplainable signs and miracles that confirmed His message. When He spoke of God, He did so with a voice of authority.

As Jesus rode into the city of Jerusalem that Sunday, His followers acclaimed Him as Messiah and king. The voices of His followers were lifted up to God in praise as they shouted, "hosanna," but as He entered the city and went into the Temple, the leaders of Israel just could not believe. They could not accept Him as Messiah and King. As He left the city, He wept. He wept not for Himself, but for the people and the city, as recorded in Luke 19:41-42:

> Now as He drew near, He saw the city and wept over it, saying, "If you had known, even you, especially in this your day, the things that make for your peace! But now they are hidden from your eyes."

They rejected and crucified Him, but the real tragedy was that in rejecting Him, they condemned themselves. Judgment would come, not just because they had sinned, but they refused to accept the only One who could deliver them from their sins. They rejected God's grace and the message of hope and salvation.

As we look again at Revelation, and the awful judgments that we find there, we must see it in this light. Judgment comes upon the people of this world not just because they are sinners, but because sinners reject God's forgiveness and grace. As we come to Revelation 11, it is almost like Palm Sunday all over again. God is speaking again to humans. Before the final trumpet sounds, announcing His judgment, He sends messengers to proclaim His truth.

This chapter begins as John is told to measure the Temple of God, even as Jesus entered the Temple on that Palm Sunday, which established God's claim upon this worship center (Luke 19:45-48). God lays claim to that which is His. In verse 2, the outer court is not measured since God in His longsuffering gives the pagans 42 more months (three and one-half years). Humans were created to worship and glorify God. They have trampled God's courtyard under their feet, yet God is gracious and longsuffering.

Throughout Old Testament days, God sent prophets to proclaim His message. Often that message was authenticated by God's miraculous power. Now before the final trumpet sounds, God sends two witnesses to proclaim His truth. Note some things about them. They come in His power (verse 3) to proclaim His message for three and one-half years. They wear the clothing of mourning and repentance. They come as Spirit-filled witnesses, a light in the darkness (verse 4). The olive trees provide a direct source of oil for the lampstands. In verse 5, God's protection will keep them, even as He protected Elijah in 2 Kings 1:10-12. The miracles that attest to the truth of their message are much like those of Elijah and Moses. Verse 6 tells us that God will support their ministry with His power, giving humans every reason to believe.

In spite of the miracles and all the evidence that these prophets are from God, we discover in verses 7-10 that their message is rejected and these messengers are put to death in the same city where Jesus was crucified (Jerusalem). Their death is actually a time for celebration and rejoicing among those who follow the antichrist. They leave the bodies in the street and rejoice over them, but this is not the end, because God is not finished. There is one more demonstration of God's power as He raises these witnesses from the dead after three and one-half days. It was an awesome sight as the enemies not only saw them rise from the dead, but they also heard the voice of God calling them home. They saw them ascend into heaven. Great fear gripped the hearts of those who saw this, and there could be no doubt that God did this.

As they watched these witnesses ascend into heaven, the city began to shake in a great earthquake. One-tenth of the city was destroyed, and 7,000 people died. Those who remained were frightened. They acknowledged God's hand in all of this, but there is nothing here to speak of repentance. They hear the truth, and the truth is affirmed by miracles. They acknowledge that God is in it, but they still do not want God to be Lord of their lives. What more can God do when they have rejected His grace, when they have refused to believe His message? The only thing that He can do is to summon the seventh angel to blow his trumpet, bringing the final judgment upon earth, so that God's kingdom might be established.

The seventh trumpet is the final one, and this last trumpet announces the seven bowls of God's wrath. The end is near. Man's kingdom is about to be destroyed, and God's kingdom will be established. As the angel sounds the final trumpet, our attention is turned to heaven. The long-awaited announcement is reverberating into every corner. The announcement is "The kingdoms of this world are become the kingdom of our Lord and of His Christ and He shall reign for ever and ever." On this earth we have seen changes in government. We have seen totalitarianism overthrown by a more democratic form of government, but we have never seen anything like this.

The kingdoms of this world become the kingdom of our Lord and of His Christ. The prophets spoke of this, and the saints have prayed for this. When Jesus rode into Jerusalem, His followers longed for this, but this could not happen until sin was put away through the sacrifice of Christ upon the cross. If sinful people are ever to be a part of this kingdom, sin must be put away. This is what our Lord came to do at His first coming. He will come again and this hope will become reality. The kingdoms of this world will become the kingdom of our Lord and of His Christ. This announcement causes all in heaven to fall before Him in worship. The 24 elders take the lead in worshipping the Lord. They fall on their faces and give thanks to God because He has taken over the government. He has exerted His power, and has placed His Son upon the throne. When He sets up His kingdom, it will bring about great changes. Justice, peace and righteousness will be the order of the day. Not everyone will be pleased when He shall reign. In the final passage of this chapter, we see how the nations of earth respond.

It may be difficult for Christians to accept, but not everyone wants to live under the righteous reign of Christ. Not all would be happy in heaven, even if they could get there. The heart is deceitful above all things, and desperately wicked. Except a man be born again, he cannot see the kingdom of God. Not only does his sin separate him from God, but he is not spiritually alive, and therefore not able to understand or appreciate the things of God. So here when God's kingdom is about to be established, there are many on earth who are angry about this. Heaven rejoices, but those who are committed to the kingdoms of this world are not happy with this change.

God has done all He can in love and grace to draw sinners to Himself. When people reject His grace, there is nothing left for God to do but to pour His wrath upon those who reject Him (11:18). The time of judgment has come for humans who are accountable to God. He will judge those who reject His grace, and He will reward those who faithfully serve Him. There is no partiality with God. It is the same whether men are small or great, important or insignificant, in the world's eyes. Human rebellion and sin have destroyed God's creation. God gave humans authority over this created earth, and they are accountable for what they have done to His creation.

When humans rule, they are not always accessible to their people. In God's kingdom, however, the door is truly open. Note that His Temple is open and there is access into the Most Holy Place, where God dwells. The veil has been torn in two for us. In this passage, it appears that it is open because God is about to speak. From His Temple, God will speak in final judgment and He is about to return to earth in the person of His Son to establish His kingdom. It is an awesome thing when God speaks. Psalm 2 speaks of man's rebellion and God's judgment as the psalmist counsels men to submit to the king and bow before Him while there is still time.

The Great Conflict – Revelation 12

In this chapter, John is given a quick summary of the spiritual conflict that has been going on since the Garden of Eden. In the Scripture, there are two great kingdoms in mortal combat. As followers of Jesus Christ, we cannot escape this battle. The kingdom of Satan has been in conflict with, and in rebellion against, the Kingdom of God. Satan swept a host of angels with him when he rebelled against God. He was able to entice Adam and Eve to join in this rebellion and, from that day on, the whole human race has been involved in this conflict. While the battle is intense and there are many casualties, the outcome is already decided (11:15).

The Lord Jesus triumphed over Satan at Calvary, and we share in His victory. Although the outcome has been decided, there are still skirmishes in our experience. John writes to the churches to reassure them that victory is certain. They were well aware of the conflict, but they needed to be encouraged with the knowledge that victory was certain. They were facing persecution and were keenly aware of the battle. For us, the conflict may be more subtle and we sometimes tend to forget that we are at war. We, at times, even seem to forget that Satan is our enemy and therefore on occasion we find ourselves in his camp, attracted to the kingdom of this world. Before we learn more about the final campaign of this conflict, we look at the brief overview of this great conflict that is given to John in this chapter.

There are two forces in this conflict, with each represented in symbolic fashion: a woman and a dragon. There is an initial appearance that they are not evenly matched, but there is more than meets the eye. This conflict began in the Garden of Eden, and that account in Genesis 3 gives us the two combatants. As Satan approaches Eve, the conflict begins. After Eve shares the fruit with Adam, the curse is announced, and with it God makes a vital statement about this conflict, and how it will end. Genesis 3:15 says,

> And I will put enmity between you and the woman, and between your seed and her Seed; He shall bruise your head,

and you shall bruise His heel.

God has a special plan for her and her seed. The conflict is not just between the woman and the serpent, but between her seed and the seed of the serpent.

This woman is a very special woman, part of God's eternal plan. While Eve is the woman in the initial conflict, the woman in Revelation 12 is identified by the description given. She is clothed with the sun, the moon is under her feet, and a crown with 12 stars is on her head. Genesis 37:9-11 helps us identify this woman with the people of Israel. Joseph had a dream recorded in this Genesis passage and his father Jacob understood the sun, moon and stars to speak of his family. So in this passage in Revelation 12 it is used to speak of Jacob's family, Israel. Israel is chosen of God to be the vehicle through which He brings the Messiah into this world. In verse 2, this interpretation is we see her giving birth to a child.

The dragon described in verses 3 and 4 is fierce and powerful, having significant authority (7 crowns on 7 heads). He has great ability to influence others, as he took with him one-third of the stars in heaven (angels). This refers back to the rebellion of Lucifer recorded in Ezekiel 28 and Isaiah 14, when a significant number of angels rebelled against God. This Dragon is identified in verse 9 of this passage, leaving no doubt that it is Satan, the Devil. As in Genesis 3:15, the two combatants are the Woman and Satan, and the struggle is intense.

The question might be asked, "Why are they fighting, what is the reason for hostility?" The answer to this question is given in verse 2 as we read that the woman is about to have a child. The hostility of the dragon is aimed at this child (Jesus Christ) and He becomes the center of the conflict (verse 4). The dragon's aim is to devour this child, to destroy Him. This attempt was made at His birth when Herod sought to kill Him. Genesis 3:15 helps us understand the reason for the hatred, as we are told that this seed of the woman is going to crush the serpent's head. Satan knows that this child will destroy him and defeat him in battle. He knows that this child will deliver humans from Satan's kingdom. Satan was told by God how the battle will end but he and his kingdom will fight to the end. In verse 5, it is clearly stated and this child will rule all nations with a rod of iron. This statement makes the identification of the child absolutely certain. This man child who will rule all nations with a rod of iron is the One who has been caught up to the Throne of God. This is certainly Jesus Christ.

Throughout the Old Testament, Satan continued to attack this woman (Israel) so as to keep her from bringing this son into the world. He tried on several occasions to destroy this seed line, as in Egypt and in the days of Queen Esther. When He could not destroy Israel, he tried to corrupt her so that God would reject her as His vehicle for giving birth to His Son. God preserved her, and when she went astray He restored her. She did bring God's Messiah into this world, in spite of Satan's attempts to thwart God's plan. When Satan could not destroy the man child, he vented his anger on the woman. In the tribulation, this will still be true so that she will be protected by God throughout this period of time (1,260 days).

This conflict is a spiritual battle that began in heaven and continues here on earth. The closer it comes to the end of the battle, the more intense it becomes. Satan knows that he is defeated, but he is not going to give up easily. He will fight right down to the end, and he will try to take as many with him as he can. Although Satan, along with those angels who followed him, was no longer a part of God's heavenly kingdom, he still had some access to heaven (as seen in Job 1-2). In the New Testament, we are told that Satan and his forces operate in the realm of the heavens (Ephesians 6:12), but the battle is not over. Here John is told how the conflict will come to an end.

In verses 7-12, we read about how the war will end. God's angels, under Michael's leadership, do battle with Satan and his demonic forces. Satan is defeated and expelled completely from heaven, and his sphere is limited to earth only. There is rejoicing on the part of God's people because of Satan's defeat and his impending doom. He has deceived the people of this world, and he has accused God's people before God, day and night. He has had a powerful influence not only on the people of this world, but even on God's people. What a joy to know that he is cast out. He can never again accuse us as he did Job. Deliverance has come for God's people, and there is great rejoicing.

In verse 11, we are told that this victory has been won through the sacrifice of Christ upon the cross. It results from the blood of the Lamb. Faith in Jesus Christ is the only way for us to have victory over Satan. Some will suffer, and even die, in this conflict with Satan, but none will ultimately be overcome. Victory is assured for all who rest their faith in Christ. While there is great rejoicing in heaven because of this victory, the same is not true on earth. In fact, the heavenly defeat suffered by Satan only intensifies his efforts here on earth. A woe is pronounced on the earth because his sphere is limited, and so is his time. When he is cast out of heaven and limited to the earth, he knows that the end is near. His time is short and his anger is intensified. He is looking for someone on whom he can vent his anger.

In his anger, he turns his attention on the woman who brought the man child into the world. He begins to persecute Israel with all of the power he has left. As we will see in what follows in the Book of Revelation, Satan will work through the Antichrist to persecute the remnant of Israel, and any others who give allegiance to God. He hates God, and will vent his anger on any who worship and serve God.

In verse 15, we see an intense assault against the woman in which Satan tries to wipe her off the face of the earth. God comes to her rescue, however, and she is enabled to escape. With the wings of an eagle, she is able to flee and find a place of refuge. God causes the earth to open and swallow the flood in which Satan would engulf her. Satan has tried on a number of occasions to destroy Israel, and it is amazing to see how God has protected her again and again. In this period of Tribulation, many from Israel will acknowledge their Messiah and, while they will suffer greatly for it, God will protect His people. God is not finished with the people of Israel, and He will not allow them to be swallowed by the enemy.

The battle that began in Genesis will continue, and the closer we get to the end, the more intense it will get. The good news here in this chapter is that the outcome is certain. Jesus Christ has won the victory, and Satan will be completely defeated. This man child, whom Satan could not destroy, has triumphed over Him. It cost Christ His own blood, but He has won the victory and now we are included in this triumph. What we see in the remainder of this book is how it all plays out on the stage of earth. Yes, there will be a powerful ruler, the Antichrist. Yes, there will be suffering for God's people, but the outcome is absolutely certain. We can celebrate, knowing that our enemy cannot defeat us as we rest our faith in the Lord Jesus Christ. Victory is assured, and as God's people we can rejoice. We still must face the enemy, but the outcome is decided.

The Real Monsters – Revelation 13

Often in our lives, we are afraid of "monsters" before discovering that such monsters are not real. In Revelation, we discover that there are some monsters that truly are real, and these are monsters of which we need to be concerned. The thing that makes these monsters so dangerous is that they do not seem to be monsters. In previous chapters we presented the two kingdoms that are seen throughout Scripture, and we identified those kingdoms as the Kingdom of God and the Kingdom of Man. We have briefly traced the conflict that has continued through the course of human history. We also have identified man's kingdom as this world system. This system with its philosophy and value system may seem to be of no real danger, and yet God's Word warns us about its potential danger to our relationship with God.

Jesus said in Matthew 6:24:

> No one can serve two masters; for either he will hate the one and love the other, or else he will be loyal to the one and despise the other. You cannot serve God and mammon [material riches].

In many other passages of Scripture we are warned about the danger of focusing on material things and what the world has to offer. In Revelation 18 this world system is seen as a great and glamorous city with many material goodies to entice us. In Revelation 17 the world system is presented as a beautiful woman who offers an enjoyable relationship with her (as a prostitute seeking to draw our love away from our relationship with God). As we look now at Revelation 13, God wants us to see this world system for what it truly is: a monster (beast).

In Revelation 12 John spoke about the Dragon and the great conflict that has been going on between the woman and the dragon. This Dragon is, of course, Satan. He has been attacking God's people since the beginning of time. The term dragon is used to help us see that Satan is a monster to be feared and to be avoided.

In Revelation 13 we see other monsters that Satan will use to vent his anger on God's people. In this chapter, John sees two beasts (monsters) that appear on the scene. As he describes what he saw, we learn that what makes these beasts even more dangerous is that they do not appear as monsters. Just as Satan does not approach us as a dragon, or as a monster with a pitchfork and horns, so these beasts do not appear to be beast-like. Satan is a deceiver, and he comes as an angel of light. John is told that these are beasts because that is their true nature, in spite of how they may appear. In verse 11, this second beast is described as a lamb. This lamb speaks like a dragon. Underneath the exterior of a lamb, he is a real monster.

John gives us a description of this first beast as a monster rising out of the sea. In Revelation 17:15, the sea represents the nations and peoples of earth. This beast is described as having seven heads and 10 horns. This description mirrors what we saw in 12:3 in the picture of the dragon. This beast is just like the dragon because it is part of Satan's kingdom. We are told in 13:2 that the dragon is the one who empowers this beast.

Before we pursue the conflict recorded here, we need further identification of this beast. We find this help in Revelation 17:9-11. In that passage, there are seven kings or seven kingdoms described. What we learn from this is that this monster has been around for a long time, and has been against God's kingdom and His people. It has shown itself in different forms (heads), but it is the same beast. Each of these seven heads represents a time when this beast was active in its hatred of God, and in its oppression of God's people.

In 17:10, we learn that five of these seven kings were in the past, looking from John's viewpoint. One was present as John was writing, and one was still in the future. In history, when the beast appeared, it was conquered by God, on behalf of His people, but later appears to come back to rear its ugly head. The message given to John focuses on the one head that will rise in the future, when Satan's time is short and his anger becomes more intense as he persecutes God's people. In the Tribulation, when Satan knows that his days are numbered, this beast will rise again with intense anger against God and His people.

The 10 crowns in 13:1 appear to represent the last form in which this beast will be seen. In 17:12 we are told, "The ten horns which you saw are ten kings who have received no kingdom as yet, but they receive authority for one hour as kings with the beast." The head of the beast speaks of the kingdom of the Antichrist, and the horns are a group of rulers who join with him. This is man's kingdom in its final evil form. This ruler is given to blasphemy, for he is opposed to all that God is and all that God is doing in this world (13:6).

We note in 13:2 that this beast has characteristics of a leopard, bear and lion. These three beasts are described by Daniel in Daniel 7:3-6. Again this is the same monster that God's people have always faced, and this last phase will embody all of the others. In the past, there were five kingdoms that were beast-like in their attacks on God's people. Three of these beasts are identified in Daniel 7 as Babylon, Persia and Greece. John sees them in reverse order compared to what Daniel saw, because John is looking back in time, compared to Daniel looking forward. Each one of these three beasts oppressed God's people, Israel. History records some of the ways that Israel suffered under these three beast-like kingdoms. Two Jewish celebrations come out of this period, remembering how God delivered them. The feast of Purim comes out of the Persian period, when an attempt was made to kill all Jews living in that kingdom, as recorded in the Book of Esther. The other feast is Hanukkah, which celebrates God's deliverance from the oppression of Antiochus Epiphanes during the Hellenistic period.

It is interesting to note that the Book of Daniel presents two visions of man's kingdom. One came in a dream to Nebuchadnezzar (recorded in Daniel 2), and the second was a vision given to Daniel and recorded in Daniel 7. The two visions speak of the same group of empires, but the form is very different. The one given to Nebuchadnezzar sees these empires as a part of a great image (statue) made up of gold, silver, bronze and iron. This vision sees man's kingdom as a glorious thing, a tribute to humans. Nebuchadnezzar was so impressed that he built an image and compelled everyone to bow down in worship. Even as we look at the great image in chapter 2 of Daniel, we are told that a great stone would hit the image in its final stage (at its feet) and destroy the entire image. This great stone that will crush man's kingdom and establish a righteous rule is the Kingdom of God under the Lordship of Jesus Christ. In Daniel's vision, these same kingdoms are seen as ferocious beasts that devour other nations and oppress people. The true nature of these empires is seen as beasts, and this description is also used in Revelation.

Since Daniel is looking forward in time, he does not mention the other two beast-like kingdoms of the past. The Old Testament, however, reveals these two heads of the beast that are past history. The first comes early in history when Jacob's family becomes a nation, while they live in Egypt for more than 400 years. After all that Joseph did to save his family, and all of Egypt, from famine, later the Pharaoh enslaved the people of Israel and even tried to destroy all the male babies born to Israeli women. The conflict became intense and God poured plagues on Egypt to defeat this beast and deliver His people. This deliverance is also celebrated in the Jewish feast of Passover. We can conclude that Egypt was one of these seven heads.

The other of the five heads would be Assyria, the nation that took the 10 northern tribes of Israel into captivity. Sometime after the tribes of northern Israel were taken into exile (722 B.C.), the Assyrian army invaded southern Israel under the leadership of Sennacherib, and laid siege to the city of Jerusalem in the time of King Hezekiah (701 B.C.). God again delivered His people from this beast-like conqueror, by

sending a death angel to destroy the Assyrian army. Adding the kingdoms of Egypt and Assyria to the three found in Daniel's prophecy, we
have a total of five of the seven heads described as being on the beast
in Revelation.

In John's day, God's people were facing the monster again in the form
of Rome. Rome oppressed the people of Israel, and later persecuted
the church as recorded in the Book of Acts and in early church history.
Many were martyred under Roman emperors, but the church continued
to grow under God's protection. Rome is the sixth head. Together with
the other five, Rome gives us six of the seven of the heads on the beast
in Revelation. This gives us some insight of what might be expected
as the seventh and final head comes to power, at a time when Satan
knows that his time is short.

This beast-like monster will rise up again and will spew out his
venom, in the time referred to as The Tribulation. Paul called this
ruler, who is the final ruler of man's kingdom, the Man of Sin (2 Thessalonians 2:3). John called him the Antichrist (1 John 2:18), and John
reminds us in 1 John 4:3 that the antichrist is already with us, in a
different form. In 1 John 2:15-17 the context connects this antichrist
with the world's system. This world system is part of Satan's kingdom,
and although it may appear in various forms, it is always hostile to God
and to His people. The beast that we find in Revelation 13 is just the
last phase of this monster system. The Antichrist is the final head on
this monster. As we will see later, this monster appears to have been
slain, yet keeps rearing its ugly head again and again.

This beast-like system is not to be taken lightly, because it does have
great power. Note that its power comes from the dragon himself. This
is Satan's kingdom, and he empowers those who sit upon the throne in
his kingdom. The recuperative powers of this beast are so great that
the people of the world are in awe, and they actually worship the beast
and the dragon who is in control behind the beast. This beast is seen as
invincible, one who causes humans to bow before him and his power
(13:4).

In 13:5-6, the power of this beast is directed against God and all that belongs to Him. Since he cannot reach God or bring Him down from His throne, he turns his anger and hostility against God's people on earth. He makes war against the saints, to overpower and destroy as many as he can. These attacks have come before, as in Egypt during the time of Moses, as in Persia in the days of Esther, and during the persecution of the church in the days of Rome. There will be another fierce attack during the last period of Tribulation. This beast will rule and will have power over the nations of the world, and those who are not of God will bow before the beast in worship. Note that the battle lines are clearly drawn here. The world system under the Antichrist will seek to annihilate those who belong to the Lamb, those whose names are in His book.

What we need to learn from this passage is the identity of this beast. It is the system of this world dominated by Satan, and in its final phase it is ruled by the Antichrist. As John tells us in his epistle, this system or monster is already with us. This system is the enemy of God and God's people as recorded in James 4:4:

> Adulterers and adulteresses! Do you not know that friendship with the world is enmity with God? Whoever therefore wants to be a friend of the world makes himself an enemy of God.

It may not look much like a monster to us now, but beware. Don't be deceived. It will rear its ugly ahead again and will show its true nature. The Scripture again and again warns us of this beast, telling us, "love not the world neither the things in the world. If anyone loves the world the love of the Father is not in him" (1 John 2:15). Don't be lulled to sleep by that which may appear harmless, or even appear attractive. In this passage, we see that in reality it is a true monster that is opposed to all that God is.

There is a challenge in verses 9 and 10 that takes us back to the challenge in chapters 2 and 3. Pay attention and hear what God is saying. It is important that you understand the true nature of this beast. We may not see this monster in its ugliest form, but do not be deceived, it is the same beast. With the challenge to listen and respond to what you see, there is also a promise for the people of God. It is true that this system has power, and that there will be casualties in the conflict. There is, however, a promise of ultimate victory. The saints are encouraged to exercise patience and faith. Don't be taken in by this evil system; don't be deceived by Satan's mighty power. God alone is worthy of our worship. God alone will rule and reign in this universe. Rest your faith in Him, and wait patiently for Him to bring glorious victory over the enemy.

The Lord will conquer this one who has taken others into captivity. God will, in the end, take him into captivity. The one who has slain God's people with the sword will be slain with the sword that proceeds from the mouth of the conquering Christ. The Lord will bring justice and vengeance upon the earth, and upon Satan and his system. The system of this world may appear attractive and may seek to entice us to follow, but we need to know that this system is doomed for destruction. Those who embrace this system will suffer the consequence. True joy and satisfaction are found only in God, and we can come into His family only through Jesus Christ. It is vital that we know God's side is the winning side.

Satan's False Prophet – Revelation 13:11-18

In this passage, we see one who is perhaps the embodiment of all that is evil in false prophets. As Satan's days grow short, and evil reaches its peak, there will be a False Prophet who will join with the Antichrist in exerting a powerful influence upon the people of earth. Satan is a liar and he works in deception, including using many false prophets during the course of human history. As we come to the last days, the time of Great Tribulation, Satan will raise up a false prophet, one that will be more devilish than any that have yet appeared. As we consider what this passage teaches about this false prophet, we can learn something about those deceivers who, even today, seek to turn people away from God's truth.

This false prophet is described in verse 11 as "another beast." The Greek term used here means another of the same kind. The false prophet is like the first beast, and is just as much a part of Satan's system as the Antichrist. Just because he is spoken of as a "lamb" does not make him less of a monster. In fact, appearing with some lamb-like qualities makes him even more dangerous. Jesus warned His disciples to beware of wolves in sheep's clothing. Satan appears as an angel of light, and his ministers also appear in this fashion. Notice here that while the beast has some likeness to a lamb, he speaks as a dragon. He is Satan's spokesman, and his message is Satan's message. Satan's false prophets wrap their lies in some of God's truth. This second beast is called the false prophet in Revelation 16:13; 19:20; 20:10. Jesus told His disciples to expect false prophets to come. In 2 Peter 2:1-3 Peter warns not only of false prophets, but also of false teachers.

We know that this one is Satan's prophet because the focus of his message is to exalt the Antichrist, pointing people to worship the beast (13:12). He is empowered by Satan, just like the first beast, and he uses all of his powers to turn people away from God and His Christ. His goal is to magnify the Antichrist and encourage people to worship him. God told His people in Deuteronomy 13:1-5 how to recognize a false prophet. If his message is not absolutely true, or if his message causes people to turn from God and worship other things, he is a false prophet. No matter what else he may say that is true, if he turns people away from the true and living God, he is a false prophet.

In 1 John 4:1-3, John tells us the same thing, except his focus is on Jesus Christ. If the message does not focus on the person and work of Jesus Christ, it is false. Salvation is found only in Christ. That message is what Satan wants to distort or destroy. In our world today, it may be acceptable to talk about God, but speaking about Jesus Christ is offensive and not politically correct. The false prophet errs on the person and redemptive work of Jesus Christ. All of the cults and false prophets go astray in this area.

In verses 13-15 we see that his deception is backed by a display of miraculous power. The beast is able to duplicate some of the miracles that God's prophets have done (11:5), such as bringing fire down from heaven. This has always been a great problem with false prophets. They seem to have the power to do miracles, as the magicians in Egypt were able to duplicate some of the miracles that Moses and Aaron did (Exodus 8:5-7). This power is so much like what God's prophets do that some people think they surely must be of God. Satan has supernatural power, and he gives power to this false prophet (16:14). In 2 Thessalonians 2:9, we again see this supernatural power:

> The coming of the lawless one is according to the working
> of Satan, with all power, signs, and lying wonders.

In Deuteronomy 13:1-5, God warned His people not to be swayed by a miracle. Not all miracles are from God, and the message is the determining factor. If someone can promise healing or some other kind of miracle, people are led astray to a false message. In Matthew 7:22-23, Jesus said that there would be some people who would do miracles, even in His name, but who did not belong to Him. God's Word is our standard for truth. If the miracle and message do not go together, according to God's Word, than the miracle is a deception. God's use of miracles authenticated His message, and we are to accept His message by faith rather than be swayed by what we see.

In verses 14 and 15, the false prophet uses miracles to encourage people to make an image of the beast and worship that image. He is even able to give life to this image, and to cause death upon those who will not worship the image. The image will be able to speak, and perhaps be able to bring death to those who will not bow. There have been other times that Satan has worked this way. In the book of Daniel, Nebuchadnezzar built an image. Those who would not worship this image were cast into the fiery furnace. Again, the message here is to not be deceived by miracles. Not all miracles are from God. If not in line with God's Word, the miracle should be ignored.

Satan's desire has always been to be worshipped as god, and to control people. In verses 16-17 we see this control as those who will not worship and support this system are denied access to the market place. There will be economic sanctions against all those who will not receive his mark and submit to his rule. In our day, we can see how easy it will be to issue a number to every person, and to stamp that identifying number on their hand or forehead. Many countries already have a national ID card. Just about everyone in our country has a social security number. It is only a further step to limit all transactions in the market place to those who have the required number.

In verse 18, we find one of the mysteries that have puzzled men over the years: trying to decipher the number 666. Many have tried to link this number to some individual, so they might identify the Antichrist. 2 Thessalonians 2:8 seems to indicate that this man of sin will not be revealed until certain other things take place. If that is true, then it is useless for us to speculate on something that God says will not yet be revealed. This number 666 may simply be a number that is "man's number". It may simply represent man's system, the system of this world.

Satan and this world have long encouraged us to look to the system to solve our problems. And in looking to the system, our dependence is turned away from God. As human government has developed over the years, we are being taught that all human needs can be met by this system. We're taught that if men will just pool their resources, all needs will be met. As god of this world, Satan wants to turn our hearts away from God. We have developed all kinds of human systems and programs to meet needs, instead of realizing our need to rely on God. We need to be wise and understand the humanistic philosophy that is embedded in the system of this world. In 1 John 5:19-21, and again in Romans 12:2, we are warned of the dangers of conforming to this system. Everything that is a part of the world system is part of the Day of Judgment.

Our God Reigns – Revelation 14

Before the bowls of God's wrath are poured upon the earth, and upon those who are a part of man's kingdom (Revelation 15-16), the reader is told again that victory is assured for those who rest their faith in Jesus

Christ. In chapter 14, we see the Lamb again and He is standing upon Mt. Zion. His people are standing with Him. Zion was one of the hills in Jerusalem, the place where David's throne was established. It appears many times in the writings of the prophets as the place where Messiah's kingdom will be situated. In Psalm 2:6 the Lord declares, "Yet I have set My King on My holy hill of Zion." God's plan and purpose cannot be thwarted and we are reminded of that fact in Revelation 14.

In Revelation 13:1 the beast rises out of the sea. The sea is a place always in motion, driven and tossed: a picture of instability. In Revelation 14:1 we see the Lamb standing on a mountain, the very opposite of the sea, a picture of stability and immovability. The Lamb is the Sovereign Ruler of this universe and He stands on Mount Zion as the conquering king. With Him are the hundred and forty four thousand who have been exposed to the hostility of Satan and of the Antichrist. They are sealed by God so that they will not be killed, but since they refuse the mark of the beast, they will have to suffer, at minimum, economic sanctions. It isn't over yet but the Lord wants them, and us, to know that He is the King and He rules and those who are His will stand with Him on the mount.

Next John hears loud voices singing and harpers playing (14:2-3). It is the music of celebration, when all heaven joins in rejoicing over the victory that has been won on earth. The Antichrist is deposed, Satan's kingdom is defeated, and the Lamb stands on top of the mount with his people. Redemption is complete, victory is assured. As the situation on earth is about to become even more intense, God's people need to know that the Lamb rules and the conflict will soon be over.

Those who stand with the Lamb are described in verses 4 and 5 as those who are virgin males, having not been defiled with women. This is not talking about celibacy as if these are all unmarried men. There is nothing defiling about a sexual relationship in marriage (Hebrews 13:4). There is, however, a spiritual fornication theme that runs throughout this book (14:8; 17:2; 18:3; 19:2). The Old Testament prophets often spoke of spiritual adultery as people are drawn away from God to worship other gods. In James 4:4, we read of this kind of spiritual adultery:

Adulterers and adulteresses! Do you not know that friendship with the world is enmity with God? Whoever therefore wants to be a friend of the world makes himself an enemy of God.

In Revelation 17 the world system is represented by a harlot woman who seeks to draw people away from God, by enticing them with the possessions and pleasures of this world. Those who stand with Christ on Zion's Hill are those who have chosen not to "be conformed to this world" (Romans 12:2), but rather have chosen to "follow the Lamb wherever He goes" (Revelation 14:4). They are further described as "redeemed from among men." They are the first fruits that belong to God and to the Lamb. They are the beginning of God's harvest and the first part of God's renewed creation.

These followers are further described in verse 5 as those who have been cleansed from all sin through the redemptive work of Jesus Christ. They have been transformed by God's power, and they are declared righteous before the throne of God. They have turned from Satan's lie and have rested their faith in God's truth. They are justified and stand before God as having no guile and no guilt.

There is an invitation from God in verses 6-7, declaring that those who will accept God's message of grace can be a part of this group that stands with the Lamb. God has a message, good news, for the whole world to hear. It is not just for a special group. You can stand with Him on the mount; you can share in the victory that He has won. The message here is similar to what the wise man Solomon concluded in Ecclesiastes 12:13-14: Fear God, bow before Him in awe and reverence. Listen to what He is saying. Put your faith and trust in the Lamb, and what He has done for you on the cross of Calvary.

God is worthy of all worship. He is worthy of all glory and honor, for He created us and has provided redemption for us through the death of His Son. You can join those who stand with Him. You can share in His victory, if you will just bow before Him and receive His gracious gift of life in Christ. As in Psalm 2, there is an invitation that is open before the wrath of God is poured upon those who reject His grace and rebel against His rule over all creation. The Lord stands on Mt. Zion as the One who is worthy to rule, and you can stand with Him.

If, however, you choose to align yourself with this world system, be aware that this world system is doomed to destruction (verses 7-8). The angel of God makes another solemn announcement as God declares that Babylon (man's kingdom) "is fallen, is fallen, that great city because she has made all nations drink of the wine of the wrath of her fornication." This world seeks to intoxicate people and draw them into an illicit love affair. The Lord desires all of our love, and the world seeks to woo us away from Him. It should be remembered that this world is destined for destruction.

In verses 9-11, the Lord's messenger makes clear what will happen to those who do cast their lot with the beast and this world system. If you choose the wine of fornication with this world, you also choose the wine of wrath when God brings judgment upon this world. There is eternal separation from God in the lake of fire. There is eternal torment for those who make this choice. Note that it is not God who chooses this, but humans who separate themselves from God and His Son Jesus Christ. If God is the source of all life, then those who cut themselves off from Him are left only with death. If God is the true source of joy and pleasure, the alternative is torment and suffering. This is the choice that each person must make.

The Lord graciously reminds us again in verses 12-13 that there is another alternative. It may seem like this world is winning in this battle, but be patient, it is not over yet. Rest your faith in Christ, and live in obedience to His commands. In the end, you will find true rest and will be rewarded for what you have done for Him. In eternity, when it is all over, you will enjoy victory with the One who is King who stands on Mount Zion. Having reassured his readers of that truth, John now goes back to his warning about the judgment that is to come.

The Lord is going to judge this world. In verses 14-20, this judgment is compared to reaping a harvest field. This is an analogy that Jesus used in His teaching. The Son of Man is the One who has won the right to judge this world. He comes in the glory cloud of heaven, with a gold crown on His head, and a sharp sickle in His hand. He is the Sovereign Lord and those who are not standing with Him will now be judged. God is long-suffering and He is willing to wait until the harvest is fully ripe. He is willing to give humans plenty of time to repent, or to allow their cup of iniquity to be full. When the time comes, He will use the sickle and reap the earth.

Some have concluded that God will not judge, and so they continue in their sin. But be assured of this, harvest time is coming, and when it does, the Lord will wield a sharp sickle. Note what Jesus said in Matthew 13:39-43, 47-50. His grain will be gathered into the barn and the grapes of the world's vines will be cut off and cast into the winepress. The winepress is called the winepress of the wrath of God. When the grapes are put into this winepress, they are then stamped upon so as to reduce them to wine.

In this passage we see the awful result of experiencing the wrath of God's winepress. We are told in verse 20 that the flowing wine is a river of blood, and that river will be as deep as the horse's bridle, flowing over a course of about 200 miles. God has told us again and again in Scripture that all humans are accountable to Him as their creator. There are two alternatives in this chapter. There is only One King who stands upon the mount and we are encouraged to stand with Him. Don't be deceived by this world and the false appearance of the world's system as winning this conflict. The truth is here in this passage, and it is here for all to know. The Lamb will stand on Mt. Zion with his followers (those who turn away from the enticements of this world). At the foot of the hill, the world lies in total destruction, with a river of blood. This refers to the awful destruction that awaits those who refuse to bow before the Lamb. God offers eternal life and rest, with rich reward, for those who choose to follow Him. For those who choose the beast and this world system, there is only torment.

Justice Must Prevail – Revelation 15-16

God's people have, for a long time, cried to God for justice. In Reve-

lation 6:9-11, we saw the souls of martyrs crying to God, as they wait
for justice to prevail. In Revelation 15, we see a scene in heaven where
God's people anticipate the Holy God executing righteous judgment
upon the earth. The scene is like one on the shore of the Red Sea,
as Moses and the people of Israel watch as God brings just judgment
upon those who have oppressed and persecuted them. The sea is seen
as surging and swelling, for it has just crashed upon the Egyptian army,
swallowing them in the swirling sea. There is a sense of relief, even joy,
filling the hearts of God's people. The awful destruction of the Egyptian
army is the final stroke of victory that brings a very difficult period
of time to a close for Israel. God intervened with a mighty miracle
by opening a path through the sea, allowing His people to pass to the
other side. Having seen Israel escape through this path in the sea, the
Egyptians attempted to pursue, only to be destroyed by the sea.

In Revelation 15, we see a similar scene as God's people celebrate a
glorious victory. They stand by a glass sea in Heaven and look back
from heaven's viewpoint to celebrate the ultimate victory that has been
won for us. Our enemy Satan is defeated, and his world system is to
be crushed under the heel of the conquering Christ. The view from
this point is filled with hope. Satan and his beast-like system have
oppressed God's people, but victory is assured through our Lord Jesus
Christ. Evil must be judged, and Christ's kingdom must prevail. We
have hope of ultimate victory.

As the scene unfolds in heaven, there are seven angels who have the
final seven plagues. These plagues express the wrath of God as it is
about to be poured upon the earth. It is a solemn scene of God's wrath
on the people who have rejected His mercy and grace. As in the days
of Moses, there is a sea, only here it is a sea of glass. There also is fire
mixed with the glass. The sea is now calm as a sheet of glass, but the
element of fire, referring to God's judgment, is there. There is a group
of people who are standing on this sea and, like Israel of old, they view
this scene from the other side of the sea. These people are identified
as those who have experienced victory over the beast, and over his
ungodly system. These people have the harps of God in their hands, as

they prepare to celebrate the victory that God has given them over this beast-like system.

Here again we come to one of the great worship scenes in the Book of Revelation. With the comparison that is drawn here, we must look back to Exodus 15 for parallel scenes. Those in heaven sing the same song as those at the Red Sea. The Song of Moses is one that celebrates the victory God has provided over the enemy. It extols and magnifies the Lamb, for He is our deliverer. It is a song very much like the song of Moses, because it celebrates God's victory. The difference is that the victory celebrated here is the one provided for us by the Lamb. It is His song that is being sung. He is worthy of praise and exaltation, because He has delivered us from bondage and set us free from Satan's dominion. From this viewpoint on the other side of the sea, the judgments of God are just and, in fact, they are to be celebrated because they bring great victory to God's people.

In verses 5-8, a heavenly scene focuses on the Temple, the very dwelling place of God. Everything about this passage has to do with worship, as God's people celebrate His glorious victory. Flowing out of the worship and coming out of the Temple are angels of God, who bear the seven last plagues to pour upon the earth in judgment. God wants us to see His wrath from heaven's viewpoint, from the other side of the sea. Men presume to question God, His judgment of sin, and of those who persist in evil.

Notice in verse 6 that these angels are dressed in pure white linen. This is the picture of righteousness, for all the judgments of God are just and holy. They also have a golden sash around their robes. This is the symbol of glory and honor. God is holy and righteous in all of His acts, including His acts of judgment. God is worthy of glory and honor, and His acts of judgment bring glory unto Him. The whole universe will acknowledge that God is just and right, when His wrath is poured upon the wickedness of this world. Each of these angels is given a bowl filled with the wrath of the Eternal God. Before we get to the description of each of these bowls and what they contain, it is important that we pause to get heaven's perspective, that is, see this from the other side of the sea.

We have seen in verses 1-4 that these judgments bring victory to the people of God as they are delivered from the beast, and from his system. Now in verses 5-8 we see that these righteous judgments bring glory to God. He is exalted as evil is defeated and sin is judged. We see this in verse 8 as the Temple is filled with the smoke of God's glory. His presence fills the Temple, and His glory and power now emanate from the Temple. All other activity in the Temple is suspended while God is at work in His righteous judgment. God is the Creator, and all of His creatures are accountable to Him. If He is holy and just, He must deal with all that is out of harmony with Himself. He is not a vindictive God. He is gracious and merciful. He has sacrificed His own Son, in order that our sins might be judged in Him. God must judge sin, but the Good News is that He has already done that at the cross of Calvary. God has judged our sin in the person of His Son. Judgment therefore is past for those rest their faith in Jesus Christ. His wrath has already been poured out, if you will accept what Christ has done for you. If you will not accept His free gift, there is nothing God can do but let you experience His wrath against sin. Either you accept Christ as your wrath bearer, or you experience it yourself. God must be just and holy. He is glorified when sin and evil are judged. This is the view from the other side of the sea, and this is the view from the other side of the cross. We celebrate the victory Christ has won for us on the cross.

One of the tragedies in our society is that justice does not always prevail. Often it appears that there is more concern for the guilty perpetrator than for the innocent victim. Our human justice system at times shows partiality in executing justice, but it is not so with God. God is holy and just, and He must judge sin righteously. Revelation 16 brings us near the end of this Tribulation period on earth and the final plagues that fall upon those on earth, upon those who continue in rebellion against God. What we see here is very similar to what happened in Egypt in the time of Moses. Pharaoh and the people of Egypt were guilty of oppressive cruelty against the people of Israel. Not only did they subject Israel to slavery, but they killed innocent babies born into

Jewish families. God rules His universe in justice, and he cannot let such wicked acts go unpunished. His justice may not always be swift, because He is longsuffering, but He surely will judge righteously. As God judged Egypt, so He will judge this world before His own righteous kingdom is established. The seven bowls of wrath that are to be poured upon the earth are very similar to the plagues that came upon Egypt.

As the bowls of God's wrath are about to be poured, the angels are directed in Revelation 16:1 to pour their bowl "upon the earth." We see justice in action as these plagues, like in Egypt, are poured upon those who are guilty. God created earth as a place for humans to dwell, and He gave them authority over this planet. They were to rule for God under His authority, but they have rebelled against God and chosen to submit to the rule of Satan and his system. So this plague strikes those who have bowed to worship the beast, Satan's man who rules on earth.

The second bowl is poured upon the sea (verse 3). God gave humans authority over the fish of the sea, and the sea has provided a number of things to add to their wellbeing. There is no mention of one-third here, as in an earlier judgment, and it appears that all of the seas are turned to blood. When the sea is turned to blood, it brings death to those who are in the sea. Man's commercial enterprises that involve the sea will be brought to a halt as God's judgment comes upon those waters.

As in Egypt (Exodus 7:20-24), the supply of drinking water is contaminated, according to verses 4-7. God has graciously supplied for the needs of the people of this world, and they have turned their backs on Him. When the third bowl is poured, the fresh water supply is contaminated. This act of God is just because these men have "shed the blood of saints and prophets." God will avenge His people who have suffered unjustly, and He will repay those who have slain His people. God declares that these wicked men are worthy of his wrath, and His justice is affirmed in heaven.

The fourth bowl, described in verses 8-9 as the sun, is involved in this judgment. Jesus reminds us that God makes the sun shine on the just and the unjust. Many people do not acknowledge the goodness of God's provision. In a previous plague (8:12), one third of the sun was darkened, resulting in a loss of light, heat and energy. Here the power of the sun is increased so there is intense heat. People are actually scorched by the heat of the sun. It is important that we take note of the response of many of those who suffer under this plague. Those who suffer from this intense heat seem to recognize that God is the source of this judgment, but they blaspheme His name and refuse to repent or bow down to give glory to Him.

These first four plagues strike the earth and the resources vital to life here on earth. We might say that they strike the natural realm where humans live. The next three plagues are more directly targeted at the rebellion of humans against God, and against the alternative kingdom that man has established. These plagues seem to strike more directly at the spiritual issue or the real heart of the problem. God has ordained humans to rule under His authority, and they are accountable to Him. Humans have usurped this authority, allowing evil to rule. Satan's man, the Antichrist, sits on the throne, and people follow and worship the beast. God brings great darkness upon this evil reign (verse 10). It is dark spiritually, devoid of all true light. Those who embrace this kingdom will experience outer darkness forever. The darkness described here is so intense that it is spoken of as being painful. That pain may be emotional in nature.

Verses 12-16 record the judgment that comes when the sixth angel pours his bowl on the Euphrates River, drying it to provide for kings from the east to move their forces. The Euphrates River is like a barrier between the Kingdom of Israel and the Kingdom of Babylon. Babylon, as we shall see later, is the heart of Satan's kingdom. Humans have chosen to acknowledge this system rather than God's rule. So God is going to remove the barrier and allow the hordes of Satan to flood across. Satanic miracles will convince the kings of the earth to unite together to fight against the Lord, and against His king who will soon descend from heaven. The battle of Armageddon will take place when the armies of this world try to resist the Lord's invasion from heaven (Revelation 19:19).

The seventh and final bowl of God's wrath is poured into the air by the angel (16:17-21). In Ephesians 2:2, we are told that Satan is the Prince of the Power of the Air. In Ephesians 6:12, we see Satan actively working in heavenly places. This is the last plague, and with it the kingdom of Satan is destroyed. Satan is defeated and the kingdom that he established on earth is also destroyed. His system is seen as a great city, the city of Babylon. The next two chapters will give us more detail regarding the overthrow of this city and the harlot woman. There are two cities in Revelation, and throughout the Word of God. One is the city that man has built, seeking to live independently of God. The other is the City of God, the one that Abraham and the patriarchs were seeking in Hebrews 11:9-10:

> By faith he dwelt in the land of promise as in a foreign country, dwelling in tents with Isaac and Jacob, the heirs with him of the same promise; for he waited for the city which has foundations, whose builder and maker is God.

With the destruction of man's city and man's system, the way is prepared for the establishment of God's kingdom.

With the outpouring of this final bowl, there is a declaration that comes from the very throne of God and the Temple in Heaven. A great voice announces "It is done." The judgment of God upon earth is complete with the destruction of Satan's kingdom and man's system. Many think that God is silent, and that He will never judge the evil of this world's system and man's kingdom. However, God will speak and, when He does, the earth and the universe will reverberate at the sound of His voice. Note the cataclysmic results of this final judgment of God as it is described in 16:18-21:

> And there were noises and thunder and lightning; and there was a great earthquake, such a mighty and great earthquake as had not occurred since men were on the earth. Now the great city was divided into three parts, and the cities of the nations fell. And great Babylon was remembered before God, to give her the cup of the wine of the fierceness of His wrath. Then every island fled away, and the mountains were not found. And great hail from heaven fell upon men, each hailstone about the weight of a talent. Men blasphemed

God because of the plague of the hail, since that plague was
exceedingly great.

Again there is no repentance on man's part, rather blasphemy directed
at God for these judgments. It is clear to any who will consider man's
incorrigibility that God is just in His judgment. Men have refused
God's grace and the sacrifice that God has made in the death of His
Son. When the judgments become more intense, there is only willful
rebellion, leaving no alternative but eternal separation from God in
the Lake of Fire. The next two chapters will give us more insight into
the true nature of man's kingdom and the world system under satanic
control. After that comes the Lord's return to establish His Kingdom
on earth.

The Great Harlot – Revelation 17

In our world, the truth is that men and women sell themselves in prostitution. Even worse, they openly seek to seduce others, enticing them
into illicit sexual activity. As we come to Revelation 17, we are reminded
that there is another kind of prostitution of which we need to be aware.
Throughout Scripture, God speaks of spiritual adultery. God made
us for Himself and He wants to be the love of our life, but the world
around us, with all of its enticements, seeks to draw us into an illicit
relationship. Enticement may take a number of different forms. Some
people are enticed by material wealth, some by political power, some
by success or fame, and some by pleasure.

In this passage, the world system is seen as a harlot woman, enticing
people to find their satisfaction in what the world has to offer (rather
than in the God who created them). There are three analogies used in
Revelation to speak of this world system. In Revelation 13, and again
here in chapter 17, we see the governmental side of this world system
described as a beast. This is because its rulers have often oppressed and
persecuted God's people. In Revelation 16:19, we see it described as a
great city, Babylon. This will be furthered developed in Revelation 18,
where this world system is seen as a self-sufficient, organized society

that offers all that a great city can provide for humans seeking satisfaction apart from God. The other figure is that of a harlot woman, who seeks to entice and seduce the people of this world with some other god, rather than fulfillment through a spiritual relationship with the true and living God.

Revelation 17:18 clearly states that this harlot and the city Babylon are both part of this same system, the same entity. The woman and the city are the same, and just two ways of looking at something. It is also important, as we begin these next two chapters, that we see these two pictures of the world system in contrast to what is written in Revelation 21:9-10. The wording found in those verses is very similar to what is found here in Revelation 17:1, 3. A comparison of these two passages will reveal that there are two women and two cities. One woman is the chaste bride of Christ, while the other is the harlot. One city is the city of God from heaven, and the other is the city of this world, Babylon. Before the Bride can be seen in all of her glory, the seductress must be destroyed. Before God's Holy City can be revealed, the world's city of Babylon must be destroyed.

John describes this harlot woman as "sitting upon many waters" (17:1). In verse 15 of this chapter, we are told that these many waters are peoples, multitudes, nations and tongues. This woman has had a great impact upon multitudes of people from all nations of this earth. Many have fallen in love with this world, with all of its allurements and gods. In verse 2, her influence also has impacted the rulers of this world, as they have lusted after all that this harlot has to offer: possessions, power and pleasure.

Many rulers have sold themselves to the system, as well as compromised moral principle to gratify their own desires with this harlot woman. Both rulers and common people have become intoxicated with the wine of her fornication. People have been intoxicated with the love of this world, and all that it has to offer. They seek satisfaction and fulfillment in the things of this world, including worshiping the gods of this world. The harlot's impact on the rulers is so great that verse 3 tells us this harlot is riding the seven-headed beast. This beast-like oppressive system of rulers may appear in different forms, but they are dominated by this harlot woman. Whatever form the political system has taken, the harlot has been in the saddle.

John describes her in verse 4 as being clothed in the finest apparel, purple and scarlet, which is the clothing of royalty. She is arrayed in such a fashion to make her attractive, alluring and seductive. She is adorned with jewelry of "gold, precious stones and pearls." In her hand is a gold cup, with the wine of her fornication. This harlot is like the harlot in the Book of Proverbs who does all she can to entice people under her spell. In verse 5, she is linked with the system that began in Babylon, the seat of idolatry in Scripture. Babylon is called the "Mother of harlots and abominations" because her pantheon of gods with all of its immorality has been adopted into succeeding cultures in this world. The gods are renamed in the different cultures but the system is the same.

This idolatrous system has long been the enemy of God and of His people. In verse 6, the writer says that she is drunk with the blood of saints and of the martyrs of Jesus. Many of God's people have been persecuted and martyred by this harlot woman. She has wielded great power over the various rulers of this world, and she is opposed to God's people. She is part of the seed of the serpent, mentioned in Genesis 3:15 and she has played a significant role in the conflict between Satan's kingdom and the kingdom of God.

John is overwhelmed by what he sees as this harlot rides the beast (verse 6), and the angel speaks to help him understand the nature of this system and not be overwhelmed by it. In order to do this, the angel provides additional information about this beast-like system upon which the harlot is riding. The final manifestation of this seven-headed beast as described in Revelation is led by both the world ruler and the false prophet who works with him. In this passage, we find additional information that was not offered in the previous passage, which helps us better understand this beast and the relationship with the harlot.

This beast-like system is described as having appeared in previous periods of history, only to reappear at a later time, and in another form.

Regardless of when it appears, its origin is made clear in verse 8 as it ascends out of the bottomless pit, and is destined to go into perdition. It is Satan's system, his kingdom on this earth. It is opposed to God, as we are told in James 3:15 and it is under the control of Satan, who is called the "god of this world" in 2 Corinthians 4:4. God's people are warned many times in Scripture of the danger of this world system.

This beast-like system has reared its ugly head on a number of occasions, oppressing and persecuting God's people and blaspheming God's holy name. The beast is conquered and seems to disappear, only to resurface at a later time. The beast has seven heads (verse 9) and these heads represent seven mountains. Some biblical students have interpreted these seven mountains as the seven hills of Rome, but this beast is more than just Rome, which is only one of the heads.

Mountains in Scripture speak of strong kingdoms (Isaiah 2:2; Jeremiah 51:25; Daniel 2:35; Zechariah 4:7). We are further helped in our interpretation by Revelation 17:10, linking these seven mountains with seven kings or kingdoms. Five of these kingdoms who fought against God's people are in the past, while one is in the present (as John writes), and one is yet to come (in the future). If we begin with the one present in John's time, it will help us identify the other kingdoms that are part of this seven-headed beast.

The one kingdom present in John's time is certainly the Roman Empire. Rome oppressed the Jews and later persecuted and martyred many of the followers of Christ. A Roman King, Herod, sought to kill Jesus when He was born. Pilate was involved in the crucifixion of Jesus, and the Emperor Titus destroyed the city of Jerusalem and leveled the Temple in 70 A.D. This destruction caused the Jews to flee and be scattered throughout many parts of our world. Church history tells us that many of the Apostles and other Christians were martyred under Roman rule.

We turn our attention next to the five kingdoms that were in the past, when John wrote this book. We turn back to Revelation 13 where John gives a description of this beast that rises out of the sea. In verse 2 of that chapter, he sees three different animals represented in this beast:

> Now the beast which I saw was like a leopard, his feet were
> like the feet of a bear, and his mouth like the mouth of a
> lion. The dragon gave him his power, his throne, and great
> authority.

The beast was like a leopard, but also had parts that were like a bear and like a lion. These three animals are found in Daniel 7, where Daniel prophesies about the nations that would oppress God's people, Israel. Daniel lists them in reverse order from John's viewpoint. Daniel is looking ahead from his time, so he begins with the lion (Babylon), then speaks of the bear (Persia), and next tells of the Greek Empire, pictured as a leopard.

These three kingdoms oppressed Israel and also blasphemed God, as they ruled over the Mediterranean world. Under Babylon's rule, people were forced to worship the image set up by Nebuchadnezzar. Those who refused were cast into a fiery furnace. King Belshazzar blasphemed the name of God by using the vessels taken from the Temple in Jerusalem to have a drunken orgy. God's response was the well-known handwriting on the wall, announcing the end of the Babylonian Empire.

Under one of the Persian kings, an attempt was made to annihilate all Jews, as recorded in the Book of Esther. God intervened through Esther and saved His people. This victory is still celebrated by Jews in the Feast of Purim. After the death of Alexander the Great, the Greek Empire was divided into four parts. Daniel records some of the struggles that would take place, as the Jewish people were caught between two of these factions. Later, one king, Antiochus Epiphanies, desecrated the Temple by offering a sow on the altar. This was known as the "abomination of desolation." God used the Maccabees to defeat Antiochus and restore worship in the Temple. This victory is remembered each year by Jewish people by the holiday Hanukkah.

The remaining two kingdoms that oppressed God's people and blasphemed the name of God are found in the Old Testament, and were prior to the time of Daniel. The first of these is at the very beginning of Israel's history as a nation. It is recorded in the Book of Exodus where we read about the Pharaoh in Egypt who enslaved the people of Israel and sought to annihilate them by killing all the male babies born to Jewish women. The plagues sent by God to deliver His people are very similar to some of the plagues found in the Book of Revelation. The conflict is with the same beast, one at the beginning of the conflict, and one at the end.

The other remaining power that oppressed Israel is Assyria, as recorded in the books of Kings and Chronicles. It was Assyria that took the 10 northern tribes of Israel into captivity (2 Kings 17:4-6). King Sennacherib also invaded Judah in the days of King Hezekiah, laying siege to the city of Jerusalem and blaspheming the name of God. God again delivered His people and destroyed the army of Assyria by the death angel in a single night (2 Kings 19:35).

These five kingdoms, Egypt, Assyria, Babylon, Persia and Greece, are the five heads of the beast that John describes as in the past. The one that was present when John wrote was Rome. Each one of these strong kingdoms persecuted the people of God. They were dominated by the harlot, and they were opposed to God's people.

There is one more head on the beast, one final phase of this system yet to come. The Antichrist will come out of that final phase. With the Antichrist, there will be ten kings, the ten horns on the beast. They will support the Antichrist and give power to him. There is a coalition of evil in this final phase. The great kingdoms of this world have always been opposed to God and His people. The system has appeared in many forms, but it is the same system. The final form may be coming together even now, or in the near future, but certainly it will raise its ugly head again. When this final form comes, it will unite the nations of this world to make war against the Lamb. The kingdoms of this world will seek to overthrow Jesus Christ, but the Lamb will overcome them. He will be the victor. This is described for us in 19:19-21:

> And I saw the beast, the kings of the earth, and their armies, gathered together to make war against Him who sat on the horse and against His army. Then the beast was captured, and with him the false prophet who worked signs in his presence, by which he deceived those who received the mark of

the beast and those who worshiped his image. These two were cast alive into the lake of fire burning with brimstone. And the rest were killed with the sword which proceeded from the mouth of Him who sat on the horse. And all the birds were filled with their flesh.

The people of God, those with the Lamb, will share in His glorious victory.

In Revelation 17:16-17, we learn that the 10 kings in league with the Antichrist will turn on the harlot and destroy her, fulfilling God's will to consolidate all power in this last head of the beast. This world system is both an idolatrous religious system pictured by the harlot, and a political and commercial system pictured by the great city. The religions of this world, and all idolatry as promoted by the harlot, will be brought to an end when God allows all worship to be focused on the beast (Revelation 13:12-15). Satan will obtain his goal of being like the Most High God (Isaiah 14:14) when worship is focused on the beast and on the dragon, Satan (Revelation 13:4).

The harlot woman in Revelation 17 is destroyed with all of her idolatry. The commercialized system, represented as a great city, also will be destroyed (as we shall see in the next chapter). These two systems are part of the world system designed by Satan to draw people away from God. Humans were created to have fellowship with God, to love and worship Him. Satan has coveted this for himself, in his rebellion as an angel. He has created a world system that seeks to steal away that which rightly belongs to God alone. John urges us in his first epistle not to love the world or the things that are in the world, for the world is going to be destroyed, and those who love it will lose everything (1John 2:15-17).

Babylon the Great is Destroyed – Revelation 18

In this chapter, we find the third analogy that pictures this world's system. It is like a harlot seeking to entice people from God, and like a beast that loves power and uses that power to blaspheme God and oppress His people. In this chapter, the world system also is pictured as a great city. This great city has lots of glamour and glitter, and offers humans power, pleasure and possessions. The truth is that it is all, as Solomon discovered, vanity and vexation of spirit (Ecclesiastes 1:14). Someone has described it as one huge soap bubble. It looks pretty, but has no lasting substance and soon will burst and be gone.

The city is called Babylon and, because of this, some have looked for the rebuilding of that ancient city. Others have identified this city with Rome, London, New York or some other great city. As we carefully read this chapter, however, we discover that when God's judgment comes upon this city, the entire world system collapses. In verses 21-23, we see there is nothing left: culturally, materially or economically. I believe that this "city" is to be understood as the world system. The whole system is pictured here.

Abraham and the patriarchs set their hearts on the eternal City of God (Hebrews 11:9-16). In our study, we are moving close to the appearing of that marvelous city. Before that eternal city can become a reality, the city of man must be destroyed. It all started in Babel (Babylon) when humans expressed a desire to create a city, tower and culture that would elevate man (Genesis 11:1-9). Babylon later became a pagan culture, worshipping a pantheon of gods and becoming the fountainhead of this world system. Other Scriptures speak of the fall of this Babylon, as found in Isaiah 21:9; Jeremiah 51:8; Revelation 14:8. When this great city falls, it is seen for what it truly is: the habitation of demonic spirits (Revelation 18:2). Satan is the god of this world, and he has inspired man to build this city. In verse 3, we see the impact that this world system has had on all nations, since they have been seduced by the allurements of this world. Through this system, people have been enslaved by their own desires for what this world has to offer.

God is just and holy and cannot allow this evil system to escape His condemnation. The angel announces God's judgment on this city and this system (18:5-8). God has seen her sins and He remembers all of her iniquities. God is just, and He must deal with this evil system. Instead of glorifying God, this system has glorified man and man's accomplishments. The system has lived for the luxuries of life, trying to find fulfillment apart from God. She (the city) has elevated herself to the status of a queen, and sought to avoid all that is unpleasant. God will rain down His plagues upon this city, and this world system will totally collapse under His mighty hand of judgment.

In verses 9-19, we hear the cries of those who have bought into this system and built their lives around what this world has to offer. They grieve greatly when the whole system is destroyed. We know that when economic disaster strikes any nation, there is great weeping. Think of what it will be when the whole world system comes to an end. John sees a number of different groups who are impacted when this system falls.

The first group mentioned in verses 9-10 is the kings of this world. The rulers of this world whether kings or presidents, have lived luxuriously and enjoyed the very finest things of life. Many have sold themselves for power, possessions and pleasure. They have been exalted by the system but, when it all collapses, they will suffer loss.

Next, in verses 11-16, we find the merchants. These are the people who have benefited greatly from this materialistic system. There are honest merchants who are not out to exploit people for personal gain, but others have focused only on personal profit. If you look at the list of things here, you will not find the basic necessities of life. The list of merchandise is that of earthly treasure, such as fancy apparel, rich furnishings, personal luxuries, fine foods, means of transportation and servants. God's Word encourages us to be content with what God has given us, but the merchants of this world try to convince us that we need far more than these basic necessities. The message is that real joy comes in the number of these things you possess. They want us to believe that we cannot live without these things. Many have sold themselves or neglected their family, in order to have the finer things of life. Some have shut God out of their lives, in their pursuit of what the world has to offer.

The third group mentioned in verses 17-19 is the shippers. This group has made a good profit in transporting the goods that will be sold by the merchants. The one thing that seems to be most important in this world is the gross national product. Imports and exports are a vital part of the system. When this materialistic system is destroyed, many will cry and lament. In 1929, when the stock market fell apart, many people committed suicide. Collapse of the system gave them no more reason to live. Their lives were so wrapped up in profit and loss that they could not go on. Those who have embraced the system have often become ensnared in it or become slaves to it. This is man's system, as he seeks to find meaning and joy in life apart from God.

The scene changes as we look at verses 20-24. In contrast to the weeping of many on earth, we now see great rejoicing in Heaven. This world system has been part of Satan's kingdom and it is an enemy of God. It has seduced many people and turned their hearts away from God. It has provided many idols for humans to worship. In the next chapter, we will read more about the celebration in heaven. Humans have been enslaved by this system, and God now brings deliverance. The system is destroyed in all of its various parts. The world's music is silenced (verse 22). The industry that produced the things that helped to entice humans is gone. The bright lights and the festivities that brought a false sense of joy and pleasure are gone (verse 23). Man has tried to invent all kinds of alternatives so he can find some source of pleasure in this world. In reality, these are all hollow and empty. They are mere soap bubbles that will be gone. Joy and fullness are to be found in fellowship with our Creator.

In verses 23-24, we see further reason why this system must be destroyed. The first reason speaks to the value system of this world. The merchants, who have been successful, have been looked up to and considered the great men of earth. A person's worth is measured by their ability to amass wealth. People have bought into this value system and have been deceived under its spell (sorceries). Secondly, we must consider that this value system produces greed and covetousness which, in turn, introduces all kinds of evil. The pursuit of the things of this world has brought about many murders, and God's people have suffered greatly. God must avenge the lives of those who have been slain because they have spoken out against this value system, but God also must execute justice on those who have taken the lives of innocent victims.

Before we leave this chapter, we must take note and focus on the challenge that is issued in verse 4:

> And I heard another voice from heaven saying, "Come out of her, my people, lest you share in her sins, and lest you receive of her plagues."

In light of God saying there will be a certain collapse of man's city, a challenge goes out to God's people. It is a challenge that is found many times in Scripture: "Come out of her my people." God warns His people of the dangers of letting ourselves get enamored with this system. Look at Jeremiah 50:8, 51:6-9, Isaiah 52:11, and 2 Corinthians 6:17: God calls His people to live here on earth without getting caught up in the philosophy of the world and seeking fulfillment from materialistic things. Our sufficiency is in God, and the true riches are those that are eternal. Why would we want to invest in a system that we know is going to be destroyed? God called on Lot and his family to leave the city of Sodom because it was doomed to destruction (Genesis 19:12-13). The angels had to take them by the hand and almost drag them out, and Lot's wife just could not let go. We should not share in her sins, or we'll share her plagues. The message of Revelation is very practical. God tells us what is going to happen, so we might invest in a kingdom that lasts. To love this world is to lose it all. To love God's kingdom is to have eternal gain.

CHAPTER 14

Vision IV

Conquering King Establishes His Kingdom
Revelation 19-20

T HE CORONATION OF A KING is a glorious time. It is a time of joyous celebration. There is not only joy, but also new hope as people look forward to the reign of a new king. Picture in your mind what it would be like to live under the rule of a wicked despot, a tyrant, one who exploited his people and even cruelly enslaved them to serve him. Think of the excitement and jubilation there would be if this wicked king was dethroned and a gracious benevolent king was crowned to take his place. You can almost hear the sighs of relief and the shouts of jubilation as the people cry out, "long live the king."

When Jesus ascended into Heaven, as recorded in Acts 1:9-11, the disciples were in awe when the angel promised that He would return in a similar manner. Jesus had promised His disciples in John 14 that He would return, and He encouraged them to live with that expectation. In Revelation 19, His long-awaited return is now described. When He rode into Jerusalem on the donkey, there were shouts of acclamation. Soon, however, those shouts were swallowed by the shouts of His enemies crying out for His crucifixion. His kingdom had to be delayed because He had to die to pay the penalty for the sins of mankind. His death and resurrection were part of God's eternal plan of redemption.

His return also must be delayed to give sinners the opportunity to hear the message of God's grace, and have an opportunity to respond to this message. This message has been preached around the world, and many have responded. Those who have not responded must also be given opportunity to bring the cup of iniquity to its fullness before God executes justice in His judgment of sin. God permits man's kingdom to reach the point where He must judge its wickedness. The world system must be judged because it has enticed many people to seek satisfaction in all that the system has to offer. We have seen this in the Book of Revelation.

The wicked ruler, called the beast, and the unbelieving people of this world worship both the beast and the dragon (Satan). In chapter 18, we see this world system judged and destroyed by the righteous judge. The religious part of this world system (the harlot) has been destroyed, as recorded in Revelation 17. With the harlot's enticements, and the materialistic culture of this world system destroyed, the one part left is the governmental ruler with all of his oppression. The ruler, the final head of this beast, is still on earth but his judgment will come with the return of the triumphant king.

Before we come to the passage that describes the return of Christ and His triumph over the beast, we see another worship scene in heaven as God's people celebrate the destruction of this evil kingdom of man and the anticipated return of the king. The word that is repeated here in this passage is the word "Hallelujah." This word is the Greek translation of the Hebrew term that means, "Praise Jehovah" or "Praise the Lord." The Jews used this word to ascribe their highest praise to the Lord as in the great "Hallel Psalms" (Psalm 113-118). These were psalms of celebration as Israel rejoiced in the deliverance of His people, in their redemption. So here in Revelation 19, we have the highest praise as God's people join with all heaven to celebrate the glorious victory of Jesus Christ over the evil enemy. They celebrate the completion of His salvation and the deliverance of His people. Four times in this passage, we hear the triumphant Hallelujah as God is praised and His king is crowned. Note the reasons why these glad and glorious hallelujahs rise from all of heaven in praise of God's Son.

First, the Lord is worthy of all praise, honor and glory (19:1). He is the "Lord our God," and God is worthy of all praise and worship. In Revelation 5, when the call went out in search for someone who was truly worthy to rule and reign over God's creation, there was no one found among all those who had lived on earth. As John grieved over this fact, his attention was pointed to One who was worthy. He was directed to the Lion of the tribe of Judah and, as He looked, he saw a Lamb that was slain. All heaven joined in acclaiming this Lamb as the only One who was worthy to rule. This is the One who is now acclaimed in Revelation 19. He is the Lord Jesus Christ. He is the Lord, our God. He alone is worthy of our praise.

In Revelation 17 and 18, we have seen the destruction of the world system that is led by the Antichrist, the pretender to the throne. He must be cast down and our attention is now drawn to the true king, the only One who is worthy to sit upon the throne. The sinful rule of Satan and man has brought nothing but frustration, rebellion, grief and misery. The promises of pleasure and fulfillment proved to be nothing but an illusion, but here is a king who can truly meet the needs of His subjects. He is someone who can bring fulfillment and satisfaction. Salvation, glory, honor and power belong to the Lord. He is worthy to receive our praise. Many people in heaven join in celebrating His praise. They shout hallelujah to the Lord our God.

Secondly, the Lord has won a great victory (19:2-4). Not only is He worthy of our praise because of who He is, but also because of what He has done. He has judged and destroyed the system that has long held people in bondage. He has overcome the harlot woman who enticed and seduced so many people to seek pleasure in what she had to offer. The world system, pictured in this harlot, and this great city, Babylon, has enticed many with the glitter of material possessions, with the offer of power, or the promise of pleasure. Many have been attracted to her charms and have turned away from God, the only One who could bring them true fulfillment. This harlot has been the enemy of God, and has been responsible for the death of many of God's servants.

Christ has triumphed over this woman and this city, which pictures this world system, as we find recorded in chapters 17 and 18. The city and the system have been destroyed, and the smoke continues to ascend forever (verse 3). Those who loved her mourn her destruction, but those who love God celebrate a glorious victory. The system is destroyed and the people are now delivered; long live the king who brought about this deliverance. Hallelujah! Those around the throne join in celebration of this great victory. The Lord is worthy of our praise because He has won a great victory over our enemy.

The third reason for praise and worship is in the reality that the Lord reigns (verses 5-6). The Lord is worthy of our worship, the hallelujahs of praise, because He now reigns. With the defeat of Satan's kingdom and the defeat of Man's kingdom, there are no more pretenders to the throne. The Lord reigns. Throughout the centuries God's people have prayed, "Thy kingdom come, Thy will be done on earth as it is in heaven." And now that prayer has become a reality, "The Lord God Omnipotent reigns." All of God's people, small and great, join together to celebrate the crowning of their king: like the voice of a great crowd shouting acclamation, like the sound of a mighty cascade of waters over a falls, like mighty sounds of rolling thunder. There really are no words to describe the volume of sound that ascends to the throne from the people of God, as they celebrate the coronation of the King of kings and Lord of lords.

Never has this world seen a celebration like this, as God's people and all the angels of God join together in acclaiming Jesus Christ as the One who is worthy to rule and reign. Hallelujah, for the Lord God omnipotent reigns. George Frederick Handel got his inspiration for his great *Hallelujah Chorus* from this passage but, as magnificent as this work is, no human composer can begin to capture the praises of God's people, as their king finally sits upon the throne. The King has been crowned, and He is ready to return to earth and establish His kingdom.

Before the King returns in all of His glory, there is one more scene in heaven that is worthy of our attention. This king is not a despot. He is, in fact, a benevolent king who delights in blessing His people and satisfying their every need. The rule of this king is one that is graciously shared. The Lamb has a bride who will share His reign. In contrast to the evil harlot woman, here is the pure and righteous bride of Christ. Because of His love and the provision He has made for her, she is clothed in beautiful white linen garments. These garments symbolically picture purity and righteousness. In Christ, sinners are cleansed and made righteous. Believers are clothed in the righteousness of Christ. His reign is shared with His bride, the love of His life. The Scripture tells us that His people are His bride.

The reign of Christ is described here as a glorious wedding feast. In Matthew 22:2, 25:1-13 and Luke 14:15-24 we see the same picture. The world, pictured by the harlot woman, offers morsels of bread to be eaten in secret. After eating, people are left as hungry as before. The Lord, however, makes us sit down at a great wedding feast, with all of the finest food, which is able to satisfy every desire that we have. There is complete fulfillment. Like at the wedding in Cana where Jesus turned the water into wine, the wine of His joy and satisfaction will never cease to flow. The picture here is that of an unending feast that leaves us totally fulfilled. John reminds us that this is all true, in contrast to the emptiness of what the world has to offer.

We will be forever satisfied with the King's love and with His gracious provision. There is no better word in response than to shout "hallelujah." John is so overwhelmed by this glorious plan that he bows in worship before the angel who revealed it all (19:10). The angel will not permit him to worship anyone but the Lord, who alone is worthy of our worship and praise. Angels are just servants of God, as we are. In this chapter, we see God's redemptive plan come to fulfillment, and it is glorious. Those who understand the message of this book, and what God is about to do in this world, join with those in this passage as they shout, "hallelujah."

The Triumphant King Returns to Earth – Revelation 19:11-21

This brings us to the climatic passage in Revelation 19:11-16, where John sees heaven open and the King descend to claim His right to the throne. Man's kingdom has been destroyed, and God's Kingdom is about to be established. The King is about to descend in triumph, and the climatic event of the ages is about to unfold. However not everyone on earth is happy about what is about to transpire. As we have found in Psalm 2, there are many who will resist the king and want nothing to do with His kingdom. The choice that they make will become their own sentence. Their desire to have no part in His kingdom will become the reality in which they must live forever. The return of the king is a glorious event for those who follow Him, but it will be a time of defeat and destruction for those who oppose Him and His kingdom.

John's attention is immediately focused on the one who rides upon a white horse. The white horse has long been the symbol of the conquering king, the triumphant champion. Jesus rode into Jerusalem as the lowly Son of Man, riding on a donkey. Now He comes as the Triumphant King, riding on a white horse. The name given to Him is "Faithful and True" (Revelation 3:14). He is The Faithful One and He is Truth. Satan's kingdom (and man's reign) is built on lies and delusions. The emphasis in man's kingdom is how things appear to others, and on managing information so that people believe what the leaders want them to believe. In contrast, here is one who is faithful and true, the one who comes in absolute righteousness.

This conquering king is further identified in verse 13 as the "Word of God" (John 1:1, 14). Also in verse 16, He is given the title, "King of kings and LORD of lords." He is the one true sovereign king, who is worthy to rule and reign over God's creation. Having identified Him, John describes His appearance. His eyes are like a flame of fire. His fiery eyes pierce into the very depths of the human heart, having full discernment of all that is there. On His head are many crowns, for all authority has been given unto Him (Matthew 28:18). His authority is over both heaven and earth. Every part of God's creation is under His rule. His name is above every other name; no one is superior to Him.

The victory that He won came at a great cost to Himself, as John describes His clothing as dipped in blood. He was "wounded for our transgressions." He suffered the agony of the cross, in order that He might provide salvation for all those who believe. When He comes, He does not come alone. There are great masses of people, and armies return with Him from heaven. He is the Captain and brings His people with Him. Each one has been impacted by His redemptive work, and they are all clothed in white linen, clean and white. They are clothed in the righteousness that He has provided through His death (verse 8).

It is important that we note what is said in verses 11 and 15 about His agenda. In the first part of this chapter, we saw great rejoicing in heaven as the kingdom of God is about to be established. While there is jubilation in heaven when the Lord returns, the scene on earth is quite different. As He comes, we note that He comes "in righteousness to judge and make war." His eyes are a flame of fire, and there is a sword that proceeds out of His mouth. Satan, the Beast and all the kings of earth, are opposed to Christ and to His rule. They have oppressed the Lord's people and have hardened their hearts against Him. They want no part of His kingdom, so He comes to execute justice and righteousness. Under human rule, there have been many injustices inflicted upon people. Rulers have oppressed people, in order to further their own cause. When the Sovereign Lord comes, He will judge righteously.

The sword proceeds out of His mouth, indicating that He has the power to judge and destroy by a simple word spoken from His mouth. With His mouth, He will slay the wicked and execute justice. He shall rule with a rod of iron. He will put down all rebellion, and all those who oppose His righteous kingdom. He will tread the wine-press of the fierceness and wrath of Almighty God. Christ came in meekness as He came to be our sin-bearer. As Lord and King, He will come to judge all who oppose the righteous rule of God. He will execute justice and judgment upon the earth.

John's attention turns now to these adversaries and the conflict, as it comes to an end with the King's return (19:17-21). In this passage, we see a second great feast. In the first part of the chapter, there is the Marriage Supper of the Lamb as God's people rejoice and enjoy His eternal provision. They will delight themselves as those who celebrate at a great feast, but those who are in opposition will themselves be part of the Great Supper of God. In this feast, it is not the people who are feasting, rather they are being feasted upon, as the birds of prey enjoy this Great Supper of God.

The arrogance of the Antichrist and the kings of earth is seen as they will gather together to try to resist the invasion of the King who comes from heaven. Not only have they rejected His message, but even when they see Him come from heaven in all of His glory, they will marshal their forces together and actually try to prevent Him from establishing His kingdom. Even though they see Him descend from heaven and witness the fact that this King comes from God, they will still resist Him and do all that they can to stop Him. Psalm 2 again fits in here as the Psalmist talks about human rulers who refuse to submit to God's authority and refuse to acknowledge His Christ. They raise their fists and make a vain attempt to stop God from accomplishing His purpose. God will only laugh at their puny efforts.

They have declared that they want no part in God's Kingdom, and so they will be removed from this earth into a place of judgment, never to see the kingdom of God or to enjoy any of His blessings. Those who join with the Antichrist and Satan's rule will be slain by the sword of His mouth, and their bodies will be devoured by the birds of prey. This is the Great Supper of God. The beast and the false prophet, the leaders of this rebellion, are cast alive into the Lake of Fire. They will later be joined by Satan and his host of evil spirits, and by all those who have rejected God's grace offered in Jesus Christ.

The Lake of Fire is a place of eternal torment and suffering. It is the only alternative when a person rejects God's goodness and grace. We can choose to enjoy all of the good things that God has prepared for those who love Him, as a great wedding feast, or we can be a part of the feast as the birds of prey devour those who reject God's grace. Like these rebellious men, you can choose to separate yourself from God's Kingdom and all of its bounty. Many do not realize all that God is graciously supplying, even now. They do not understand the awful desolation when a person chooses to have nothing more to do with God and with His gracious provision. Each person has a choice to make, determining his own destiny.

The King Reigns and Judges – Revelation 20

As Jesus taught His followers to pray, the first request in what is called *The Lord's Prayer* is: "Thy kingdom come, thy will be done on earth as it is in Heaven." God's people have often spoken these words and, for many of Christ's followers, it is the cry of their heart. In Revelation 19, we see that cry answered when Jesus Christ descends from heaven to judge and to make war. He comes to fight against this world system, and to defeat Satan and his followers. When Christ returns to earth, He will defeat the armies of earth and will cast the beast and the false prophet into the Lake of Fire (19:20). In Revelation 20 we see Him deal with Satan, the god of this world, and the one who has given power to this beast-like system. If the Kingdom of God is to be established, and if righteousness and peace are to prevail on earth, Satan must be dealt with and removed from the scene.

This chapter begins with the binding of Satan in the bottomless pit (20:1-3). This is necessary, in order to establish a kingdom of righteousness and peace. An angel from heaven is given authority from God and is sent on a special mission. His authority is seen in the fact that God gives him the key to the bottomless pit. With the key to the pit, he also has a great chain. His mission is to bind the dragon, Satan, with the chain. He is to remain bound for 1,000 years. After he is bound, he is cast into the bottomless pit. The pit is sealed so that there is no possibility of escape.

If God's kingdom is to be established, Satan must be restrained and his influence upon humans must be immobilized. From the Garden of Eden to the present day, Satan has been active in his work of deception. He has deceived the nations for thousands of years, and they have followed him in this deception. If Christ is to reign and righteousness is to prevail, this deceiver must be incapacitated. Jesus told the people of His day that you cannot enter into a strong man's territory unless you bind the strong man. Jesus defeated Satan at the cross, but the final conclusion of that victory still waits for His return. As we see in 20:1-3, Satan is bound for 1,000 years, when humans will not be under attack from the evil one. While that is a considerable period of time, it is a limited period. It is stated that he will be set free again for a short period of time.

The people of God have long suffered at the hand of Satan, and by those who were a part of his kingdom. There were many casualties in this spiritual conflict. Some of God's people were actually put to death for their faith. It often seemed as though Satan and his forces would prevail. God kept promising His people that, in the end, they would share in His glorious victory. Now we see it. Satan is bound in the pit, and people of God are seated on thrones along with the King of kings and Lord of lords. Authority to judge is given to God's people. The believers are raised from the dead and they will reign with Christ for 1,000 years.

This resurrection of the dead is called the first resurrection. It is a resurrection unto life. The hope to which believers have been committed is now a reality. Many have endured the sufferings and struggles of this life, with the hope of what God has promised. From this passage, we are reminded that we do not need to fear what the unbelieving world may do to us, or what Satan and his forces may do. In the end, Satan is bound and the people of God are upon the throne ruling with Christ for 1,000 years.

The unbelieving dead will not be raised until after the 1,000 years are over, and at that time they will be raised to face the final time of judgment. In verse 6, we see there is a special blessing for those who are raised in this first resurrection. Those who are part of this resurrection will never experience the second death, which is described in the latter part of this chapter. Those who are in Christ have eternal life, and never need to fear this second death. Jesus Christ experienced death for us as He was separated from the Father on the cross. We will never have to experience this separation since we are in Him and share His life. Again we are told that God's people will rule and reign with Christ for 1,000 years. His people also enjoy the privilege of serving God as His priests. The future position and relationship that we will enjoy with Him far outweighs any suffering we might have to endure here and now.

This is the ultimate victory. It may appear in our present life that we are overmatched, and that God's people may seem to be on the losing side. In these verses, however, is a brief glimpse of the final outcome. Do not be discouraged. Continue to be faithful, for in the end we will prevail.

Very little information is given in this passage to describe the nature of this millennial reign of Christ, but the promises given to the Old Testament prophets provide this information in great detail. In these prophecies we are told of the removal of the curse so that the desert will "blossom as a rose" (Isaiah 35:1). We are also told that the "wolf and the lamb shall feed together" (Isaiah 65:25) and "every man will sit under his own fig tree" (Micah 4:4). There will be righteousness and peace along with prosperity and an extended life-span. The promises God made through these Old Testament prophets will all be fulfilled.

In the next paragraph (20:7-10), we are given information that may seem impossible to even imagine. Certainly, we might think, "If humans have the opportunity to live under the righteous rule of Christ, they will want that to continue forever. If only humans could know peace, justice and the satisfaction of all their needs, surely they would be content." But wait, do we really know that for a fact? Do not those, who are living under Christ's reign, need to be given an opportunity to make their own choice? Do all those who are born during this 1,000 year reign love Christ and submit to Him willingly, or do they only do so because there is no other alternative? God will give those who live under the rule of Christ an opportunity to choose for themselves.

In the Book of Revelation, it is interesting to note that God will allow humans, living on earth, to experience a taste of eternity. In Revelation 9, during the time of the tribulation, God allows humans to experience the torment of hell as demons are released from the pit to torment men for five months. God graciously limits the time and does not allow the demons to kill these people, but they still refuse to repent. In the passage here in Revelation 20, God allows humans to experience what we might describe as "heaven on earth" as they live under the righteous, peaceful reign of Christ for 1,000 years. At the end of this wonderful period of time, many of these humans still choose to reject the reign of Christ.

Satan will be released from his imprisonment and allowed to offer humans an alternative. The amazing thing is that when he goes out to every corner of the earth, he will gather a huge following. There are many who still will choose not to live under the reign of Christ. Satan and this host of people will actually try to attack the capital city of God's kingdom. They will try to overthrow the rule of Christ. There is still rebellion in their hearts, and when they are given the opportunity and a leader to rally around, they seize that opportunity. Of course Satan and his forces can never prevail over God's kingdom, but they will still try.

We may wonder about this: Is it true that people who have lived under the perfect rule of Christ will still rebel against Him? Is it true that people living in perfect conditions, almost heaven on earth, will still be dissatisfied? Jesus gave us the answer in John 3:3, when He said, "Except a man be born again he cannot enter into the kingdom of heaven." The human heart is deceitful and desperately wicked, and it is not changed by simply changing one's environment. We blame the conditions around us, we blame Satan for our sinful acts, and we blame the fact that the government is corrupt. During the 1,000-year period, none of these will exist, but the heart is still unchanged apart from the new birth. The fact is, the natural man is dead spiritually (Ephesians 2:1, 5), and is not capable of functioning in the spiritual realm. Unbelievers in the kingdom or in heaven would be like fish out of water, and just waiting for an opportunity to return to the realm where they feel comfortable.

When Satan and humans continue in their rebellion against God, there is no alternative but for them to be forever separated from God. To be totally separated from God, who is the source of life, leaves nothing but what we might call eternal death. Since God is also the source of all that is good, if a person is totally separated from Him, he is left with nothing but misery and evil. In verse 10, Satan is cast into the Lake of Fire – totally separated from God, to experience eternal torment.

Humans also will spend eternity in that place, according to the last part of this chapter. God does not force anyone to live in fellowship with Him. He created us to live in fellowship with Him, but He allows us to choose for ourselves what we will. We should know this: those who choose to separate from Him choose death and torment. Those who choose to submit to His Lordship and live under His rule will enjoy life eternal and find full satisfaction. Those who follow Christ will rule and reign with Him, enjoying ultimate victory. So although it may appear at the present time that God's people are on the losing side, this passage assures us that His people will prevail.

God has warned humans again and again in Scripture that there is a Day of Judgment. God has created all humans, and holds us accountable for what we do. The Bible tells us clearly that "it is appointed unto men once to die, but after this the judgment" (Hebrews 9:27). Jesus told His listeners that a day of judgment was coming and they needed to be prepared. Peter warned his readers that they should not interpret delay as an indication that God would not judge (2 Peter 3:1-9). As we come to Revelation 20:11-15, John is taken into the future where he sees the Throne of Judgment, and where he sees humans stand before God to give an account. God not only holds humans accountable for their sins, but He also provides a way of escape so that they do not have to fear this time of judgment. God gives humans a choice, but then He holds them accountable for the choice they make.

What John sees in this vision is awesome, for he sees the Throne of God, and it is described as a Great White Throne. We use the word "great" very loosely in our world, but in God's Word "great" means great. It is majestic and awe-inspiring. It is the Throne of God. Next we find the word "white," calling our attention to the fact that it is absolutely pure, righteous and just. There is not even a hint of injustice or unfairness here. It is absolutely pure and holy. So it is great and it is white. To this John adds the word, "throne." It is the seat of authority, the place of sovereign power. Absolute rule is present at this throne.

John then is focused on the One who is seated on this throne. It is great, white and supreme because it is God who sits upon this throne.

There is no higher authority in this universe than that of the Creator. There is no other court to which we can appeal. God sits upon this throne and He is the final authority. This scene is so awesome that the earth and heaven fled from His presence. Even God's creation is insignificant in the presence of God Himself. Nothing, and no one, can stand in His awesome presence. So with everything else stripped away, it is just humans and God, one man or one woman standing before the Holy God.

Those who stand before Him are the "dead." If we compare this with verses 4-6, it seems clear that these dead are those who did not share in the first resurrection. They were not among those who were raised to rule and reign with Christ during the 1,000 year kingdom. It seems then that these are the unbelieving dead, and they are now raised to stand before God and give an account. Note here that none is exempt, whether small or great, whether rich and powerful or poor and insignificant. Those who have died at sea will be raised, and those who were buried or cremated will be raised. The souls who have been held in hell, the place of torment, are now called forth to stand before the Throne of the Holy God. None will be overlooked at this court appearance. It is indeed a solemn and awesome scene as humans stand before the Righteous God, to give an account to Him.

When God passes judgment, He is not arbitrary. He does not show favoritism or prejudice. His evaluation is always based upon truth and facts. So here in verses 12-13, we see that the books are opened. These books contain an accurate record of what humans have done. A person's life record is contained in these books. The evidence is all there, and there is no way to escape the facts that are revealed. It is important that we note here that the dead are judged out of those things which are written in the books, according to their works. God deals in truth and righteousness. Each person will be judged fairly on the basis of their works (what they have done).

It is important that we do not miss what is happening here. Every person in this world has some concept of right and wrong. This concept may be very different based upon one's knowledge and one's cultural setting. Some have greater knowledge than others, but all have a concept of right and wrong. The question that might be asked is, "What person in this world has perfectly lived up to their standard of right and wrong?" Everyone in this human family would have to admit that they have done something that is a violation of their own standard of right and wrong. Romans 3:23 teaches us that sin is failing to measure up to God's standard of right and wrong. It is falling short of the glory of God. Sin is a lack of conformity to the holiness and righteousness of God. Surely every human being comes short of God's holy standard, but even if humans are judged on the basis of their own standard, they are guilty. Humans are condemned, even in the light of their own standard of right and wrong. Their own works will judge them to be guilty. Some may appear to do better than others, but all are condemned as guilty.

Sin is exposed when the unbelieving dead stand before the throne of God. As Psalm 1:5-6 states, sinners will not be able to stand in the judgment. No one can stand in the presence of God as those who are not guilty. There is another book here also, and this book is man's only hope. This book is called *The Book of Life* or *The Lamb's Book of Life* (13:8, 17:8, 21:27). In this book are the names of all those who are "in Christ." We are all guilty sinners, but Christ died for the sins of the whole world. The price of redemption has been paid in full. God has provided the gift of eternal life through the shed blood of Jesus Christ. All who come to Christ by faith have their names written in The Book of Life (John 5:24).

This brings us to the real issue. It is true that all are guilty before God, and all are condemned on the basis of what they have done. All have sinned and fallen short of God's holy standard. All have even failed to measure up to their own standard of righteousness. The penalty of sin is death, what is described here as the "second death," which is eternal separation from God in the Lake of Fire. This is the only sentence that can be pronounced upon those who have rebelled against God. There is another book that is present at this Great White Throne. That book is The Book of Life.

While it is true that all are guilty and deserve the Lake of Fire, it is also true that God has provided life for those who are dead. God sent His Son Jesus Christ into this world to take our sin upon Himself, to go to the cross and experience death and separation from God, on our behalf. Christ experienced death for us, in order that we might have eternal life. All those, who rest their faith in Him, are listed in the Lamb's Book of Life. This book contains the names of those who have put their trust in Jesus Christ as their Savior. The real issue at this judgment is not just who is guilty; all are guilty. The real question is, "Is your name recorded in His *Book of Life?*" People will spend eternity separated from God in the Lake of Fire because they have not only sinned, but because they have not accepted the sacrifice of Christ as full and complete payment for their sin. God has offered the gift of life to those who are dead in trespasses and sins. If they do not accept God's gift, the only alternative is that they experience eternal separation from God. The ultimate issue is, have you accepted what Christ has done for you?

Vision V

Eternal Son Reigns over God's New Creation
Revelation 21-22

WITH THIS FINAL VISION the exaltation of Jesus Christ comes to its fullness as God brings His New Creation into being and His Son sits upon the throne in God's Eternal Kingdom. The creation described in Genesis has been corrupted by sin and the rebellion of both humans and angels (under Satan's Leadership). But in spite of this rebellion God's creative plan and purpose will be fully realized. In Revelation 20:11 we are told that the present "earth and heaven fled away." Peter speaks of this in 2 Peter 3:10-12.

Satan has been cast into the lake of fire where the beast and the false prophet are, to be eternally tormented (Revelation 20:10). At the Great White Throne (20:11-15) humans are also judged and those who are not found in the book of life (not trusted Christ as their Savior) are cast into the lake of fire. With all evil judged and forever separated from God's presence the eternal plan of God is ready to unfold.

All that God purposed in Genesis will be fulfilled as the New Creation comes into being and God and humans dwell together in eternal fellowship. All of this has been made possible through the redemptive work of Jesus Christ on the cross of Calvary. God now highly exalts Him as the one who is worthy to reign forever in God's eternal kingdom. In this final vision we see a description of this glorious kingdom as all glory and honor is given to God's Son.

God's final revelation closes with a gracious invitation for all who read this book, calling humans to rest their faith in Jesus Christ and be assured of having a part in this glorious Kingdom of God. Be assured that God will prevail and His plan will come to fulfillment, and God graciously invites humans to respond in faith to His invitation.

All Things New – Revelation 21:1-8

There is something exciting about something that is new: a new house, car, baby, or a new job. There is a sense of freshness, a sense of beginning, a sense of hope that goes with newness. There is a hope that somehow what is new will be better and that it will make a real difference in our lives. Like Solomon, we soon discover that in this present life there is "nothing new under the sun." There is nothing in our world that is truly new. There is nothing not affected by the curse of sin. That new baby is still a self-willed sinner. That new car still rusts and breaks down. The new home is subject to the same laws of deterioration as the old one. The new job still has problems and some of the same frustrations, and also still requires sweat and toil, wearisome labor. Man works to improve his lot in life. He looks for ways to escape the curse, but newness is soon gone and the same old problems resurface again. Try as he may, man cannot escape sin or sin's curse. Thanks to God, there is hope. There is deliverance. There is One who can bring new out of the old.

In Revelation 21:1-8, we see this hope realized. We now discover true newness. Sin has been put away through the sacrifice of Christ and, with His return, there is restoration and all things become new. This world system is destroyed. All that is evil has been put away. Satan is cast into the Lake of Fire, and God has judged all those who have rejected Jesus Christ. With the judgment and removal of all that is evil, God can now bring into existence a creation that is truly new. Those who have trusted Christ have already come to know something of this new creation. We have spiritually experienced the fact that old things pass away, and all things become new (2 Corinthians 5:17). There is, however, so much more to God's new creation.

In the beginning, God created the heavens and the earth. His purpose was that He might fellowship with those whom He created to dwell on this earth. Heaven and earth were to live together in concert, but sin entered: humans joined with Satan in rebellion against God. Sin separated humans from the God who made them, and the curse came upon all creation as a consequence of that sin. With the curse came decay, disintegration and finally death. All creation suffered as a result, being made subject to bondage (Romans 8:21). Thank God the story does not end there, for God, in love, sent His own Son to die in our place. In His death He paid in full the penalty of sin and provided deliverance for humans, and deliverance for the creation from bondage.

With sin put away, God's design for His creation can now come to fulfillment. God's plan and purpose cannot be thwarted. As we look at Revelation 21, we see God bringing to completion all that He planned. What He began in Genesis, He brings to completion in Revelation. As we approach the Eternal State, as it is described here, we may have to put aside some of our stereotyped concepts. When we think of eternity, we tend to think only of heaven, and when we think of heaven, we tend to think of rest and inactivity. This is not what we find in this passage.

What John sees next was "A New Heaven and a New Earth," as recorded in Revelation 21:1. The word for "new" in this passage does not mean "new in point of time" or "recent." Instead, it is the word that speaks of newness in quality: something that is fresh and unlike what we have experienced up to this point. It is truly new. The creation, involving both heaven and earth, is recreated in absolute perfection. The curse of sin is gone, and everything is without the slightest blemish. Again note that it is not just heaven, but heaven and earth. God had a plan when He created the earth, and He will see His plan come to completion. This earth was made to be inhabited, and it will be. It was and is part of God's plan.

One of the interesting changes in this new creation is that there will be no sea. The seas have long divided humans, creating barriers between those who dwell on earth. The sea in Scripture also pictures a restlessness and turmoil (Isaiah 57:20, 21). The sea is a place of danger and even death to humans (20:13). It is the place where the Leviathan dwells and those creatures that have terrorized humans. In 13:1 we saw the beast rising up out of the sea. We may ask, "Is not water needed to sustain human life?" The answer is yes, but in 21:6, and again in 22:1-2, we see that God supplies all the water that is necessary to sustain life. In this New Creation, God will provide for every human need.

With a new heaven and a new earth, John's attention is turned to the New Jerusalem in verses 2 and 3. Jerusalem was the holy city for God's covenant people, Israel. It was the capital city, the seat of the Theocracy (God's rule). It was the place where the Temple was located, and the place where God dwelt in the midst of His people. This ancient city of Jerusalem however has been marred and scared with sin. It was a city often given to disobedience and rebellion. It was there that the prophets were slain, and the apostles imprisoned. It was in that city that God's Son, Jesus Christ, was rejected and put to death (Revelation 11:8). Again, God's purpose cannot be thwarted and He will have a city where He can dwell in the midst of His people. It is here called the New Jerusalem, a truly Holy City. It comes down from God out of heaven. This is God's city. It is the city that captured the attention of Abraham and the other patriarchs (Hebrews 11:9-16). With earth's city, Babylon, being destroyed, there is a new city, a holy one, gloriously arrayed as a bride adorned for her husband. God is the creator, the One who prepares this city. It will be unlike anything that we have ever seen. It will be a city of beauty and glory.

In verse 3, we are told that this city provides a place where God can dwell with humans. This city comes down from heaven in order to provide a tabernacle, a meeting place, a point of contact between God and humans. In the Old Testament, God dwelt behind a veil in a tent (Tabernacle), and later He dwelt in the Temple. God's presence in those dwelling places was represented by a glory cloud. In John 1:14, we see that God dwelt with men in the person of His Son, Jesus Christ. In Ephesians 2:21-22, Paul declares that the Church is now God's Temple, wherein He dwells in a spiritual presence today. In the New Creation, with sin and the curse removed, there is nothing to separate humans

from God. In the Garden of Eden, God came down to walk and fellowship with Adam and Eve in the evening (Genesis 3:8). God's purpose
will be fully realized as He lives among His people. He will be their
God, and they will be His people. They will live together in harmony.

In this New Creation and in this New City, there will be a new order
of things (21:4-8). Every vestige of sin and of its curse is forever gone.
All things will be perfect and complete. It is difficult for John to describe
this newness, because it is beyond what we have experienced in this
life. One way he can help us understand is to tell us that all the things
that were wrong in the old order are gone forever. There are no more
tears. The tears currently seen on earth are the tears of pain, suffering
and sorrow. God will wipe away all of those tears. There is no more
death. There will be no reason for death to exist, because the reason
for death (death, as the consequence of sin) has been put away by the
sacrifice of Christ.

There will be no more sorrow, because sin is the source for all sorrow
in this life. All grief and sorrow will be forever gone. John again is told
that there will be no more crying. God cannot emphasize this enough
to comfort our hearts. He also adds that there will be no more pain,
because all pain is again tied to the curse caused by sin. God is not the
author of pain. Pain finds its source in sin. In verse 5, God speaks from
the throne, assuring us that indeed this New Creation will be totally
new. These words are true and faithful, and you can rest your hope in
them. It is an absolute certainty.

When we read the words "It is done" in verse 6, we are reminded of
the words of Jesus from the cross. He announced the completion of the
work of redemption by saying, "It is finished" (John 19:30). With the
same certainty, it is now announced that the New Order in God's New
Creation is absolutely sure. God started it all, as recorded in the Book
of Genesis. He is the Alpha, and He will bring it to completion. He is
the Omega. He is the sovereign God, and what He started in Genesis
will be completed in Revelation. No one can thwart God or keep Him
from completing His work.

God will fully satisfy the thirst of man with living water, as Jesus promised to the Samaritan woman in John 4. God alone can provide for those whom he has created, and He alone will give all that is needed to sustain life eternally. What He supplies will not only sustain life, but it will bring complete satisfaction, as well. Those people who belong to Him will inherit all things, and they will share His reign (verse 7). In the beginning, man was to have dominion over all the earth and, in the end, this will be fully realized.

There are those who will have no part in this glorious fulfillment of God's purpose. In verse 8, John reminds us that not all will share in the glory of this new creation:

> But the cowardly, unbelieving, abominable, murderers, sexually immoral, sorcerers, idolaters, and all liars shall have their part in the lake which burns with fire and brimstone, which is the second death.

In fact, they will be separated from all that God has provided through His Son. They have chosen another path. They have rejected God's grace, refusing to accept what God has offered. The only alternative is for them to be eternally separated from God, and all that He provides. Their place will be in the Lake of Fire.

The City of God – Revelation 21:9-22:5

There are two kingdoms presented in God's Word, and these two kingdoms are in conflict. Within the concept of these two kingdoms, there is also the concept of two great cities. These cities are very different in their culture, as well as how they provide for the needs of their people. Each of these cities offers their citizens something to bring fulfillment and satisfaction into their lives. The one city is built around materialistic values, seeking to draw men away from the true and living God. The other city focuses on spiritual and eternal values, seeking to draw men into a closer relationship with God.

Abraham and Lot are good examples of how a city can impact a person's life. These two men were from the same family and background, yet they went in two different directions. In Genesis 13:12, Lot pitched his tent toward Sodom, and it wasn't long before he and his family moved into the city. The sad thing was, not only did they move into Sodom, but Sodom moved into their lives. The city had a great influence on Lot and his family. On the other hand, Hebrews 11:9-10 tells us that Abraham's heart was fixed on another city, and he was so influenced by that city that he was content to live as a pilgrim in a tent. His heart was fixed on the City of God, and he refused to be satisfied with anything less.

Not only are these two cities different in nature and in how they impact people, but they are different in time. Man's city is temporal, and as we have seen in Revelation 18, it is doomed for destruction. This earthly city built by humans, called Babylon, is doomed for total destruction with all of its pleasures and allurements. The heavenly city, the City of God, is eternal, and those who love and long for this city will be blessed forever. In Revelation 21:9-22:5, God gives John a vision of this eternal city, and he tries to describe what he saw for us so that our hearts might be drawn away from man's city and we might fall in love with the City of God.

It is significant to note the similarities that we find in the record, as each of these cities are described for us. As we compare 21:9-10 with 17:1, 3, we note the following similarities and differences. Both cities are described as a woman. One is a harlot, and the other is the Lamb's wife. One is in the wilderness, while the other is on a high mountain. The one is built by man, and the other comes down from God. The one is doomed for destruction; the other is eternal. These two cities are given to us in this fashion so that we might make a wise choice.

As we look at the description of this eternal city, we find the use of pictorial language that emphasizes the radiant glory of this great city. We first see that this New Jerusalem is built upon a solid foundation, which gives it permanence (verse 14). The city has twelve foundations, emphasizing not only stability but also permanence. If it is going to stand, the foundation must be firm and secure. Man's cities may appear to be secure, but an earthquake, tornado, or simply the decay of time, can cause huge buildings to crumble and fall. God's City can never be moved; it will stand for all eternity.

In verses 10-20, we discover that there is not only firmness, security and permanence, but there also is great beauty, as the foundations are garnished with all kinds of precious stones. The stones that are listed in this passage are like those found in the breastplate of the High Priest. The colors of these stones cover the entire spectrum of the rainbow, which speaks of the radiance of God's glory. The character of God is represented here as this city is built upon His integrity. It can never fall. It will stand forever, because the foundations rest upon God Himself.

As the city is further described in verse 12, the focus is on the wall that surrounds the city and provides protection for its citizens. Ancient cities were built with walls around them for protection. The wall is said to be great and high, and these words are not exaggerated when we read the dimensions that are given. In verse 16, we find that the height is the same as the length and the breath. The dimension given is 12,000 furlongs, which is about 1,400 miles, and that's a high wall. Another dimension is given in verse 17, 144 cubits, which would be about 200 feet. About the only dimension left to fit here is the thickness of the wall. Absolute protection is seen here. Nothing can ever penetrate God's City, and verse 27 assures us of this point. So there is absolute protection from any enemy.

While he describes complete safety and security, he also makes it clear that there is freedom of entry for God's people. This point is made as we discover that in this great wall there are 12 gates (verses 12-13). These gates are described as being like 12 pearls in all of their beauty (verse 21). These gates will never be closed to God's people, giving them complete access to this city (verse 25). Anything that defiles is forever excluded from this eternal city, but there is also access for God's people.

The city is described in its perfection as it is described as being foursquare, of full dimensions in every direction. There is nothing lacking, no matter which way you go. It is like a giant cube, providing space for all of God's people. It is perfect also in its beauty, for it is described as a great jasper or diamond (verse 11). Its beauty is further enhanced in verse 18, as it is described as being pure gold. The writer is limited in trying to paint a true picture of what he has seen. It is like nothing we have ever seen in this world. He selects some of the most beautiful and most glorious things that are known to man, as he tries to describe that which is truly indescribable. This city is absolutely perfect in every way.

John has tried to describe this city in all of its perfection, but there is something else that makes this city truly great. It is the City of God, and God Himself dwells there in all of His glory. The true beauty and glory of this city is found in the presence of God (21:11, 22-26; 22:3-5). God's glory so radiates throughout the city that there is no need for sun or moon (verse 23). There is no night in that city, because God is there in all of His glory (21:25; 22:5). No other light is needed in this city, because God is light, and in Him is no darkness at all. God's light radiates throughout the whole city.

The presence of God is seen also as John notes the fact that there is no temple in this city (verse 22). The temple was a place on earth where God's presence was represented by a glory cloud as He dwelt among His people. In this city, God Himself is there dwelling in all of His glory. What is said of God is also true of the Lamb, God's Son. Jesus Christ is the exalted one and God's glory radiates from Him. Verses 23-26 tells us that people from all nations, those who are saved, will live in the light of God's glory. All honor and glory will be given to Him as the kings of earth bow before Him. All glory and honor belongs to the Lord, and every knee will bow, including those who have ruled on earth. This city is wonderful and beyond our ability to fathom. Its true greatness is found in the fact that God dwells there in all of His glory.

The description continues in 22:1-3, as John sees how God provides for all of the needs of His people. All life comes from God, and in His city the life is eternal life. Not only is He the source of life, but He is the sustainer of life as well. One of the needs that we have to sustain life is water. In this passage, we are told that there is a pure river of the water of life, and it flows out of the Throne of God and of the Lamb. This water is absolutely pure, clear as crystal.

The Tree of Life is also there (Revelation 22:2). God planted the Tree of Life in the Garden of Eden to provide for humans the opportunity to live forever. When Adam and Eve sinned, they forfeited this opportunity and death came upon the human race. In Genesis 3:22 God graciously protected the Tree of Life from His fallen creatures so that they would not life forever in their fallen state. In Revelation 22 we discover that the Tree of Life is flourishing in the City of God. Not only is life sustained in this eternal city but it makes provision for the full enjoyment of life. We note that this tree will provide a different kind of fruit every month. Everything that we could ever want, or will ever need, is provided for us by God. Life is sustained by the provision of God.

Many have sought and searched for true meaning and purpose in life. One of the frustrating things in Man's City is that people continually search for meaning and purpose. God had a plan and purpose for us when He made us. That purpose was for humans to live in fellowship with God, and to serve and glorify Him. Sin has kept us from seeing that purpose fulfilled in our lives. Even as believers, we fall short of the full realization of God's purpose for us. With the curse removed (verse 3), there is nothing to hinder our fellowship with God, or to interfere with whole-hearted service to Him. As we seek to serve Him in this life, there are often problems with purity of motivation, and we are limited by weariness and other factors. In God's City, we will be released from all effects of sin and the curse, and we will be free to serve Him, fully realizing the purpose for which we were created.

In verse 5, we read about reigning for ever and ever. God's purpose for humans was that they might reign with Him over His creation (Genesis 1:26-28, Hebrews 2:8). God's purpose was for humans to have dominion. They were to serve God as His regents, ruling over this created world. God has not abandoned His purpose. Christ has won a great victory for us, and the purpose of God can now be fulfilled in our lives as we live eternally in His City. We will rule and reign with Him, and enjoy all that God intended when He first created humans.

The Book of Revelation sets two cities before us. The city of man,

Babylon, is this world system, and it is headed for total destruction. The City of God is the eternal city, with all that God has prepared for those who follow Him. We must set our hearts on one of these two cities. Abraham was content to live as a pilgrim in this world because he was looking for a City which had foundations, and one whose builder and maker is God. The Lord has given us the Book of Revelation to help us choose wisely. He has described the glamour of man's city, and compared it with the glory of God's city. He has told us that man's city is headed for certain destruction, while God's city is to continue forever. The choice is ours to make.

God's Final Message to Man – Revelation 22:6-21

The Bible is the most unique book ever written, because it is God's message to humans. God created humans, and He fellowshipped with Adam and Eve in the perfect environment of the Garden of Eden. Adam and Eve rebelled against God, however, and sin separated humans from God. The curse of sin brought great consequences to life here on earth. God loved those whom He had created, however, and He began communicating through prophets so that humans might know how they could be restored to fellowship with God. When God sent His Son into our world, He spoke of Him as "the Word" (John 1:1-14) because He came to reveal God to us and to provide the way through His sacrifice, so humans might be restored to fellowship with God (John 14:6).

As we come to Revelation 22:6-21, we reach not only the conclusion of this book, but the conclusion of God's revelation to man. This is God's final message to humans and, as it concludes, the Lord personally speaks to John to emphasize the importance of this final message. God urges those who have read this book not to miss the importance and eternal significance of what has been written. God has spoken, and now those who hear must respond to what they have read and heard.

As the book begins, God promises a special blessing for those who read and respond to what they find in this book (Revelation 1:3).

Throughout the book, we find the repeated statement, "Those who have ears to hear, let them hear." There are eternal implications in the message of this book, and there are grave consequences for those who ignore or reject what God says in this concluding passage.

In this final passage, there is a threefold emphasis that the Lord brings to our attention. First, He wants to assure all who read this book of the integrity of this message (Revelation 22:6). The message in this book is absolutely true. The Lord Himself wants us to know it is His message. What is recorded in the Book of Revelation "must shortly be done." There are symbols and analogies, but it is important that we do not miss the message as we try to wrestle with the symbols. What is described in this book is beyond our human experience, and beyond our finite minds. The only way that it can be conveyed to us is to make comparisons with what we have experienced.

The second thing that the Lord emphasizes in this message is to assure us of His return (verses 7, 12, 20). This book is all about the unveiling of Jesus Christ, as He returns as King of kings and Lord of lords. We need to be ready, and living in anticipation of His return at any time. When Jesus says that He will come quickly, it does not necessarily mean that it will be soon. Many have stumbled over this and have begun to doubt that He will return at all. The word used here is a word that means "with suddenness." When He comes, it will be quickly so that there will be no time to make adjustments in preparation for His coming.

Jesus deals with this concept in verse 11, when He says that those who are unjust will be unjust when He returns. Those who are righteous will be found in righteousness when He returns. The same is true of those who are filthy or holy. There will be no time for change when He returns. Jesus spoke of this in Matthew, when He said that there will be no time to gather things together at His return. Jesus spoke about the suddenness of His return and urged His hearers to be prepared (Matthew 24:44).

The third point that the Lord wants to emphasize, as He closes this message, is that the invitation is still open. The Lord calls upon humans to respond to God's gracious invitation. Don't ignore God's message or delay in responding to His gracious invitation. Too much is at stake for anyone to take God's message lightly. We look now at this concluding passage.

The Lord speaks to John to reassure him that the message that has been revealed to him is absolute truth (22:6-9). The same God who spoke through the holy prophets has spoken again, and this is His final message. This message is truth, and when it comes to pass, it will be with suddenness. God will move swiftly as He brings all of these things to fulfillment. As He said at the beginning of this revelation, He repeats again: there is a special blessing for those who keep what is revealed in this book. What is revealed here is not just to give us information about the end times. The message of this book is to impact our lives and our value system.

If it is true that this world system is going to be destroyed, then a person who builds his life around the values of this world is a fool. There is a blessing for those who set their hearts on God's eternal kingdom, and who live their lives in harmony with that which has eternal significance. If we really believe that Christ is coming back, and that it could be at any time, then this should affect how we live from day to day. We must respond to what we have heard in this book, and we must respond in the right way.

John's first response was to fall before the angel who brought the message and worship him. He is immediately rebuked and reminded that the one who brings the message is only a servant. God alone is to be worshipped. As we respond to His truth, our focus must be on Him. Many people today get enamored with the messenger. The servant who delivers the message is often elevated to a special status. Sadly, there are messengers today who seem to encourage this kind of elevation. The messenger is only God's servant. He may do an excellent job in his delivery of the message, but only God is worthy of exaltation and worship. The servant only delivers the message of his Lord. He is not the author of that message. The call is made for those who read this message to respond to God's truth, bow before Him, and seek to live in obedience to what He says. It is then that you will experience His promised blessing.

As the Lord speaks to John, He tells him that the message of this book is for now, so it is not to be sealed. When Daniel received his word from God, he was told to seal the book because its message was for a later time. Now John is told that the time is at hand (22:10-16). The message of this book is vital to all those who are living in this last age. We need to know what is in this book and understand how it applies to us. Christ will come suddenly, even when people are not expecting Him, and then it will be too late to make any necessary adjustments. Those who are unjust and filthy will not have time to make any change. Those who are righteous and holy will be found as they are.

Jesus said in the Gospels that when He comes, those who were working in the field or on the roof would not have any time to make any adjustments (Matthew 24:38-51). You must be prepared now, because you do not know when He will come. When He comes, His obedient servants will be recipients of His blessing. They will have access to the Tree of Life, and they will dwell with Him in His eternal city.

Those who are not prepared for the coming King will be forever shut out of this Eternal City (22:15). The dogs represent those who have no appreciation for the things of God. Sorcerers are those who seek power from Satan's kingdom. Whoremongers are those who live to gratify their own fleshly lusts. Murderers are those who have no respect for human life, which is made in the image of God. Idolaters are those who worship something other than the true and living God. Those who lie are those who deviate from God's truth and buy into Satan's lie. In verse 16, Jesus attests to the fact that this message is from the One who sits in the seat of authority, and whose word is to be given highest honor.

In the last of the Lord's threefold message (22:17-19), we are told that there is still an opportunity to respond to the message of this book. The Holy Spirit is still graciously calling for sinners to accept God's invitation. And the Bride, the church, is commissioned to extend this invitation to those who will respond. Those who have heard, responded and accepted God's invitation now share that invitation with others.

Those who are thirsty, looking for something to satisfy, are invited to come. All those who will respond are invited to drink of the water that God has supplied in Christ.

This is the message and the invitation is still open, but we do not know how much longer. It is not wise to delay in responding to God's message. This message is from the Lord, and it is to be taken seriously. This message is so special that we are warned about altering it in any way (22:18-19). We should not add anything or take anything away from it. God's truth is not to be altered by humans. Who are we to presume to add something to what He says, or to take away, as though unimportant, something that God has said? One of the great problems today is that humans have presumed to add, detract and change what God has said in His Word. This is so important that a curse is pronounced upon those who presume to make such an adjustment.

The Lord closes His revelation with another reminder that He is coming again, and His coming will be with such suddenness so that we will not have time to make any adjustment. We must be prepared. We need to take seriously what He says in this book. Now is the only time to respond to His invitation. John responds for all true believers when he says, "Even so come, Lord Jesus." Those who know Him should be looking forward to his return, and living each day with this expectation. This ought to be the prayer of our hearts as we live from day to day. This is the eternal perspective that we get from this book, and we need to live it in our daily lives. John is aware that we can do that only by the grace of our Lord Jesus Christ, and so this is His benediction for us.

CPSIA information can be obtained at www.ICGtesting.com
Printed in the USA
LVOW10s0313150816

500373LV00001B/1/P